Rational Emotive Behaviour Therapy:
Advances in Theory and Practice

Rational Emotive Behaviour Therapy: Advances in Theory and Practice

Michael Neenan
and Windy Dryden

Whurr Publishers
London

© 1999 Whurr Publishers Ltd
First published 1999 by
Whurr Publishers Ltd
19b Compton Terrace, London NI 2UN, England

British Library Cataloguing in Publication Data
A catalogue record for this book is available from the British Library.

ISBN: 1 86156 104 0

Printed and bound in the UK by Athenaeum Press Ltd, Gateshead, Tyne & Wear

Dedication

To Albert Ellis, a true pioneer in the field of psychotherapy

Contents

Dedication   v

Preface   ix

Chapter One   1

Rational Emotive Behaviour Therapy (REBT): An Overview

Chapter Two   11

Trends in REBT: 1955-95

Chapter Three   37

REBT and the Question of Free Will

Chapter Four   52

An Elaboration of the REBT Concept of Ego Disturbance

Chapter Five   61

Beyond Low Frustration Tolerance and Discomfort Disturbance: The Case
for the Term 'Non-ego Disturbance'

Chapter Six   92

Some Reflections on Rational Beliefs

Chapter Seven   101

The Use of Chaining in REBT

Chapter Eight   107

The Intricacies of Inference Chaining

Chapter Nine   119

When Laddering and the Downward Arrow can be used
as Adjuncts to Inference Chaining in REBT Assessment

Chapter Ten   129

Further Methods of Identifying the Critical A

Chapter Eleven   145

Blundering into Disputing: The Perils of Inadequate Assessment,
Overzealousness and Insensitivity

Chapter Twelve   161

Structured Disputing of Irrational Beliefs

Index   175

Preface

At first blush, Rational Emotive Behaviour Therapy (REBT) appears simple to practise. Its well-known model of emotional disturbance and change, ABCDE, describes a clear, direct and uncluttered approach to therapy: find a problem at A, discover the individual's rigid beliefs (B) about this problem which, in turn, lead to her disturbed emotional reactions at C, dispute (D) these disturbance-creating beliefs in order to develop a new and effective (E) philosophy of living. No wonder that some REBT students think that REBT will be a therapy that is easy to absorb and implement. However, we would argue that REBT is deceptively simple. The easy progression implied by the model belies the often extremely difficult tasks that the therapist has to execute in each component of the model in order to facilitate this progression. For example, if a client's presenting problem is 'my whole life', the therapist has to help the client translate this amorphous problem into a specific one and then link it to goals that are behavioural, measurable and observable. In REBT terms, asking for a problem is certainly not the same thing as understanding it.

Some commentators have criticised the ABC model for its simplicity both as a scientific theory (Eschenroeder, 1982) and in detailing the complexities of human behaviour (Ziegler, 1989). Though Albert Ellis, the founder of REBT, and the other REBTers have been revising and adding to the model since the 1950s, he agrees that the ABC model is 'oversimplified and omits salient information about human disturbance and its treatment' (Ellis, 1985, p. 313). Elsewhere, Ellis (1991, 1993, p. 3) strikes a balance between simplicity and complexity in his assessment of REBT: 'The ABCs of rational emotive [behaviour] therapy seem to be very simple and can easily be explained to disturbed people who want to help themselves, but they are exceptionally interactional and therefore in many ways complex.'

For this book, we have decided to opt for complexity in detailing some of the advances in REBT theory and practice. This decision is not to deter would-be readers interested in this therapeutic approach, disillusion novice REBTers or elevate ourselves above our readership, but to do justice to a system of psychotherapy that is both sophisticated and efficient in tackling emotional disturbance. We also hope to provide further proof that REBT is not about turning out REBT clones or neglecting clients' feelings in favour of an exclusive focus on their thinking (for rebuttals of these and other criticisms, see Dryden, Gordon and Neenan, 1997). In this book, then, we consider some of the complexities of REBT that are inevitably created by continual refinement and revision of its conceptual and clinical domains.

In Chapter 1, we provide an overview of REBT so that readers can grasp some of the main features of its theory and practice as well as commenting on its current empirical status. This chapter supplies a framework for the complexities that follow. Chapter 2 describes REBT's complex 40-year development from being a pioneering form of cognitive–behavioural therapy (CBT) in 1955, through evolution of its theory and clinical interventions, to its present-day trend as an integrative therapy. We also speculate on possible future directions REBT might pursue. Given REBT's view of largely self-induced emotional disturbance, Chapter 3 argues that individuals have a significant amount of free will which allows them to choose their reaction to any given situation. As the dialogues show, convincing clients that they have some freedom of choice and their behaviour is not totally constrained by biological, environmental, cultural, etc., factors can be a lengthy and complex procedure in therapy.

In Chapters 4 and 5, we explore and elaborate on the two major forms of psychological disturbance: ego disturbance and discomfort disturbance/low frustration tolerance (LFT). Chapter 4 details the many forms of self-depreciation in ego disturbance and cautions REBTers not to push their self-downing clients into the catch-all category of 'shithood', i.e. no matter what clients call themselves it is synonymous with labelling themselves as 'shits'. It is important to use the client's term of self-depreciation throughout therapy. We explore how these self-damning beliefs are activated in negative interpersonal contexts and the compensatory strategies individuals employ to restore a positive self-image. Chapter 5 considers the concepts of discomfort disturbance and LFT and argues that these terms are too narrow in accounting for the complex category that we call 'non-ego disturbance'. Over 40 types of such disturbance are identified and briefly explored. While much attention has been given to irrational beliefs in REBT theory, the concept of rational beliefs has been comparatively neglected. In Chapter 6, we redress this imbalance and consider the complexities of rational beliefs which are the cornerstone of psychological health in REBT theory.

The process of linking or chaining cognitions and/or emotions and sometimes behaviours in order to represent the interconnectedness and frequent complexity of clients' presenting problems is examined in Chapter 7. Several types of chains are discussed. One of these, an inference chain, is analysed in Chapter 8. The aim of inference chaining is to locate the most clinically relevant part of the client's presenting problem (also known as the critical A). This can be an exceedingly difficult task for the therapist and we chart the false starts, mistakes, detours and premature termination of the chain before unravelling it for the reader. Chapter 9 continues to explore inference chaining and how the use of techniques from other therapies can assist when chaining grinds to a halt or begins to lose its clinical direction. Other methods for uncovering the critical A are outlined in Chapter 10 including asking the client to relive the problem or experience in therapy and 'taking a wild guess' as to what she is most upset about with regard to her presenting difficulties.

Musts and shoulds in REBT can lead novice therapists into a morass of meanings: which ones are harmless, pathological or irrelevant to therapy? Which ones to dispute? Without a proper assessment of the meaning of such words, blunders inevitably occur. This is the subject of Chapter 11 and includes ways to avoid or minimise such blunders. We also urge therapists not to ram REBT down clients' throats (clients do not *have* to accept its tenets) and that sensitivity in therapy is important in REBT as elsewhere if progress is to be made. Finally, in Chapter 12, we outline a structured approach to disputing irrational beliefs. Building on DiGiuseppe's (1991) seminal work on disputing, we elaborate on this central therapeutic activity in REBT practice. In particular, we compare the value of questioning irrational beliefs and rational beliefs consecutively with questioning them concurrently.

In conclusion, a complex subject does not have to be treated in a complex manner; to do so usually reveals a failure of imagination in how to reach a wider readership or an intellectual arrogance to exclude it. We hope that in this book we have displayed some imagination and avoided arrogance in order to present these complicated areas of REBT in a lucid and informative way.

References

DiGiuseppe, R. (1991). Comprehensive cognitive disputing in RET. In: M. E. Bernard (Ed), Using Rational–Emotive Therapy Effectively. New York: Plenum Press.

Dryden, W., Gordon, J. & Neenan, M. (1997). What is Rational Emotive Behaviour Therapy? A Personal and Practical Guide, 2nd edition. Loughton, Essex: Gale Centre Publications.

Ellis, A. (1985). Expanding the ABC's of rational-emotive therapy. In: M. Mahoney & A. Freeman (Eds), Cognition and Psychotherapy. New York: Plenum Press.

Ellis, A. (1991). The revised ABC's of rational-emotive therapy (RET). Journal of Rational–Emotive & Cognitive–Behaviour Therapy, 9, 139–72.

Ellis, A. (1993). Fundamentals of rational-emotive therapy for the 1990s. In: W. Dryden & L. K. Hill (Eds), Innovations in Rational–Emotive Therapy. London: Sage Publications.

Eschenroeder, C. (1982). How rational is rational–emotive therapy? A critical appraisal of its theoretical foundations and therapeutic methods. Cognitive Therapy and Research, 6, 381–92.

Ziegler, D. J. (1989). A critique of rational-emotive theory of personality. In: M.E. Bernard & R. DiGiuseppe (Eds), Inside Rational–Emotive Therapy: A Critical Appraisal of the Theory and Therapy of Albert Ellis. San Diego, CA: Academic Press.

Acknowledgements

We wish to thank the following for granting permission to reprint material in this book: Counselling, the Journal of the British Association for Counselling (Chapter 1), Journal of Rational–Emotive and Cognitive–Behaviour Therapy (Chapters 7 and 8) and Sage Publications (Chapter 2).

Chapter One
Rational Emotive Behaviour Therapy (REBT): An Overview

Background

Rational emotive behaviour therapy (REBT) was founded in 1955 by an American clinical psychologist, Albert Ellis. Ellis (1994) originally practised as a psychoanalyst but became increasingly disenchanted with this approach as he considered it to be long-winded, time-consuming, anti-scientific, needlessly passive and fundamentally wrong in its view that present emotional problems have their roots in early childhood experiences. Having abandoned psychoanalysis in 1953, Ellis, now calling himself a 'psychotherapist', experimented with active-directive approaches to therapy informed by his abiding interest in philosophy, particularly the Stoics, Epictetus and Marcus Aurelius. It is a quote from Epictetus that forms the cornerstone of REBT: 'People are disturbed not by things, but by the views which they take of them.' In other words, emotional distress is largely determined by our perceptions, meanings and evaluations of events rather than by the events themselves. REBT is primarily concerned with how individuals maintain their problems through their belief systems, rather than how these problems were acquired. Since its inception, REBT (called rational-emotive therapy until 1993) has evolved into a sophisticated model of psychotherapy and is one of the leading approaches within the cognitive–behavioural movement.

Basic theory

REBT sets out a primarily cognitively orientated theory of emotions through its ABCDE model of emotional disturbance and its amelioration (Ellis and Dryden, 1987). In the model:

A = activating events (actual or inferred; past, present or future occurrences; internal or external;

B = evaluative beliefs which mediate the individual's view of these events;

C = emotional and behavioural consequences largely determined by the
   individual's beliefs about these events;
D = disputing disturbance-producing ideas, particularly irrational beliefs;
E = a new and effective rational outlook.

REBT hypothesises that rigid and absolute beliefs in the form of musts,
shoulds, have tos, got tos, oughts are usually to be found at the core of
emotional disturbance, e.g. the anxiety-inducing belief 'I must never make
a mistake otherwise I'm pathetic'. Flowing from these primary musts,
shoulds, etc. are three major derivatives: awfulising–defining negative
events as so terrible that they cannot be comprehended within a human
and therefore realistic scale of grimness; low frustration tolerance (LFT)–
the perceived inability to endure discomfort or frustration in one's life and
to envisage any happiness while such conditions exist; damnation of self
or others–assigning a global negative evaluation to one-self and/or others
based on a particular action or trait as in the above example. These rigid
beliefs are called irrational (self-defeating) because they are illogical,
unrealistic, block or interfere with individuals realising their goals for
change and generate a good deal of emotional disturbance. By forcefully
and persistently disputing these distress-inducing ideas through a variety
of multi-modal (cognitive, behavioural, emotive, imaginal) methods a
rational and effective philosophy of living can be internalised.

Beliefs based on flexible preferences, wishes, wants, desires are seen as
rational (self-helping) because they are logical, realistic, aid goal-attain-
ment and usually reduce the individual's specific or general level of
emotional disturbability, e.g. the concern-producing belief 'I would greatly
prefer not to make a mistake, but there is no reason why I must not do so.
If I do make one, I can acknowledge the mistake without condemning
myself on the basis of it.' Flowing from these primary preferences, wishes,
etc., are three major derivatives and constructive alternatives to the above:
anti-awfulising–negative events are evaluated along a continuum of
badness that lies within the realm of rational comprehension; high frustration tolerance–the ability to tolerate or withstand a great deal of difficulty
or discomfort in one's life and still achieve some measure of happiness or
stability; acceptance of self and others–human beings are seen as fallible
and in a state of flux, therefore it is futile to assign to them a single, global
rating (though they can rate their individual traits or actions if they so
choose).

Two types of disturbance

REBT posits two types of emotional disturbance that underpin most, if not
all, neurotic problems: ego and discomfort (Ellis, 1979a, 1980). The
former type relates to demands made upon oneself, others or the world,
and the resulting self-depreciation when these demands are not met, e.g.

'As I can't have your love, which I must have, this means I'm no good.' The latter type involves demands made upon oneself, others or the world that comfortable life conditions must exist and the consequent frustration when they do not, e.g. 'I can't stand any longer this turmoil in my life. It shouldn't be this way!' Ego and discomfort disturbance are discrete categories but frequently overlap in emotional distress as when, for example, a man berates himself as weak for being unable to cope with a stressful work environment.

Constructing an emotional vocabulary

Dryden (1995) suggests that emotional reactions to adverse life events can be divided into unhealthy and healthy negative feelings with their cognitive correlates of, respectively, demands and preferences (see Table 1). This is not meant to be prescriptive in the sense of telling clients how to feel but a means of establishing which emotions may require therapeutic attention in order to alleviate the client's suffering, e.g. focusing on a woman's prolonged damning anger and depression over being rejected by her partner rather than on her non-damning anger at queue-jumpers. Transforming unhealthy negative emotions into healthy ones through attitudinal change can help individuals to bear what they perceive to be unbearable and thereby help them to adapt constructively to harsh or grim reality.

Table 1 A Vocabulary of Unhealthy and Healthy Negative Emotions

Unhealthy	Healthy
Anxiety	Concern
Depression	Sadness
Guilt	Remorse
Shame	Regret
Hurt	Disappointment
Damning anger	Non-damning anger
Jealousy	Concern about one's relationship
Envy (malicious)	Non-malicious desire to possess another's advantages

Practice

REBT therapists teach clients two forms of responsibility: (1) emotional–that they largely construct their emotional disturbance which they may blame on others for causing; and (2) therapeutic–that in order to overcome their problems they need to carry out a variety of tasks often on a lifelong basis if they wish to maintain their therapeutic gains (Dryden and Neenan, 1995). In order to help clients absorb these responsibilities, REBTers use an active-directive approach that sorts out clients' presenting problems into their ABC components and which includes encouraging them to move away from A–C thinking (e.g. 'He makes me anxious') to embracing B–C thinking (e.g. 'How do I make myself anxious about him?'). Such a paradigmatic shift in understanding emotional causation can come as a shock to some clients as well as act as a major reason for them to terminate therapy prematurely. The following case example illustrates some of the steps in the REBT counselling sequence.

Early problem-solving focus

While REBT therapists pay attention to developing a therapeutic alliance through warmth, empathy and unconditional acceptance of their clients, they also wish to encourage them to start tackling their problems as quickly as possible. This can often engender a sense of empowerment as clients bring clarity to chaos, order to confusion. In the following interchange we show how the REBT therapist helps the client to do this:

Therapist: Which problem would you like to start with?

Client: I get knots in my stomach every time I have to do any public speaking.

Therapist: Can you describe a specific example?

(REBT therapists argue that analysing specific examples helps clients to be clear about self-defeating emotions and behaviours and the irrational beliefs that underpin them).

Client: Yes, I had to give a presentation to some senior managers and my stomach was churning, heart racing, my head was spinning...that sort of thing. I felt physically sick. I don't know how I got through it. It's always the same.

Therapist: So you were highly anxious, bordering on panic.

(Early on in the therapeutic process REBTers help their clients to identify their unhealthy negative emotions).

Client: Exactly.

Therapist: Do all of your colleagues experience similar anxiety when they give presentations?

Client: A few do but most of them don't. Some of them are as cool as a cucumber. That's how I want to be, if possible.

Therapist: We can say then that it isn't the talks themselves that make you anxious otherwise all your colleagues would be, but some ideas that you bring to these talks themselves that really are the culprits. Would you agree with this assessment?

(Here the REBT therapist helps the client to understand that it is not A–i.e. giving a talk–that determines his anxiety, but the beliefs he holds about giving the talk at A.)

Client: Yes, I would but I don't know what these ideas are. My panic just seems to descend upon me and I can't do anything about it.

Therapist: Well, let's find out what's going on.

What is the client most disturbed about and how to start dealing with it?

At the core of the client's anxiety is, REBT hypothesises, a rigid and unqualified irrational (self-defeating) belief in the form of a must or should. At this stage of the assessment the therapist is unclear as to what the client is most disturbed about at A (known as the critical A) and seeks to elicit it through a process known as inference chaining, i.e. linking the client's personally significant assumptions about giving presentations. This process combines speed with depth in moving the client from the periphery to the centre of his anxiety by encouraging him to assume the worst:

Therapist: Now close your eyes and imagine standing in front of your senior managers. How are you feeling?

Client: Very anxious!

Therapist: Now what is anxiety-provoking in your mind about giving the presentation?

(Here the therapist initiates the inference chain).

Client: I might make a mistake.

Therapist: Let's assume that you do. Then what?

(In inference chaining, the therapist does not challenge the client's inference; rather she uses it to go deeper into the chain).

Client: They might think I'm incompetent.

Therapist: And if they do...?

Client: (starting to panic) Oh! God. I can see them rejecting me.

(This seems like the critical A because the client begins to panic).

Therapist: So you are standing there alone and rejected. What's going through your mind at that very moment?

Client: I'm totally unlikable, useless, no one wants me. I might as well kill myself.

Therapist: Okay, open your eyes now. Out of those things that you fear might happen to you, which is the most fearful?

(Here the therapist double checks with the client concerning the nature of the critical A).

Client: That I'll lose their approval and end up worthless.

Therapist: In their eyes or yours?

Client: Ultimately mine. But none of this has happened yet.

Therapist: But it might do and that's what drives you to anxiety.

At this point the therapist might contrast, among other options, the emotional and behavioural outcomes of a philosophy based on demands with one based on preferences and ask the client which one is present in his thinking:

Therapist: What do you think you are demanding at this point?

Client: I'm demanding that I must have their approval otherwise I'll see myself as worthless.

(Having identified the critical A, the therapist helps the client to identify his major demand about this A).

Therapist: Now if you want to be, as you said earlier, 'as cool as a cucumber' when you give these presentations, what do you need to change?

Client: That rigid belief of mine. It hasn't done me much good over the years.

Therapist: Well, we'll do something about that through a variety of disputing methods which will encourage you to examine this belief in great detail. Now let me start by asking you how, in your mind, does losing their approval through a poor presentation make you worthless?

(Here the therapist begins to dispute the client's self-downing derivative from his demand).

Client: I've always been like that – looking to others to make me feel good about myself.

Therapist: Okay, so you've subscribed to this belief for a long time. In REBT, we believe it is more important to focus on how the belief is being maintained rather than how it was originally acquired in order to start dismantling it as soon as possible. So let me ask you again, how are you a worthless person because you've lost their approval?

Client: Well, no one wants to be disliked, do they?

(In disputing, it often happens that the client responds to a question about his irrational belief with the evidence in favour of his rational belief. The therapist notes this and then returns to the original enquiry).

Therapist: Probably not, but not every person condemns him- or herself on the basis of being disliked by others. You're giving power to others, whether they know it or not, to control your feelings rather than you controlling them.

Client: But I can't seem to have faith in myself that I'm still okay if others reject me. I've nothing inside of me to fall back on.

Therapist: That's because self-esteem, which REBT sees as based on conditional self-worth, often vanishes when things go wrong or people reject us, whereas unconditional self-acceptance, which I want to teach you, is an enduring means of support irrespective of how others are treating you and is always something 'to fall back on' as well as the basis for addressing the problems in your life.

(In disputing clients' irrational beliefs, REBTers often use a blend of Socratic questions – which the therapist in this interchange began with – and short didactic explanations about rational concepts as in the above therapist response).

Client: I can see how that would be a better way but I don't think I could ever be like that. I'm too set in my ways.

Therapist: That may be true, but shall we put it to the test and review the situation after six sessions?

Client: Okay, I'll give it a try.

The therapist outlines some of the potential problems involved in the process of change, such as feeling strange or unnatural as individuals start to undergo personality change – called the 'I'm not me' syndrome or cognitive–emotive dissonance (Grieger and Boyd, 1980), –and a major reason why some clients may drop out of therapy at this point. Also that sustained hard work and practice will be needed to effect such change and can trigger low frustration tolerance (LFT) beliefs, e.g. 'Change is too hard, as it must not be, and I can't stand it!' Ellis (1979b) advises clients that force and energy rather than milk-and-water methods are usually required to remove irrational ideas and internalise rational ones. This can be difficult for clients to achieve who believe that they have to go very slowly in tackling their problems and therefore may actually reinforce their emotional disturbance, e.g. 'I'm so fragile I have to go at this pace'.

At the end of the first session, as at the end of every session, homework tasks (or whatever term the client prefers to use) are negotiated with the client in order for him to practise strengthening his rational beliefs and weakening his irrational ones and thus developing both competence and confidence in facing his problems as well as minimising the potential for him to become dependent upon the therapist. The therapist is also alert to the client seeking her approval which, when it occurred, she challenged and placed within the context of his presenting problems. The therapist elicits sessional feedback from the client to determine which aspects of counselling he finds both helpful and unhelpful. This will assist her to tailor therapy to his requirements, but not if the client's suggestions appear to exacerbate his psychological problems, e.g. the client seeks continual reassurance that the therapist likes him.

Course of therapy

In striving for unconditional self-acceptance as a fallible human being, the client found the following methods instrumental in realising this goal. Bibliotherapy – reading self-help literature such as Paul Hauck's *Why Be Afraid?* (1981) and *Hold Your Head Up High* (1991).

Imagery – e.g. feeling highly anxious as he imagines being rejected for giving a poor presentation and then, with no alteration of details, feeling concerned about what has occurred but without rejecting himself. Behavioural – such as giving as many presentations as possible in order to habituate himself to the discomfort involved in carrying them out, as well as developing his public speaking skills. Emotive – principally, shame-attacking exercises (Ellis, 1969) in which he acts in a 'shameful' way (e.g. taking an imaginary dog for a walk) in order to invite public ridicule, criticism or disapproval and distinguish between condemning an action but refraining from condemning himself on the basis of it. Such exercises helped him to remove the 'horror' (emotional disturbance) of losing others' approval. All these methods were used in the service of cognitive change as the client repeatedly and forcefully chipped away at his irrational ideas.

The client's approval needs were present in other areas of his life (e.g. with his partner, friends, neighbours) and tackling his core belief enabled these other problem areas eventually to be addressed concurrently rather than consecutively. The client stayed beyond the agreed six sessions and actually attended for 12. At the end of therapy, his anxiety had greatly reduced because he was striving to be much more self-accepting in the face of potential or actual rejection. Practical benefits experienced in developing a rational outlook included delivering presentations in a highly competent manner as he was much less afflicted by performance-diminishing anxiety.

At the follow-up appointments (three, six and twelve months), he said he felt a greater sense of autonomy in his life which enabled him to take hitherto avoided risks, such as seeking promotion and leaving his unsatisfactory relationship. He realised that maintaining and deepening his therapeutic gains would be a lifelong commitment which would continue to include relapses but 'using the ABCDE of REBT usually gets my life back on the rails again'. The client had become his own therapist, which is the ultimate aim of REBT.

Applications of REBT

Ellis and his colleagues have produced many books on REBT including a growing number on its clinical application to specific emotional and behavioural problems such as substance abuse (Ellis, et al., 1988), anxiety (Warren and Zgourides, 1991), and those experienced in childhood and adolescence (Ellis and Bernard, 1983; Bernard and Joyce, 1984). REBT is applied in various treatment modalities: individuals (Dryden and Yankura, 1993), couples (Ellis, et al., 1989), and families (Huber and Baruth, 1989). REBT is used non-clinically in business and industry where the word 'therapy' is dropped and the 'focus in [industrial] training is always on the relation of self-defeating thinking to low productivity, not on irrationality and emotional consequences' (DiMattia, 1991, p. 309).

Research findings

Silverman, McCarthy and McGovern (1992) in a review of 89 outcome studies of REBT carried out between 1982 and 1989 supported earlier research (DiGiuseppe and Miller, 1977; McGovern and Silverman, 1984) that REBT 'has constantly verified its role as an efficacious therapy applicable in a variety of problem situations' (p.169). However, a number of conceptual and methodological flaws in REBT research need to be addressed if REBT is to improve its scientific status as an empirically based psychotherapeutic approach. This task is underway as REBT seeks responsible criticism, both from within and without, in order to increase its therapeutic efficacy (Kendall, et al., 1995).

References

Bernard, M E. and Joyce, M. R. (1984). Rational–Emotive Therapy with Children and Adolescents. New York: Wiley.

DiGiuseppe, R. A. and Miller, N. J. (1977). 'A review of outcome studies on rational-emotive therapy' in A. Ellis and R. Grieger (Eds). Handbook of Rational-Emotive Therapy, New York: Springer.

DiMattia, D. J. (1991). Using RET effectively in the workplace in M. E. Bernard (Ed). Using Rational-Emotive Therapy Effectively: A Practitioner's Guide (pp. 303–17), New York: Plenum Press.

Dryden, W. (1995). Preparing for Client Change in Rational Emotive Behaviour Therapy, London: Whurr.

Dryden, W. and Neenan, M. (1995) Dictionary of Rational Emotive Therapy, London: Whurr.

Dryden, W. and Yankura, J. (1993) Counselling Individuals: A Rational-Emotive Handbook, 2nd edn, London: Whurr.

Ellis, A. (1969) Suggested Procedures for a Weekend of Rational Encounter, New York: Institute for Rational-Emotive Therapy.

Ellis, A. (1979a) 'Discomfort anxiety: a new cognitive-behavioural construct'. Part 1, Rational Living, 14, 2, pp. 3–8.

Ellis, A. (1979b) 'The issue of force and energy in behaviour change', Journal of Contemporary Psychotherapy, 10, pp. 83–97.

Ellis, A. (1980) 'Discomfort anxiety: a new cognitive-behavioural construct', Part 2, Rational Living, 15, 1, pp. 25–30.

Ellis, A. (1994) Reason and Emotion in Psychotherapy, 2nd Edn, New York: Carol Publishing.

Ellis, A. and Bernard, M. E. (Eds) (1983) Rational-Emotive Approaches to the Problems of Childhood, New York: Plenum Press.

Ellis, A. and Dryden, W. (1987) The Practice of Rational-Emotive Therapy, New York: Springer.

Ellis, A., McInerney, J. F., DiGiuseppe, R. and Yeager, R. J. (1988) Rational-Emotive Therapy with Alcoholics and Substance Abusers, New York: Pergamon Press.

Ellis A., Sichel, J. L., Yeager R. J., DiMattia, D. J. and DiGiuseppe, R. (1989) Rational-Emotive Couples Therapy, New York: Pergamon Press.

Grieger, R. and Boyd, J. (1980) Rational-Emotive Therapy: A Skills-Based Approach, New York: Van Nostrand Reinhold.

Hauck, P. (1981) Why Be Afraid? London: Sheldon Press.

Hauck, P. (1991) Hold Your Head Up High, London: Sheldon Press

Huber, C and Baruth, L. (1989) Rational-Emotive Family Therapy: A Systems Perspective, New York: Springer.

Kendall, P. C., Haaga, D., Ellis, A., Bernard, M. E., DiGiuseppe, R. and Kassinove, H. (1995) 'Rational-emotive therapy in the 1990s and beyond: current status, recent revisions, and research questions', Clinical Psychology Review, 15, pp. 169-86.

McGovern, T. and Silverman, M. (1984) 'A review of outcome studies on rational-emotive therapy' Journal of Rational-Emotive Therapy, 2, pp. 7-18.

Silverman, M. S., McCarthy, M. and McGovern, T. (1992) 'A review of outcome studies of rational-emotive therapy from 1982–1989', Journal of Rational-Emotive and Cognitive-Behaviour Therapy, 10, 3, pp. 111-86.

Warren, R. and Zgourides, G. (1991) Anxiety Disorders: A Rational-Emotive Perspective, New York: Pergamon Press.

Chapter Two
Trends in REBT: 1955–95

Rational emotive behaviour therapy (REBT) is a system of psychotherapy that teaches individuals how their belief systems largely determine their emotional and behavioural reactions to life events (Ellis and Bernard, 1985). More specifically, it is rigid, unrealistic, and absolute beliefs couched in the form of musts, shoulds, have tos, got tos, oughts, which lie at the core of emotional and behavioural disturbance, e.g. the depression-inducing belief, 'I must have the love of my partner otherwise I will be worthless'. Such beliefs are targeted for challenge and change through a variety of multimodal methods (cognitive, emotive, behavioural and imaginal) in order to develop a rational philosophy of living based on preferences and desires. REBT hypothesises that a preferential belief system is more likely to produce emotional stability and constructive behaviour that will aid goal attainment than a belief system based on dogmatic demands.

Albert Ellis, an American clinical psychologist, originally practised as a liberal psychoanalyst but became increasingly disillusioned with what he regarded as the inefficiency and ineffectiveness of this discipline in tackling emotional disturbance, as well as with his own inability to make its tenets more scientifically based. After experimenting with different therapeutic methods, he launched REBT in 1955 as a mixture of philo-sophical insight and behaviour therapy. This chapter examines some of the trends that have shaped the development of REBT over the last 40 years.

Rational therapy: 1955–61

REBT was originally called rational therapy (RT) to emphasise its use of reason and the intellect in combating emotional distress. (Ellis later came to regret the use of the term 'rational' because it suggested to people that he was advocating cognition to the exclusion of affect.) As the originator of the first of the cognitive or cognitive-behaviour therapies (Ellis, 1994a), Ellis went back to a first-century Stoic philosopher, Epictetus, to provide the major underpinning of his new approach: 'People are disturbed not by

11

things, but by the views which they take of them.' Such an outlook clearly placed primary responsibility on individuals for their emotional disturbance rather than on early childhood influences (psychoanalysis) or environmental conditioning (behaviourism). Ellis developed an active-directive, confrontational style in attacking the illogical and unrealistic aspects of clients' belief systems and therefore eschewed the passive, non-directive approaches of psychoanalysis and Carl Rogers's client-centred therapy.

Clients were urged to adopt a scientific approach to tackling their problems by being open-minded and flexible in searching for evidence to confirm or disconfirm their beliefs and to treat their beliefs as hypotheses about reality rather than as grounded in fact. Ellis (1958a) distinguished between two types of belief: irrational ones were usually rigid, disturbance-producing, and goal-blocking; rational ones were more likely to be adaptable, disturbance-reducing, and goal-oriented. At this stage of REBT's development, Ellis did not 'fully realise that neurotic beliefs include explicit or implicit absolutist musts or demands' (1994a, p. 17) and therefore advanced 11 irrational ideas (e.g. the idea that it is awful and catastrophic when things are not the way one would very much like them to be) as the major source of neurosis. In the 1970s, these ideas would be subsumed within three musturbatory (musts) categories. As well as bifurcating beliefs into rational and irrational, Ellis (1958a) also divided emotions into disturbed or self-defeating (e.g. anger, depression) and non-disturbed or self-helping (annoyance, sadness) states. Emotions were designated in this fashion if they, respectively, blocked or aided people's goal-seeking behaviour. The use of reason for personal problem-solving was not meant, as some critics believed, to remove all human emotions because 'many kinds of negative emotions (e.g. sorrow, regret) are perfectly legitimate reactions to deprivation and frustration' (Ellis et al., 1960, p. 16). REBT never encouraged or encourages clients to feel passive, apathetic or emotionless in the face of adverse life events. In *Reason and Emotion in Psychotherapy* (1962), Ellis began to describe affective states as appropriate or inappropriate negative emotions. For over 30 years, Ellis adhered to this appropriate vs. inappropriate division before adopting in 1994 Dryden's (1990) taxonomy of unhealthy and healthy negative emotions.

Ellis (1958a; Ellis et al., 1960) offered to his clients a relatively simple model of the development and maintenance of emotional disturbance, ABC: A represents the activating event which is mediated by irrational beliefs at B which, in turn, largely create emotional and behavioural consequences at C. (In the early 1970s, D for disputing in order to create a new and effective philosophy at E would be added to the ABCs.) As humans have the ability to think about their thinking, the model also demonstrates how they frequently develop secondary and/or tertiary emotional disturbances about their primary ones (e.g. anxiety about becoming depressed;

ashamed of feeling anxious about being anxious) and thereby block or make it more difficult for themselves to work on these primary issues. In 1962 Ellis stressed the importance of routinely searching for these second- and third-order problems during assessment but stressed it even more later (Ellis, 1994a).

From the outset, REBT emphasised its humanistic and existential aspects, which included placing rationality in the service of achieving human happiness; favouring long-range rather than short-range hedonism to achieve a healthy balance between the pleasures of the moment and realising long-term goals; stressing that humans have considerable, but not total, free will and choice in determining how they live their lives; assuming that humans are neither superhuman nor subhuman but fallible and can choose to accept themselves as worthwhile simply because they exist and not because of any external achievements. However, this concept of self-acceptance was still a measurement of sorts (e.g. an individual can say she is worthless because she is alive) and therefore conditional. Ellis (1971, 1973a) would later remove this pitfall and emphasise uncondi- tional self-acceptance.

During this period, Ellis was still prone to accept the psychoanalytic view that an individual's fallacious and disturbance-creating ideas were instilled by his parents and the wider society and he then kept reindoctri- nating himself with them. Even though he emphasised human's biological predisposition to crooked thinking, Ellis did not fully develop this viewpoint until later decades when he hypothesised that our innate ability to disturb ourselves about familial and societal ideas is the real culprit rather than the ideas themselves (Ellis, 1976a, 1978a). In subsequent years REBT would largely concentrate on the perpetuation rather than the acquisition of emotional disturbance.

From the inception of REBT, Ellis sought to tackle a wide range of emotional disorders and offer his new therapeutic approach to the general public (as opposed to Beck's cognitive therapy, founded in the early 1960s, which initially focused on depression within a clinical setting). Some of his early titles aimed at a public audience include *How to Live with a Neurotic* (1957) and (with Robert Harper) *A Guide to Rational Living in an Irrational World* (1961). In 1959 Ellis founded the Institute for Rational Living (located in his own apartment), 'dedicated to treating and educating the public in Rational Therapy' (Wiener, 1988, p. 96). As well as originating and promulgating REBT, Ellis continued his career as a pioneering and outspoken sex therapist whose books on this subject, from the mid-1950s onwards, contained REBT principles and practices; these include *Sex without Guilt* (1958b) and *The Art and Science of Love* (1960). This aspect of Ellis's work diminished in the early 1980s.

Some critics of this new therapeutic approach accused it of ignoring emotions and behaviour as vehicles for constructive change in its 'narrow' concerns with only thought processes; others saw it as a form of rationalism (the philosophical view that knowledge of the world is obtained through reason alone). Both groups of critics were mistaken because REBT 'always had very strong evocative-emotive and behavioural components and from the start favoured activity-oriented, therapeutic homework assignments, *in vivo* desentisization, and skill training' (Ellis and Bernard, 1985, p. 2). In order to try and avoid this confusion and convey more accurately his therapeutic method, Ellis in 1961 changed rational therapy's name to rational-emotive therapy (RET) because 'the term implies, as the theory of rational-emotive psychotherapy holds, that human thinking and emotions are, in some of their essences, the same thing, and that by changing the former one does change the latter' (Ellis, 1962, p. 122).

Rational-emotive therapy: 1961–93

The year 1962 was a milestone in REBT's development, with the publication of *Reason and Emotion in Psychotherapy* which pulled together and revised Ellis's earlier articles on REBT. This synthesis 'represented his first attempt to present his ideas on therapy in a systematic and comprehensive form, and can be considered an early classic with respect to modern cognitive-behavioural therapy' (Yankura and Dryden, 1994, p. 14). This book remains the main text for REBT practitioners (Ellis, 1994a) and, along with other REBT literature, 'led to the "cognitive revolution" in modern psychotherapy, which followed about 10 years after I started teaching REBT in 1955' (Ellis, 1994a p. xiii). *Reason and Emotion in Psychotherapy* also set down three major insights into human disturbance which ever since have provided clients with a concise account of REBT and act as a lifelong guide to emotional problem-solving. These insights are: (1) emotional disturbance is largely created by irrational ideas: we mainly feel the way we think; (2) we remain disturbed in the present because we continually reindoctrinate ourselves with these ideas; (3) the only enduring way to overcome our problems is through persistent hard work and practice – to think, feel and act against our irrational ideas. These insights were later augmented by other ways humans perpetuate their psychological problems, e.g. the process of change is too hard to undertake (low frustration tolerance); secondary emotional problems (e.g. shame) block individuals from tackling their primary ones (e.g. anxiety); individuals predict failure before carrying out a goal-directed task (self-fulfilling prophecy).

While REBT was gathering more adherents, both professional and public, Ellis continued to refine its theory and practice. An early paper on the differences between intellectual and emotional insight showed that understanding of one's problem is usually insufficient to effect deep-rooted change unless accompanied by vigorous and sustained action against one's irrational ideas; in this way, one can both think and feel the efficacy of newly acquired rational beliefs (Ellis, 1963a). In the same year, Ellis used the medium of film to demonstrate REBT by appearing in *Gloria*. Along with Carl Rogers and Fritz Perls, he sought to provide therapeutic help for the eponymous client. *Gloria* has generally not provided good publicity for REBT because of Ellis's 'aggressive' and overly intellectual style in the film. Later films demonstrate Ellis's much more relaxed therapeutic style and the use of a multimodal approach to tackling emotional problems; these films are a more accurate depiction of REBT in practice (Bernard, 1986). Ellis later judged *Gloria* as 'the worst session of recorded psychotherapy I ever had' (Palmer and Ellis, 1993, p.173). However, some counselling trainees and professionals still judge Ellis and REBT by what occurred over 30 years ago.

In 1965 Ellis moved the Institute out of his apartment and into a six-storey building in Manhattan. The building was now called the Institute for RET and has remained so ever since, despite RET's conversion to REBT in 1993. The Institute offers training programmes for mental health professionals, and workshops and courses for the general public including a Friday night workshop entitled 'Problems of Daily Living' (see Dryden and Backx, 1987). This workshop asks for volunteers from the audience to come on to the stage to discuss their problems with Ellis while the rest of the audience can absorb from this session REBT principles and practice to tackle their own problems. At the end of the session questions and discussion are invited from the audience. Such workshops underscored Ellis's belief that REBT was primarily a psychoeducational approach rather than a merely therapeutic one. Because of 'the ubiquity of emotional disturbance' (Ellis, 1980a, p. 10), Ellis hypothesises that a 'public education policy of disseminating some of the main elements of RE[B]T to the general populace would effect a great deal of prophylaxis and treatment of emotional ills' (Ellis, 1980a, p. 11). Indeed, Ellis has frequently suggested that the 'psychoeducational aspects of RE[B]T are more likely to be important in the future than the psychotherapeutic aspects. It [REBT] had better encourage public education and public acceptance of its principles and practices' quoted in Bernard, 1986, p.271).

In 1966 REBT set up its own journal, which was called *Rational Living* until 1983, when it changed its name to the *Journal of Rational-Emotive Therapy*; in 1988 it became the *Journal of Rational-Emotive and Cognitive Behaviour Therapy*. The journal 'seeks to provide a forum to stimulate research and discussion into the development and promulgation of Rational-Emotive Therapy (RET) and other forms of cognitive-behavioural therapy' (from the journal's statement of intent). Published by the Institute until 1984, in the following year it was taken over by Human Sciences Press but remains sponsored by the Institute for RET.

As well as seeking to educate emotionally the general public, Ellis (Ellis and Blum, 1967) also turned his attention to the workplace and advocated rational training as a method of helping 'people function more effectively in their work by actively teaching them certain basic principles of interpersonal relations which promote better self-understanding as well as increase insight into others'. The aim of rational training is to facilitate the development of more productive relations between management and labour. In the early 1970s, Ellis wrote a book for business executives, *Executive Leadership*, to show them how to deal effectively 'with the inanities and insanities of the organizational world' (1972a, p.15) and to discover how they sabotaged their potential effectiveness. Eventually the Institute for RET established its own corporate affairs division to introduce the concepts of REBT into management training as well as, more ambitiously, to influence corporate cultures. REBT – when used in industry it is commonly called rational effectiveness training – focuses 'always on the relation of self-defeating beliefs to low productivity, not on irrationality and emotional consequences' (DiMattia, 1991, p. 309). Using the word 'therapy' in training programmes usually deters more potential applicants than it attracts.

REBT has always been eager to increase its stock of therapeutic techniques to help clients undermine and remove their often tenaciously held self-defeating beliefs. While others still saw REBT as mainly a cognitive approach, Ellis, before and after 1962, was busily introducing emotive-evocative methods into his practice: these included imagery (Maultsby and Ellis, 1974), role-playing, forceful coping statements, forceful disputing, humour, unconditional acceptance of clients as fallible human beings but not always of their behaviour (Ellis,1965, 1973a), and his famous shame-attacking exercises (Ellis, 1969). These exercises encourage clients to act in a 'shameful' way (e.g. walking backwards down the street) in order to attract public ridicule or disapproval while at the same time learning to accept themselves for acting in such a manner. Behavioural methods added to REBT's armamentarium include exposure, *in vivo* desensitisation (rapid rather than gradual), rewards and penalties, skill training, and assertiveness training. REBT was developing into a truly multimodal approach to constructive change, in contrast to Ellis's declaration in *Reason and Emotion in Psychotherapy* that 'this book will one-sidedly emphasize the rational techniques, while admitting the possible efficacy of other legitimate means of affecting disordered human emotions' (1962, p.41).

REBT was increasing not only its range of techniques but also its therapeutic application. Influenced 'by the experiential and encounter movements of Will Schutz, Fritz Perls, and others', Ellis, in the late 1960s, 'incorporated some of their methods in individual and group sessions of REBT and, especially, in one- or two-day rational encounter marathons' (Ellis, 1994a, p.48). The aim of the marathon is twofold: 'first, to provide maximum encountering experiences for all the group members; and second, to include a good measure of cognitive and action-oriented group psychotherapy that is designed not only to help the participants feel better but also to get better' (Ellis and Dryden, 1987, p.180). The length of the marathon was eventually reduced from two days to a single day of 14 hours, as any longer did not produce any discernible benefits.

The 1970s

In *Reason and Emotion in Psychotherapy*, Ellis (1962) suggested that helping the parents of a disturbed child to become rational and problem focused was usually the best way to help the child. However, by the late 1960s he had become more optimistic about directly helping children to overcome their problems, and in 1970 he launched an ambitious project in emotional education and preventive psychotherapy, the Living School. This private school was located at the Institute for RET in New York and designed to teach ordinary schoolchildren the basic principles and practices of REBT alongside their normal academic curriculum. Such an emotional education programme, it was hypothesised, would help the children: 'if they work within this program for several years, they will have a significantly lesser chance of developing mild or severe personality maladjustment than they might otherwise commonly develop' (Ellis, 1973b). The school's teachers were supervised by REBT therapists. The experiment lasted only five years due to a high turnover rate as parents sent their children to bigger and better equipped schools–the Living School wanted to monitor the progress of the children from the first grade (6 years old) to the eighth. Such a turnover rate interfered with the long-term follow-up studies (also there was no control group to compare the children with), so the school was closed in 1975. REBT educational materials such as Ann Vernon's (1989) *Thinking, Feeling, Behaving* are used in more traditional American schools and there is nowadays a greater emphasis within REBT on working with children and adolescents in general (DiGiuseppe, 1977; Knaus, 1977; Knaus and Haberstroh, 1993).

REBT had always sought to teach clients self-acceptance rather than self-esteem, as the latter concept placed intrinsic worth on external achievement. However, as we noted previously in this chapter, Ellis's earlier formulation of self-acceptance still contained an element of self-measurement. This was finally eliminated when Ellis (1971, 1973a) advocated that clients should strive for unconditional self-acceptance, i.e. they should refuse to rate themselves in any way whatsoever, but only rate their specific traits, actions and performances. This kind of rating helps individuals to decide if particular traits or deeds aid or interfere with their goal-seeking behaviour. Unconditional self-acceptance became the 'elegant' solution (Ellis, 1976b) to the problem of self-worth as Ellis advises individuals to 'abolish most of what we normally call your human ego and retain those parts of it which you can empirically verify and fairly accurately define' (1976b, p. 6). The 'inelegant' solution to self-rating (if individuals were unable to achieve the elegant one) was to choose to rate themselves as good or worthwhile simply because they were human and alive. The elegant solution to human emotional disturbance remains one of the most difficult concepts for clients not only to understand but also to internalise.

REBT has long argued that its aim in therapy is not merely the removal of clients' presenting symptoms, but to effect a deep-seated change in their basic philosophies of living (Ellis, 1963b). To this end, REBT teaches clients not only how to feel better through amelioration of disturbed emotional states (e.g. depression, guilt) but also how to get better by identifying and removing the core disturbance-creating beliefs (Ellis, 1972b). Feeling better usually produces a palliative and short-term solution to clients' problems, while getting better frequently brings about a philosophical and enduring one. As we shall see later, therapies that only emphasise feeling better can be considered inefficient and potentially harmful.

Ellis (1973c) stresses that the REBT therapist is primarily a teacher who shows clients the ABCDE model of the acquisition, maintenance and eventual remediation of emotional disturbance. Such a process puts the therapist in the role of an authoritative (but not authoritarian) teacher, although some REBT therapists might demur at the thought of teachers making 'a forthright, unequivocal attack on his [client's] general and specific irrational ideas and to try to induce him to adopt more rational views' (Ellis, 1962, p. 94) and prefer an approach more subtle and less forceful than full-frontal assault. Although Ellis (1962, 1977a) argues that a vigorous and challenging active-directive approach to therapy rather than a passive, non-directive one is more likely to help clients overcome their problems, REBT therapists generally adopt an approach that suits their preferences and personality styles.

A notable addition in the 1970s to REBT's emotive-evocative methods was rational-emotive imagery (Maultsby and Ellis, 1974) which Ellis adapted from Maultsby. In Ellis's version, a client is asked, for example, to imagine vividly being rejected by his girlfriend and to let himself experience what he spontaneously feels (such as anger) and then really implode that emotion. Without changing any details of the imagined rejection, the client is then asked to feel only displeased at what is happening rather than angry about the rejection. When asked by the therapist how he accomplished this, the client ideally responds that he modified his disturbance-producing cognitions. Rational-emotive imagery 'can serve as an in-session demonstration to clients that they can exert control over their feelings, and that focusing on changing some aspect of their thinking represents the most effective and efficient way of doing so' (Yankura and Dryden, 1990, p. 16). This technique is frequently given to clients as a homework task.

One of the major philosophical influences on the development of REBT was the work of the general semanticists (e.g. Korzybski, 1993).

They considered the important ways in which language influences thought, which, in turn, affects emotions. The imprecise or careless use of language can lead to overgeneralisation, as when individuals equate themselves with an action, trait or event: e.g. 'I am a failure because I failed my driving test.' Known in general semantics as 'the is of identity', this form of linguistic inaccuracy would be changed by omitting the verb 'to be' and the preferred mode of expression might be, 'It is true that I failed my driving test but this fact does not make me a failure as a person.' The written form of this semantic position is called e-prime and during the 1970s Ellis wrote four books in this style (e.g. *Anger–How to Live With and Without It*, 1977a). According to Wessler and Wessler, 'while this practice underscored his position against global evaluations of anything, especially of the self, it proved to be an awkward mode of writing, and he later abandoned the practice. Although e-prime is a cumbersome mode of writing, and nearly impossible to speak, the basic notion remains an important feature of RE[B]T' (1980, p. 249).

Ellis originally created REBT on the basis of logical positivism, 'a modern view of science which was prevalent in the US and Europe in the 1950s' (Ellis, 1994a, p. 405). This doctrine argued that any statement or proposition would be excluded as meaningless if it was not directly verifiable: for example, it would be impossible to prove conclusively an individual's universal claim that 'I'm always going to be rejected in life'. Although REBT has always attempted to be scientifically minded in constructing its theories and monitoring its practice, Ellis eventually came to the conclusion 'that scientific statements are not empirically confirmable' (quoted in Jacobs, 1989, p. 184) and therefore abandoned logical positivism. Since 1976, 'it [REBT] is close to Popper's (1962, 1985) critical realism...which focuses on critically assessing theories and trying to learn by falsifying them rather than on striving for their "truth" or "validity"' (Ellis, 1993a, p. 10). In the above example, it only takes one instance where the individual is not rejected to falsify her claim and thus allow the therapist to start 'chipping away' at her irrational beliefs. The principle of falsifiability is also applied to her rational beliefs (wishes and desires): these are seen as self-helping and goal-oriented until the time experience and evidence suggest the opposite.

From the inception of REBT, Ellis has argued that human beings have a biologically rooted propensity towards crooked thinking and emotional disturbance (although in REBT's early phase, Ellis emphasised a largely environmentally based view of disturbance). This theory of biological predisposition to irrationality set REBT apart, then and now, from other major psychotherapeutic approaches which usually stress environmental conditioning or social learning theories. Accumulated clinical experience, among other factors, reinforced Ellis's biological view of disturbance and in a 1976 paper he presented evidence to support his hypothesis. This evidence includes the following: virtually all humans subscribe, at some time or another, to a greater or lesser degree, to some form of irrational thinking, e.g. the belief that people cannot be happy without love; no society or culture which has ever been studied is devoid of irrational beliefs; many of the self-defeating ideas that individuals hold run counter to the self-helping teachings of parents, peers, the mass media, etc., e.g. parents may teach their children to work hard to get ahead in life but instead of heeding this advice, some choose to pursue a downward path of apathy and idleness; just because individuals acknowledge that they adhere to dysfunctional beliefs and behaviours does not necessarily mean they will relinquish them, e.g. 'I know it is silly to think you can be a perfect human being but why not?'; people revert to self-destructive patterns of behaviour after working hard to give them up, e.g. alcoholism. Ellis also hypothesised that we have a second biologically based tendency to think rationally and therefore are able to examine our irrational ideas in order to counteract their influence on our lives.

Another important development in REBT that was not clearly seen and articulated until the 1970s was the centrality of the musts in emotional disturbance. Ellis (1994a) realised from the start of REBT that underneath clients' irrational ideas lay rigid musts and shoulds, e.g. 'If I don't do well at this task, as I absolutely must do, then I'm a complete failure', that seemed to create and maintain these irrational ideas. But, he says, he only saw this 'musturbatory' influence faintly and incompletely. When he compared REBT with Beck's cognitive therapy and its emphasis on automatic thoughts (distorted negative inferences) and illogical thinking but which accorded no particular significance to musts in mainly creating emotional disturbance, 'I [Ellis] clearly (and strongly) began to realise the primacy of people's Jehovian musts and saw how they usually underlay their other dysfunctional beliefs' (1994a,p xvii).

Ellis (1977b) eventually collapsed his 10 or so major irrational beliefs into three basic musturbatory categories: demands on self–'I must...'; demands on others – 'You must...'; demands on the world/life conditions – 'Life conditions must...'. Ellis suggests that what 'we normally call "emotional disturbance", "neurosis", or "mental illness", then, largely consists of demandingness – or what I now refer to as musturbation' (1977b, p. 27). From these basic musts flow three major derivatives (although these were not seen as logical deductions from the musts until the 1980s): awfulising – seeing events as worse than they could conceivably be; I can't-stand-it-itis (low frustration tolerance) – the perceived inability to tolerate discomfort in life; damnation – labelling oneself or others as worthless, useless, inadequate, etc. on the basis of failures and rejections in life. Derivatives play an important role in contributing to self-defeating emotions and behaviours, but REBT generally regards them as secondary and musts as primary in the creation of emotional disturbance.

In order for people to achieve a profound philosophical change in their lives (surrendering musturbatory thinking and replacing it with a preferential outlook), Ellis (1977b) advocated the logico-empirical method of scientific debate in challenging irrational beliefs and identifies several important steps in this. First, detecting – this refers to discovering one's disturbance-producing ideas, mainly in the form of rigid musts and shoulds; as Ellis's franglais has it: '*cherchez* [look for] *les* "musts", *cherchez les* "shoulds"'. Second, debating – this requires individuals to challenge their detected musts and shoulds to determine if they are logical, realistic and pragmatic (helpful) and discard them if they are not. Third, discriminating–this consists of distinguishing between irrational beliefs with their self-defeating consequences and rational beliefs with their self-helping nature. Fourth, defining – this refers to semantic precision in the use of language and the avoidance of disturbance-generating overgeneralisations. For example, 'Because I failed to get this job, I'll never get another one' is more accurately translated as, 'It is a fact that I didn't get this job but this certainly does not mean that I will never get another one.' Ellis (1979a) later devised a formal method of challenging self-defeating ideas known as DIBS (Disputing Irrational Beliefs) which uses forms to guide clients though the ABCDE model of emotional disturbance and its amelioration.

One of the major causes of human disturbance, Ellis (1977c) hypothesises, is individuals taking themselves and their ideas too seriously. An important means of undermining clients' irrational thinking is by poking fun at it (but not at the clients themselves). Humorous techniques include puns, witticisms, irony, slogans, reduction to absurdity of dysfunctional ideas, and paradoxical intention. Humour in therapy can help clients to, among other things, 'lighten the load' while still absorbing rational concepts; become more objective observers of how they disturb themselves and less liable to keep on repeating this process; build rapport with the therapist and thereby construct a productive working alliance. When humour is used it should be guided by a clinical rationale, not used for the purpose of the therapist's enjoyment. Humour should be omitted from therapy if the client objects to it. One of Ellis's (1977d) most famous comical interventions is his rational humorous songs. These are popular songs with lyrics rewritten in order to impart a self-helping philosophy of living or to attack a self-defeating one, e.g. 'Perfect Rationality' set to the tune of Luigi Denza's 'Finiculi Finicula'. The songs, like advertising jingles, are designed 'to repetitively go around and around in your patients' heads...and thereby to have their messages sink in and influence the person who sings them aloud or internally "hears" them' (Ellis and Abrahms, 1978, p. 147). The songs Ellis has rewritten are of a certain vintage, and REBT therapists may need to use modern songs for their younger clients.

Ellis (1962, 1973b) has long argued that a forceful and confrontational approach to therapy is usually the best means of promoting constructive change; the assumption in REBT is that those of its practitioners who have certain characteristics will produce better client outcomes than REBT therapists who lack them. Ellis (1978b) suggests what some of these characteristics might be including: the ability to work comfortably within a structured (but not inflexible) format; having a philosophical bent towards disputation and being scientifically minded in analysing the evidence for and against clients' beliefs; working generally in a strong active-directive manner in helping clients to tackle their problems; not needing the love or approval of clients, and fearing neither therapeutic failure nor taking calculated risks if impasses in therapy occur; working comfortably within a multimodal approach to therapy and not adhering rigidly to any one modality. Despite Ellis's preferred therapeutic approach, some REBT practitioners may lack some of the above characteristics or may modify REBT to suit their own personality traits, so 'whether such modification of the preferred practice of RE[B]T is effective is a question awaiting empirical enquiry' (Ellis and Dryden, 1987, p. 32).

While REBT has always implied a theory of personality originating from its theory of personality disturbance and change (Ellis, 1962, 1977e), it was not until the late 1970s that Ellis (1978a) explicitly offered one. First, he suggests how crooked thinking impairs many personality theories, e.g. environmental prejudices – because an individual has learned to behave badly she is not responsible for continuing to act badly, or environmental conditions have to change before she can; overemphasis on dramatic incidents from the past – the belief that a past trauma (e.g. sexual abuse) accounts completely for an individual's present self-defeating behaviour rather than other additional factors. REBT's theory of personality formation rests largely on how individuals appraise themselves, others and the world and 'hypothesises that probably 80% of the variance of human behaviour rests on biological bases and about 20% on environmental training' (1978a, p. 41). For example, we usually accept and follow familial and societal standards, but because of our innate ability to disturb ourselves we may transmute these standards into dogmatic musts and shoulds that eventually prove more self-defeating than self-helping: e.g. cultural encouragement that being slim equates with confidence and sexual success is converted into a demand that one must be thin to be happy, which then leads to the development of anorexia nervosa. REBT's 'emphasis on the importance of the biological bases of human behaviour attempts to balance the environmentalist position, which has dominated personality and therapy theory for the last half century' (1978a, p.43).

From the outset of REBT, Ellis emphasised the centrality of ego disturbance in clients' problems, i.e. damning themselves on the basis of their failures and rejections in life. Through clinical observation he developed another equally important theory of disturbance: discomfort anxiety or low frustration tolerance (Ellis, 1979b, 1980b): the worry that individuals experience when anticipating pain or unpleasantness and therefore demand that this discomfort must not occur. Discomfort anxiety was

eventually absorbed into a broader category called 'discomfort disturbance' when it was realised that other disturbed emotional states had low
frustration tolerance aspects, e.g. discomfort depression (Dryden, 1987)
and discomfort anger (Dryden, 1994). Ego and discomfort disturbance are
discrete entities but frequently interact, as when an individual damns
herself as a failure because she is unable to tolerate difficult working
conditions. Ellis asserts that ego and discomfort disturbance are the 'two
main sources of just about all neurosis' (quoted in Dryden, 1991, p. 28).

Clients can become so habituated to irrational ideas that they cling
tenaciously to them while acknowledging how counterproductive they
are, e.g. a client who believes 'I must be liked otherwise I'm no good'
always tries to please everyone even though he remains friendless. In
order to tackle this problem, Ellis (1979c) advises therapists to teach their
clients how to combat their self-defeating ideas through the use of force
and energy. Such an attack can be launched on a multimodal front: cognitive (powerful disputation), emotive (shame-attacking exercises), behavioural (flooding), imaginal (rational-emotive imagery). Clients who only
challenge their dysfunctional beliefs in a milk-and-water fashion rather
than in a vigorous way run the considerable risk of being marooned at the
level of intellectual insight (rational beliefs lightly and intermittently held)
instead of reaching emotional insight (rational beliefs deeply and consistently held).

The 1980s

The year 1980 produced a clutch of excellent and influential REBT texts
aimed at trainee and experienced REBT practitioners (most of the REBT
books up to that point had been directed at a non-professional audience).
These works include *The Principles and Practice of Rational-Emotive
Therapy* (Wessler and Wessler, 1980), *Rational-Emotive Therapy: A Skills-
Based Approach* (Grieger and Boyd, 1980), *A Practitioner's Guide to
Rational-Emotive Therapy* (Walen et al., 1980) and *Brief Counselling with
RET* (Hauck, 1980). The Wesslers introduced an expanded ABC model
called the emotional episode which is broken down into eight steps. Part
of the activating event (A) includes inferences people make about As and
these inferences can be linked. However, it is appraisals (rigid or flexible)
at B of these inferences that actually determine people's emotional and
behavioural reactions at C. Grieger and Boyd, echoing Ellis (1979c),
largely eschewed traditional clinical assessment procedures (such as
extensive history-taking and projective tests, e.g. Rorschach) in favour of
understanding clients' presenting problems within the ABC framework.
Such a process can take, 'depending upon the therapist's expertise and
the complexity of the client's problems...from 10 minutes to several
sessions' (Grieger and Boyd, 1980, p. 52). Walen et al., provided the first
manual for the therapist-in-training as 'leading a client successfully

through the RE[B]T maze often sounds a lot easier than it actually is' (1980, p. xiii). Hauck presented the best rational arguments to deploy against clients' irrational ideas, 'which are so reasonable, so irrefutably right, that an opposing idea cannot exist once the rational one has been grasped' (1980, p. 117). These books also demonstrated a broadening REBT authorship rather than the narrow focus on Ellis as largely the sole exponent of REBT.

As a pioneering form of cognitive-behaviour therapy (CBT) and one of the most influential within the field – Mahoney (1987) lists 17 current cognitive therapies – Ellis (1980c) details the differences between REBT and other CBT approaches. These differences include: seeking enduring and profound philosophical change (uprooting musturbatory thinking) rather than mere symptom removal through inferential change, thereby leaving disturbance-producing ideas intact; stressing unconditional self-acceptance and avoiding conditional self-esteem; according low frustration tolerance a central rather than a relatively peripheral role in the creation of emotional disturbance; discriminating keenly between self-defeating (e.g. anxiety) and self-helping (concern, the healthy alternative) emotions which are, along with their cognitive correlates, located on separate continua rather than along a single continuum; standing alone among other CBT approaches in emphasising the biologically rooted nature of human irrationality and the consequent need to fight against it with force and energy. While agreeing with most of these differences, the authors would like to stress that Beck's cognitive therapy also strives for enduring and fundamental attitudinal change.

Because of Ellis's profound disenchantment with what he regarded as psychoanalysis's inefficiency and ineffectiveness, he left the fold and eventually founded REBT. In striving for efficiency in therapy, REBT seeks to identify, challenge and change as rapidly as possible clients' disturbance-creating ideas in order to, ideally, effect profound philosophical change in their lives. Ellis (1980d) lists what he considers are the characteristics of efficient therapy. *Brevity* – achieving constructive change within a relatively short timescale. *Depth-centredness* – focusing on the deeply rooted causes of clients' presenting problems as well as increasing their understanding of how they disturb themselves; in REBT, this would be core musturbatory ideologies they adhere to. *Pervasiveness* – dealing not only with clients' presenting symptoms but also with other problem areas in their lives; in this sense, REBT equips them with a lifelong therapeutic approach. *Extensiveness* – helping clients through 'intensive' therapy to reduce their emotional distress and through 'extensive' therapy to maximise their potential for a happier and more fulfilling life. *Thoroughgoingness* – selecting multimodal methods (cognitive, emotive, behavioural and imaginal) to help therapists achieve better client outcomes. *Maintenance of therapeutic progress* – helping clients to achieve symptom removal and enduring constructive change after formal therapy has ended. *Prevention* – showing clients how they disturb themselves and how to tackle it in order to achieve emotional stability in facing future problems. Homework tasks are an important feature of efficiency as they encourage clients to gain both competence and confidence in facing their problems outside of therapy sessions and decrease the likelihood of clients becoming dependent on the therapist; homework also provides the bridge between intellectual and emotional insight into their problems. Ellis's zest for efficiency in psychotherapy may derive from his somewhat humorous claim that 'I have a gene for efficiency' (1993a, p. 12).

As well as expounding on the characteristics of efficient therapy, Ellis (1982) describes therapeutic methods which he considers to be inefficient, unhelpful or iatrogenic (symptoms induced or exacerbated inadvertently by the therapist or his/her treatment). Such methods include the following: giving excessive warmth and approval to clients may reinforce their dire needs for these things and increase their dependence on the therapist; allowing clients to talk incessantly about their feelings instead of encouraging them to examine the ideas largely creating these feelings; expressing suppressed emotions (e.g. anger) often in dramatic ways to achieve catharsis, which may provide respite from but not removal of these emotions as the disturbance-creating ideas are strengthened through frequent catharsis; employing gradual desensitisation techniques rather than implosive ones can reinforce clients' low frustration tolerance of feared objects or situations; putting the locus of control for change on to an external force or higher power (e.g. Alcoholics Anonymous) rather than within the individual. Such methods distract, interfere with or prevent clients from becoming their own self-therapist; this role usually enables them to achieve effective results from present and future problem-solving.

Like any other therapeutic approach, REBT has its share of failures with clients. Ellis (1983) lists the characteristics of clients who failed in REBT (even though some of them initially appeared good candidates for therapy) including clients who were: highly disturbed and therefore unable or unwilling to show any persistence in disputing their irrational beliefs; angry, rebellious, or resistant to what was required of them (e.g. taking responsibility for their emotional problems) and generally avoiding the hard and uncomfortable work involved in the change process. Failures in REBT also result from therapist errors, actions or characteristics such as lack of force and energy in encouraging clients to surrender their musturbatory thinking; getting quickly discouraged or impatient with difficult clients because of their own low frustration tolerance beliefs; focusing too heavily on REBT's cognitive aspects and thereby neglecting its multimodal approach to facilitate optimum change. Ellis suggests that more research needs to be undertaken in the area of REBT failures so that its efficacy and efficiency can be significantly improved.

REBT's group therapy activities were expanded in 1984 with the creation of day-long rational-emotive training intensives. These draw upon the est (Erhard Seminars Training) movement and other intensive group procedures, 'but throwing out the cultish and mystical procedures that they often include' (Ellis, 1994a, p.49), and frequently attract over 200 participants. Group members receive cognitive lectures and undertake experimental and behavioural tasks. As preliminary research findings 'on several hundred participants indicate, [these methods] can produce favorable results in a single eight-hour large-scale intensive' (Ellis and Dryden, 1987, p. 155).

Although Ellis had vast clinical experience of resistance in therapy, it was not until the 1980s that he 'trained his sights' on the subject in his writings and suggested that overcoming clients' resistance to therapeutic change is in some ways the most important problem of psychotherapy' (1985a, p. 1). Ellis distinguishes between healthy and pathological forms of resistance. An example of the former is a client who refuses to accept the therapist's rigid insistence that her present depression is caused by her parents' divorce. The latter include fear of discomfort – that change is too hard and uncomfortable to endure; fear of disclosure and shame – that by revealing shameful thoughts and deeds clients will be condemned by their therapist; fear of success – actually, fear of subsequent failure after initial therapeutic success. Ellis also examines therapists' resistance which can impede progress if they subscribe to certain irrational beliefs, e.g. 'I have to be successful with all my clients practically all the time'; 'I have to be greatly respected and loved by all my clients'. If therapeutic movement rather than impasse is to occur, Ellis urges both clients and therapists to use force and energy in challenging and changing their resistance-creating beliefs.

REBT asserts that a philosophy based on preferences (including wishes, wants, desires, hopes) will usually lead to psychological health because these beliefs are adaptable, will minimise emotional disturbance and aid goal attainment. Over the previous decades Ellis had been establishing and increasing the criteria underpinning psychological health (or, rather, his version of it) until he reached 13 (Ellis and Bernard, 1985). The 13 criteria are:

1. *Self-interest* – usually putting one's own interests ahead of others.
2. *Social interest* – making one's goals both personally and socially responsible.
3. *Self-direction* – taking responsibility for one's own life without depending heavily on the support of others.
4. *High frustration tolerance* – the ability to endure discomfort and stress in one's life without becoming emotionally disturbed about it.
5. *Flexibility* – being open-minded and adaptable in one's thoughts and actions.

6. *Acceptance of uncertainty* – that one can remain relatively happy despite not knowing for sure what the future will bring.
7. *Commitment to creative pursuits* – having external interests rather than indulging in excessive introspection.
8. *Scientific thinking* – examining the evidence for and against our beliefs in order to introduce a greater self-helping objectivity into our lives.
9. *Self-acceptance* – choosing to accept ourselves unconditionally rather than linking such acceptance to external factors.
10. *Risk-taking* – making life more exciting or adventurous through calculated rather than foolish risks.
11. *Long-range hedonism* – achieving a balance between enjoying the pleasures of the moment and planning constructively for the future.
12. *Non-utopianism* – accepting what is empirically evident and achievable in life rather than pursuing the chimera of finding utopia or reaching self-perfection.
13. *Self-responsibility for own emotional disturbance* – accepting that one is largely responsible for creating one's emotional upsets instead of blaming others or environmental conditions.

The above list is not meant to be definitive and no doubt will be added to.

While Ellis has always advocated the use of vigorous methods (e.g. shame-attacking exercises) to challenge clients' self-defeating ideas, Dryden (1986) introduced the concept of vivid methods for the same purpose. Vivid REBT is aimed at approaching therapy in a striking, lively, fresh and memorable way. Examples of vivid REBT include: flamboyant therapist actions – e.g. the therapist flinging herself to the floor and barking like a dog in order to teach the client that behaving stupidly does not make you a stupid person; therapist as raconteur – using stories, jokes, parables, poems, aphorisms, etc., to communicate rational concepts to clients; in-session simulation – attempting to recreate in therapy the conditions or circumstances which engender the clients' problems, e.g. asking a client to maintain eye-contact when he is anxious to avoid it in order to uncover his anxiogenic thinking. The indiscriminate use of vivid REBT methods can lead some clients to feel overwhelmed by such a 'dazzling' display and so it will have little or no therapeutic impact on them.

REBT therapists agree that empathy, genuineness and unconditional positive regard (or REBT's version of this last quality, unconditional acceptance) are the core conditions of therapy. Golden and Dryden (1986), influenced by the work of Bordin (1979), suggest other components which are also needed to construct a therapeutic alliance. These are: *bonds* – a bonded relationship between the therapist and client is established in the latter's preferred interpersonal and learning style in order to promote constructive change, e.g. a formal counselling approach based on the therapist's expertise; *goals* – the client's goals for change are made clear and specific rather than vague or assumed, e.g. 'I want to overcome this guilt' as opposed to 'I want to discover my true self'; *tasks* – both the therapist and the client have tasks to perform, e.g. the therapist structures the counselling process and the client carries out homework assignments. REBT hypothesises that greater therapeutic benefits are more likely to be achieved if therapists pay attention to the requirements of these alliance domains.

REBT therapists encourage their clients to, ideally, strive for an enduring and profound philosophical change in their lives, i.e. surrendering musturbatory thinking and internalising a rational outlook. In order to achieve a philosophical change at the specific or general level, Ellis and Dryden (1987) advise clients to recognise that they largely create their own psychological disturbances; realise that they have the ability to reduce significantly their disturbances; understand that these disturbances largely stem from irrational thinking; detect these irrational ideas and discriminate them from rational ideas; dispute the rational ideas by using the logico-empirical methods of science; work hard to internalise their newly acquired rational beliefs through multimodal methods of change; realise that the change process is a lifelong commitment. Clients who are unable, for whatever reason, to effect a philosophical change are switched to a non-philosophical approach, e.g. challenging and changing a client's inference such as 'My wife is going to leave me' rather than the irrational belief from which it derives: 'My wife absolutely must not leave me'.

As Ellis has always been interested in providing clients with efficient therapy, he turned his attention in 1989 to the issue of consumerism in psychotherapy, i.e. the extent to which clients' interests are served by the profession of counselling. He identifies several forms of ineffective consumerism. Self-defeating consumerism of clients – they pick a therapy which will help them to feel better but not to get better, so their disturbance-creating ideas are left intact. Ineffective consumerism of psychotherapists – e.g. clients may actually get worse in therapy because therapists, who believe they need the approval of their clients, will refuse or be reluctant to push clients to undertake the hard work usually associated with constructive change. Ineffective consumerism in cognitive-behavioural therapies – e.g. unlike REBT, these approaches usually involve only disputing clients' distorted and negative inferences rather than removing the philosophical core (absolute musts and shoulds) of their emotional disturbances. Drawing upon his own practice in REBT, Ellis suggests various ways of tackling ineffective consumerism in psychotherapy, including: therapists paying attention to the counselling research literature in order to be aware of which techniques are deemed to be effective and which are not; therapists being alert to and challenging clients' desires for therapeutic methods that usually only bring relief from but not removal of their psychological problems. By following these guidelines, Ellis avers, therapists can maximise their helpfulness to clients.

During the 1980s and early 1990s REBT produced practitioner guides to tackling various clinical problems: alcohol and substance abuse (Ellis et al., 1988); anxiety disorders (Warren and Zgourides, 1991); childhood and adolescence (Ellis and Bernard, 1983; Bernard and Joyce, 1984). Guides were also produced on REBT's application to different treatment modalities: individual therapy (Dryden, 1987), couples counselling (Ellis et al., 1989), family therapy (Huber and Baruth, 1989). The self-help literature continued to flourish including Ellis's (1988) *How to Stubbornly Refuse to Make Yourself Miserable About Anything–Yes, Anything!* This book sought to teach, or at least its title reflected, a super-elegant solution to rational living (Weinrach and Ellis, 1980). This solution involves a decrease in the level of distress usually found in any presenting problem as well as individuals becoming less disturbable in the future because they have achieved an enduringly profound philosophical change. As no human being, including Albert Ellis, the founder of REBT, is expected to become totally undisturbable for any sustained period, the book is likely to help readers to make themselves less disturbable but hardly undisturbable.

A novel application of REBT was its uses in underpinning the programme of rational recovery (RR), a self-help group for individuals recovering from alcoholism and a rival to the dominant approach in the field, that of Alcoholics Anonymous (AA). Differences between the two groups include the following: RR puts the locus of control for change within the individual while AA invests it in a higher power (e.g. God, the AA group); RR sees alcoholism as a self-destructive personal philosophy of living as opposed to the AA's view of it as a disease process; RR emphasises individuals getting over alcoholism but still remaining vulnerable, while the AA stresses that they are lifelong recovering alcoholics, thereby confirming their self-image. Trimpey (1989) urges his readers in *The Small Book* to 'see how quickly we can let the nation know that it's time for a Rational Recovery (RR) program everywhere an AA group is found' (1989, p. 7). Although RR now focuses less on REBT methods, a new organisation, Self-Management and Recovery Training (SMART), is closely involved with REBT.

The 1990s

During the late 1980s, Ellis became embroiled in a controversy when some cognitive-behavioural theorists (Guidano, 1988, Mahoney, 1988) asserted that cognitive psychotherapy could be divided into two camps: rationalist and constructivist. REBT has been placed in the rationalist camp, which Ellis takes great exception to as REBT 'is not only non-rationalist but...in several important respects more constructivist...than just about all the other cognitive therapies, including those of Guidano (1988) and Mahoney (1988)' (Ellis, 1990, p.169). Evidence to buttress Ellis's counter-assertion includes the following: REBT 'posits no absolutistic or invariant criteria of rationality' (Ellis, 1990, p. 176) but, instead, views rationality as relative and self-helping to each person's goal-directed beliefs; Ellis (1962) has always emphasised that thinking, feeling and behaving are interdependent processes for acquiring and validating knowledge rather than reason alone; REBT strives to effect deep personality change in individuals by encouraging them to surrender their core disturbance-creating musts and shoulds rather than focusing on disputing their distorted inferences to achieve only superficial change. Ellis suggests that this dichotomy of cognitive psychotherapy is neither helpful nor accurate.

The ABCDE model of the acquisition, maintenance and eventual amelioration of emotional disturbance is the cornerstone of REBT theory and practice. However, the sequential steps involved in applying this model were not always clearly delineated. In order to bring greater clarity to this process, Dryden and DiGiuseppe (1990) developed the 13-step REBT counselling sequence. The sequence is: ask for a problem(s) and assess its A and C elements (steps 1–5); teach the B–C connection that beliefs largely lead to emotional consequences and relate this to the client's emotional disturbance (steps 6–8); dispute the client's irrational beliefs and show him how to deepen his conviction in his newly acquired rational beliefs through homework tasks which are reviewed at the next session (step 9–12); in order to internalise his new rational outlook, the client challenges his irrational beliefs in a variety of problematic situations (step 13). Dryden (Dryden et al., 1993, p.10) states that the 13 steps 'comprise the effective and efficient practice of RE[B]T'.

Ellis (1962) had divided emotions in REBT into 'appropriate' and 'inappropriate' negative states (see p. 214). Not all REBT therapists agree with, and some object to, this emotional classification. Dryden (1990) offers his own taxonomy of unhealthy and healthy negative emotions (e.g. anxiety vs. concern; depression vs. sadness) as a more sophisticated account of individuals' reactions to unpleasant or stressful life events. Unhealthy negative emotions interfere with or block goal attainment, decrease the ability to enjoy life, and lead to self-defeating behaviour. Healthy negative emotions, on the other hand, while still signalling some degree of emotional upset, act as a stimulus towards goal attainment, increase the ability to enjoy life, and lead to self-helping behaviour. Ellis eventually adopted Dryden's classification system in 1994 after being persuaded of its merits.

Disputing clients' irrational ideas is the principal activity of REBT therapists but can be undertaken, by both trainee and experienced counsellors, in a haphazard, cursory or arbitrary fashion rather than by following clearly defined disputing strategies. DiGiuseppe (1991) proposes comprehensive cognitive disputing as a method of 'provid[ing] a blueprint for the process of disputing' (p. 173). This blueprint entails challenging clients' irrational beliefs along logical, empirical and pragmatic lines and constructing rational alternatives (the nature of the dispute); using

Socratic, didactic, humorous and metaphorical interventions because the form of the argument presented is as important as its content (rhetorical disputing styles); tackling irrational beliefs held in specific contexts and at the general plane (level of abstraction); disputing clients' musts (demand-ingness) and the relevant derivatives from the musts without assuming that challenging one irrational idea will automatically or necessarily lead to rational changes in other irrational beliefs (multiple irrational belief process). DiGiuseppe suggests that comprehensive cognitive disputing is a powerful addition to the therapist's armamentarium.

When the ABC model was initially presented (Ellis, 1958a, 1962) it was a relatively simple explanation of emotional disturbance. Since that time the model has been expanded and refined (DiGiuseppe, 1986; Ellis, 1969, 1973a; Wessler and Wessler, 1980); but Ellis (1985b, p.313) noted that the model was still 'oversimplified and omits salient information about human disturbance and its treatment' and therefore he expanded again the ABCs of REBT. Ellis (1991), among other things, teases out the complex interac-tions of As, Bs and Cs, e.g. a woman who believes (B) 'I must always be approved of by others' turns a friend's mild rebuke at A into outright rejec-tion and thereby experiences depression rather than sadness at C; a man's prior irrational beliefs (e.g. 'I must always succeed') are brought to new As (e.g. a delay in receiving his examination results) and encourage him to distort his view of them thereby strengthening his disturbance-producing ideas (in this example, his fear of failure). Ellis speculates that one day he may write a book on the ABCs of REBT in order to do full justice to them.

Rational emotive behaviour therapy: 1993–

The name change in 1993 from rational-emotive therapy to rational emotive behaviour therapy brought REBT full circle 'because it [RET] really has always been highly cognitive, very emotive and particularly behavioural' (Ellis, 1993b, p. 2). The new name accurately reflects REBT's long-standing trimodal approach to tackling emotional disturbance, namely, that individuals have to think, feel and act against their irrational beliefs if constructive change is to occur in their lives. Ellis suggested that some REBT practitioners would not be enthusiastic about the name change and is characteristically forthright in his reply: 'Tough–but not awful!'

In 1994 Ellis produced a collection of papers on major clinical dis-orders. An REBT theory of post-traumatic stress disorder (PTSD) recog-nises, along with other cognitive-behavioural therapies (CBT), 'that PTSD victims (e.g. of rape, a car crash) at least partly create their severe distress by holding dysfunctional or irrational Beliefs (iBs) and that to alleviate their overwhelming fears they had better be treated with cognitive restruc-turing plus exposure' (Ellis, 1994b, p.13). Ellis asserts that most CBT approaches to PTSD follow an information-processing model which only challenges client's unrealistic and illogical cognitive distortions (e.g. 'Because I was out on my own late at night, it's my fault I was raped') rather than focusing on and removing the underlying rigid musts and shoulds from which these distortions derive (e.g. 'Because I was out on my own late at night, which I absolutely should not have been, it's my fault I was raped and therefore I'm a totally worthless person'). Ellis suggests that 'REBT hypotheses about the "deeper" causes of PTSD would be inter- esting ones for empirical investigation' (1994b, p. 21).

As REBT is a cognitive approach to counselling, it is recommended that some clients may need an assessment of their cognitive functioning because 'cognitive deficits [e.g. attention, memory, thought organisation] may have a neurological basis which may be responsible not only for the psychological problems but social skill deficits as well' (Walen et al., 1980, p. 34). Working with personality disorders, particularly borderline person- alities, is notably difficult because they 'almost always have cognitive, emotive [e.g. highly-strung, histrionic], and behavioural [e.g. hyperactive, impulsive] organic deficits for various reasons, including hereditary predispositions' (Ellis, 1994c, p. 102). Added to these existing problems, such individuals may severely denigrate themselves on the basis of these innate deficits. Besides persistently and forcefully employing the usual multimodal methods, REBT therapists are advised to employ skill training as a means of ameliorating these deficits in order to improve both cogni- tive competence and therapeutic outcome.

Ellis (1962) originally considered obsessive-compulsive disorder (OCD)to be largely caused by individuals' demands for certainty (e.g. in order to be absolutely certain that she is both clean and approved of, a woman engages in endless handwashing after getting her hands dirty). Ellis's (1994d) view of the causation of OCD is now much more complex. He hypothesises that individuals with OCD, like other personality disor- ders, usually have biological deficits (cognitive, emotive and behavioural), 'including the strong tendency to overfocus on a particular problem and to compulsively perform ritualistic and/or other habits (such as compul- sively checking, handwashing, and locking doors)' (1994d, p. 123). OCDers exacerbate their original problems by developing low frustration tolerance (LFT) about them and condemning themselves for having these problems in the first place; in addition, they frequently develop secondary emotional problems (e.g. anxiety, depression) in relation to their OCD. Individuals with OCD are also prone to self-denigration and LFT over non- OCD-related frustrations and failures in their lives. Such a catalogue of problems and the usually considerable persistence needed in therapy to effect change in their lives leads Ellis to call them VDCs (very difficult customers). However, the use of REBT's multimodal methods often combined with antidepressant medication can 'help clients reduce and minimize, but rarely entirely eliminate, their OCD behaviours' (Ellis, 1994d, p. 132).

Conclusion

The above chronological commentary on trends in REBT over the last 40 years is not meant to be exhaustive but to provide a guide to some or most of the important developments during this period. Some trends have remained constant over the decades such as REBT's strong desire to reach the widest possible audience with its psychoeducational principles and practices; others have been abandoned, e.g. its former adherence to logical positivism as a basis for challenging clients' irrational ideas; and new ones are beginning to emerge or at least be hinted at, such as Dryden's observation that 'to date no one has offered an integrated model that systematically applies rational-emotive concepts to the broad area of psychology' (1994, p. 5). As REBT moves towards the millennium, its dynamic and innovative approach to understanding and tackling human disturbance shows no signs of diminishing.

References

Bernard, M.E. (1986). Staying Rational in an Irrational World: Albert Ellis and Rational-Emotive Therapy. Carlton, Australia: McCulloch.

Bernard, M.E. and Joyce, M.R. (1984). Rational-Emotive Therapy with Children an Adolescents. New York: Wiley.

Bordin, E. (1979). The generalizability of the psychoanalytic concept of the working alliance, Psychotherapy: Theory, Research and Practice, 16, 252–60.

DiGiuseppe, R. (1977). The use of behaviour modification to establish rational self-statements in children, in A. Ellis and R. Grieger (Eds), Handbook of Rational-Emotive Therapy, Vol. 1. New York: Springer.

DiGiuseppe, R. (1986). The implications of the philosophy of science for rational-emotive theory and therapy, Psychotherapy, 23(4), 634–9.

DiGiuseppe, R. (1991). Comprehensive cognitive disputing in RET, in M.E. Bernard (Ed), Using Rational-Emotive Therapy Effectively: A Practitioner's Guide. New York: Plenum.

DiMattia, D. (1991). Using RET effectively in the workplace, in M.E. Bernard (Ed), Using Rational-Emotive Therapy Effectively: A Practitioner's Guide. New York: Plenum.

Dryden, W. (1986). Vivid methods in rational-emotive therapy, in A. Ellis and R. Grieger (Eds), Handbook of Rational-Emotive Therapy, Vol. 2. New York: Springer.

Dryden, W. (1987).Counselling Individuals: The Rational-Emotive Approach. London: Taylor & Francis.

Dryden, W. (1990). Rational-Emotive Counselling in Action. London: Sage Publications.

Dryden, W. (1991). A Dialogue With Albert Ellis: Against Dogma. Buckingham: Open University Press.

Dryden, W. (1994). Invitation to Rational-Emotive Psychology. London: Whurr.

Dryden, W. and Backx, W. (1987). Problems in living: the Friday night workshop, in W. Dryden (Ed), Current Issues in Rational-Emotive Therapy, London: Croom Helm.

Dryen, W. and DiGiuseppe, R. (1990). A Primer on Rational-Emotive Therapy. Champaign, IL: Research Press.

Dryden, W., Neenan, M. and Doggart, L. (1993). Professional rationality: an interview with Windy Dryden, The Rational-Emotive Therapist: Journal of the Association for Rational-Emotive Therapists, 1(1), 5–11.

Ellis, A. (1957). How to live with a neurotic. New York: Crown.

Ellis, A. (1958a). Rational psychotherapy, Journal of General Psychology, 59, 37–49.

Ellis, A. (1958b). Sex without guilt. Secaucus, NJ: Lyle Stuart.

Ellis, A. (1960). The Art and Science of Love. Secaucus, NJ: Lyle Stuart.

Ellis, A. (1962). Reason and Emotion in Psychotherapy. Secaucus., NJ: Lyle Stuart.

Ellis, A. (1963a). Toward a more precise definition of "emotional" and "intellectual" insight, Psychological Reports, 13, 125–6.

Ellis, A. (1963b). Rational-Emotive Psychotherapy. New York: Institute for Rational-Emotive Therapy.

Ellis, A. (1965). Showing clients they are not worthless individuals, Voices, 1(2), 74–7.

Ellis, A. (1969). Suggested procedures for a Weekend of Rational Encounter. New York: Institute for Rational-Emotive Therapy.

Ellis, A. (1971). Growth through Reason. North Hollywood, CA: Wilshire Books.

Ellis, A. (1972a). Executive Leadership; A Rational Approach. Secaucus, NJ: Citadel Press.

Ellis, A. (1972b). Helping people get better rather than merely feel better, Rational Living, 7(2), 2–9.

Ellis, A. (1973a). Humanistic Psychotherapy: The Rational-Emotive Approach. New York: McGraw-Hill.

Ellis, A. (1973b). Emotional Education at the Living School. New York: Institute for Rational-Emotive Therapy.

Ellis, A. (1973c). My philosophy of psychotherapy, Journal of Contemporary Psychotherapy, 6(1), 13–18.

Ellis, A. (1976a). The biological basis of human irrationality, Journal of Individual Psychology, 32, 145–68.

Ellis, A. (1976b). RET abolishes most of the human ego, Psychotherapy: Theory, Research and Practice, 13, 343–8. (Reprinted New York: Institute for Rational-Emotive Therapy.)

Ellis, A. (1977a). Anger–How to Live with and Without it. Secaucus, NJ: Citadel Press.

Ellis, A. (1977b). The basic clinical theory of rational-emotive therapy, in A. Ellis and R. Grieger (Eds), Handbook of Rational-Emotive Therapy, Vol. 1. New York: Springer.

Ellis, A. (1977c). Fun as psychotherapy, Rational Living, 12(1), 2–6.

Ellis, A. (1977d). A Garland of Rational Songs (cassette recording). New York: Institute for Rational-Emotive Therapy.

Ellis, A. (1977e). RET as a personality theory, therapy approach, and philosophy of life, in J.L. Wolfe and E. Brand (Eds), Twenty Years of Rational Therapy. New York: Institute for Rational-Emotive Therapy.

Ellis, A. (1978a). Toward a theory of personality, in R.J. Corsini (Ed), Readings in Current Personality Theories. Itasca, IL: Peacock. Reprinted in W. Dryden (Ed) (1990). The Essential Albert Ellis. New York: Springer.

Ellis, A. (1978b). Personality characteristics of rational-emotive therapists and other kinds of therapists, Psychotherapy: Theory, Research and Practice, 15, 329–32.

Ellis, A. (1979a). The practice of rational-emotive therapy, in A. Ellis and J.M. Whiteley (Eds), Theoretical and Empirical Foundations of Rational-Emotive Therapy. Monterey, CA: Brooks/Cole.

Ellis, A. (1979b). Discomfort anxiety: a new cognitive-behavioural construct (Part 1), Rational Living, 14(2), 3–8.

Ellis, A. (1979c). The issue of force and energy in behavioural change, Journal of Contemporary Psychotherapy, 10(2), 83–97.

Ellis, A. (1980a). An overview of the clinical theory of rational-emotive therapy, in R. Grieger and J. Boyd, Rational-Emotive Therapy: A Skills-Based Approach. New York: Van Nostrand Reinhold.

Ellis, A. (1980b). Discomfort anxiety: a new cognitive-behavioural construct (Part 2), Rational Living, 15(1), 25–30.

Ellis, A. (1980c). Rational-emotive therapy and cognitive-behaviour therapy: similarities and differences, Cognitive Therapy and Research, 4, 325–40.

Ellis, A. (1980d). The value of efficiency in psychotherapy, Psychotherapy: Theory, Research and Practice, 17, 414–19.

Ellis, A. (1982). Must most psychotherapists remain as incompetent as they now are?, Journal of Contemporary Psychotherapy, 13(1), 17–28.

Ellis, A. (1983). Failures in rational-emotive therapy, in E.B. Foa and P.M.G. Emmelkamp (Eds), Failures in Behaviour Therapy, New York: Wiley.

Ellis, A. (1985a). Overcoming Resistance: Rational-Emotive Therapy with Difficult Clients. New York: Springer.

Ellis, A. (1985b). Expanding the ABCs of rational-emotive therapy, in M. Mahoney and A. Freeman (Eds), Cognition and Psychotherapy. New York: Plenum.

Ellis, A. (1988). How to Stubbornly Refuse to Make Yourself Miserable About Anything–Yes, Anything! Secaucus. NJ: Lyle Stuart.

Ellis, A. (1990). Is rational-emotive therapy (RET) "rationalist" or "constructivist"?, Journal of Rational-Emotive and Cognitive-Behaviour Therapy, 8(3), 169–93.

Ellis, A. (1991) The revised ABCs of rational-emotive therapy (RET), Journal of Rational-Emotive and Cognitive-Behaviour Therapy, 9(3), 139–72.

Ellis, A. (1993a). Fundamentals of rational-emotive for the 1990s, in W. Dryden and L.K. Hill (Eds), Innovations in Rational-Emotive Therapy. London: Sage Publications.

Ellis, A. (1993b). Letter to mental health professionals, Catalogue of the Institute for Rational-Emotive Therapy, 1993–4, p. 2.

Ellis, A. (1994a). Reason and Emotion in Psychotherapy, 2nd edn. New York: Carol Publishing.

Ellis, A. (1994b). Post-traumatic stress disorder (PTSD): a rational emotive behavioural theory, Journal of Rational-Emotive and Cognitive-Behaviour Therapy, 12(1), 3–25.

Ellis, A. (1994c). The treatment of borderline personalities with rational emotive behaviour therapy, Journal of Rational-Emotive and Cognitive-Behaviour Therapy, 12(2), 101–19.

Ellis, A. (1994d). Rational emotive behaviour therapy approaches to obsessive-compulsive disorder (OCD), Journal of Rational-Emotive and Cognitive-Behaviour Therapy, 12(2), 121–41.

Ellis, A. and Abrahms, E. (1978). Brief Psychotherapy in Medical and Health Practice. New York: Springer.

Ellis, A. and Bernard, M.E. (Eds) (1983). Rational-Emotive Approaches to the Problems of Childhood. New York: Plenum.

Ellis, A. and Bernard, M.E. (1985). What is rational-emotive therapy (RET)?, in A. Ellis and M.E. Bernard, (Eds), Clinical Applications of Rational-Emotive Therapy. New York: Plenum.

Ellis, A. and Blum, M.L. (1967). Rational training: a new method of facilitating management and labor relations, Psychological Reports, 20, 1267–84.

Ellis, A. and Dryden, W. (1987). The Practice of Rational-Emotive therapy. New York: Springer.

Ellis, A. and Harper, R.A. (1961). A Guide to Rational Living in an Irrational World. Englewood Cliffs, NJ: Prentice-Hall.

Ellis, A., McInerney, J.F., DiGiuseppe, R. and Yeager, R.J. (1988). Rational-Emotive Therapy with Alcoholics and Substance Abusers. New York: Pergamon.

Ellis, A., Wilson, R.A. and Krassner, P. (1960). An impolite interview with Albert Ellis, The Realist, 6(1), 9–14; 17, 7–12. (Reprinted New York: Institute for Rational-Emotive Therapy.)

Ellis, A. Sichel, J., Yeager, R.J., DiMattia, D. and DiGiuseppe, R. (1989). Rational-Emotive Couples Therapy. New York: Pergamon.

Golden, W.L. and Dryden, W. (1986). Cognitive-behavioural therapies: commonalties, divergences and future developments, in W. Dryden and W. Golden (Eds), Cognitive-Behavioural Approaches to Psychotherapy. London: Harper & Row.

Grieger, R. and Boyd, J. (1980). Rational-Emotive Therapy: A Skills-Based Approach. New York: Van Nostrand Reinhold.

Guidano, V.F. (1988). A systems, process-oriented approach to cognitive therapy, in K.S. Dobson (Ed), Handbook of Cognitive-Behavioural Therapies. New York: Guilford.

Hauck, P (1980). Brief Counseling with RET. Philadelphia, PA: Westminster Press.

Huber, C. and Baruth, L. (1989). Rational-Emotive Family Therapy: A Systems Perspective. New York: Springer.

Jacobs, S. (1989). Karl Popper and Albert Ellis: their ideas on psychology and rationality compared, Journal of Rational-Emotive and Cognitive-Behaviour Therapy, 7(3), 173–85.

Knaus, W.J. (1977). Rational-emotive education, in A. Ellis and R. Grieger (Eds), Handbook of Rational-Emotive Therapy, Vol. 1. New York: Springer.

Knaus, W.J. and Haberstroh, N. (1993). A rational-emotive education program to help disruptive mentally retarded clients develop self-control, in W. Dryden and L.K. Hill (Eds), Innovations in Rational-Emotive Therapy. London: Sage Publications.

Korzybski, A. (1993). Science and Sanity. San Francisco: International Society of General Semantics.

Mahoney, M.J. (1987). Psychotherapy and the cognitive sciences: an evolving alliance, Journal of Cognitive Psychotherapy: An International Quarterly, 1, 39–59.

Mahoney, M.J. (1988). The cognitive sciences and psychotherapy: patterns in a developing relationship, in K.S. Dobson (Ed), Handbook of Cognitive-Behavioural Therapies. New York: Guilford.

Maultsby, M.C., Jr. and Ellis, A. (1974). Techniques for Using Rational-Emotive Therapy. New York: Institute for Rational-Emotive Therapy.

Palmer, S. and Ellis, A. (1993). In the counsellor's chair: interview with Albert Ellis, Counselling: The Journal of the British Association for Counselling, 4(3), 171–4.

Popper, K.R. (1962). Objective Knowledge. London: Oxford University Press.

Popper, K.R. (1985). Popper Selections, David Miller (Ed), Princeton, NJ: Princeton University Press.

Trimpey, J. (1989). Rational Recovery from Alcoholism: The Small Book, 2nd edn. Lotus, CA: Lotus Press.

Vernon, A. (1989). Thinking, Feeling, Behaving. An Emotional Educational Curriculum for Children Grades 7–12. Champaign, IL: Research Press.

Walen, S.R., DiGiuseppe, R. and Wessler, R.L. (1980). A Practitioner's Guide to Rational-Emotive Therapy. New York: Oxford University Press.

Warren, R. and Zgourides, G.D. (1991). Anxiety Disorders: A Rational-Emotive Perspective. New York: Pergamon.

Weinrach, S.G. and Ellis, A. (1980). Unconventional therapist: Albert Ellis (interview). Personnel and Guidance Journal, 59, 152–60.

Wessler, R.A. and Wessler, R.L. (1980). The Principles and Practice of Rational-Emotive Therapy. San Francisco, CA: Jossey-Bass.

Wiener, D.N. (1988). Albert Ellis: Passionate Skeptic. New York: Praeger.

Yankura, J. and Dryden, W. (1990). Doing RET: Albert Ellis in Action. New York: Springer.

Yankura, J. and Dryden, W. (1994). Albert Ellis. London: Sage Publications.

Chapter Three
REBT and the Question of Free Will

Introduction

Clients frequently believe that they are at the mercy of all-powerful forces and therefore are unable to exert any control or influence over their lives. These forces can be described as biological, physiological, hereditarian, neurological, psychological, familial, environmental, cultural and socio-logical – clients might subscribe to one or more of these theories of causation. An REBT therapist attempting to explain to the client the concept of emotional responsibility (Dryden and Neenan, 1995) may feel daunted in the face of this deterministic onslaught. Indeed, how is the REBTer to make meaningful such concepts as responsibility, self-direction, self-control, commitment, freedom and self-determination when the client feels compelled to act in the way that she does?

The debate in philosophy between free will and determinism is centuries old. Free will means having the ability to make uncaused, uncompelled choices, that the future is not fated and that given the same conditions or circumstances individuals can act other than they did. Determinism, on the other hand, postulates that all events, including human actions, are predetermined and therefore behaviour which appears to be self-willed is, in fact, inevitable. Vesey and Foulkes (1990) suggest three possible solutions to this problem:

1. Not everything is physically determined – physical indeterminism allows for human actions to be determined mentally, by the will.
2. Everything is determined, and freedom is an illusion.
3. Free will and determinism are compatible.

Where does REBT stand in this debate? Ellis (1990, p. 46) opts for a balance between free will and determinism: 'Indeterministic theories put emphasis on self-direction and place control within the person. RE[B]T stands mainly in the indeterministic camp. But it sees choice as *limited*. It hypothesizes that the more rationally people think and behave, the less deterministically they act. But rationality itself has its limits and hardly leads to complete free, healthy, or utopian existences!' Elsewhere, Ellis (1980, pp. 21–2) calls this REBT viewpoint 'soft determinism' because it 'assumes that all human behaviour, including emotional disturbance, is largely determined by hereditarian and environmental conditions or influences and that therefore pure free will does not seem to exist'. However, humans are still capable of exercising a significant degree of free will or choice within these predetermined limitations. One of the unique features of REBT is that 'it particularly emphasises the importance of will and choice in human affairs...' despite our constrained behaviour (Ellis and Bernard, 1985, p. 22). Therefore with hard work and effort people can alter rather than fundamentally change how they think, feel and act.

A case in point is a person's temperament. Definitions of temperament usually refer to its distinct nature or natural disposition thereby implying its biological origins. This biological basis of temperament has been supported by, among others, Thomas and Chess (1980). An individual who, for example, has a temperamental tendency to act before he thinks may be able to rein in such impulsivity without removing it from his personality. As Dryden and Yankura (1995, p. 128) observe: 'You can certainly work to curb the excess of these [temperamentally based] patterns but...you will not be able to change the "pull" of your temperament.' This is an example where individual behaviour is party determined and partly free. Some clients might argue that this is circumscribed freedom but REBTers would argue that this is still freedom of a sort and therefore these clients can choose to work in therapy at tackling their long-standing (and seemingly inevitable) emotional disturbances and thereby striving to lead healthier and happier lives.

Other clients may come to therapy claiming to have no will-power to effect change in their lives. The therapist can point out that the client's will-power is latent, untapped, underused, neglected, etc. The collaborative task of the therapist and client is to help the latter locate and mobilise it. Will-power in REBT 'is defined not merely as the determination to change but the determination to *work* at changing oneself and the *actual work* that one does to follow up this determination' (Ellis, 1980, p.22). In this chapter we demonstrate some ways of dealing with clients' seeming inability to change because of their beliefs that their fate has been predetermined and therefore their will is neither free nor present.

The following dialogues show how clients can, to some extent, change the way they think, feel and act. This seems to be, initially, a more important point to make than focusing on specifically how their absolute thinking (rigid musts and shoulds) diminishes self-determination while flexible thinking (rational preferences and wishes) increases it. This stage of REBT can be initiated once clients accept that they have some degree of free will and wish to exercise it in order to tackle their problems.

Susceptibility is not inevitability

Clients with substance abuse problems often claim, for example, that they are 'born addicts' or they could not resist their family history of alcoholism. Both points of view have some validity. As Ellis et al. (1988, pp. 16–17) point out: 'A number of reasonably well-controlled twin studies have demonstrated a hereditary or genetic component to alcoholism...the greater the family history [of alcoholism], the greater the risk of progressive, serious alcohol dependency.' While genetic predisposition and familial patterns of excessive drinking may indicate a gloomy prognosis for the client, the REBT therapist needs to provide some hope that change can occur rather than pessimism that none can:

Client: I was born an alcoholic. My father is a drunk, so was his father and my brother is a drunk. My mother has her moments too!

Therapist: Anybody who isn't a 'drunk'?

Client: My sister seems to have avoided it.

Therapist: We can discuss possible reasons why later. Now with your own case, do you see treatment being of any help?

*Client:*It hasn't helped before – I just kept on drinking. I'm a drunk and that's the way it's always going to be.

Therapist: This is because you believe you have a biological impulse towards drinking because of your family history.

Client: That's right.

Therapist: Have you ever considered that your life doesn't have to be this way: you could reduce your alcohol intake or even achieve sobriety?

Client: It's true there have been times in my life when I've thought to myself 'I don't want to end up like my father and brother' and have tried to stop drinking.

Therapist: So that sounds like you can see the possibility of making a choice between carrying on drinking and stopping. What happens when you actually stop drinking?

Client: Well, I stop for a few days, weeks or, sometimes, for a few months but then I run into problems in my life like hassle from the neighbours and I think 'why bother?' and I start drinking again.

Therapist: Could you clarify something for me: when you say 'why bother?' is that because you believe you are being biologically driven towards your next drink or that you don't believe you can cope with problems in your life and therefore seek solace in alcohol?

Client: Both really. Does it make a difference?

Therapist: I think so. If you were to cope better with your emotional and behavioural problems, would you be less likely to have a drink?

Client: Well I probably wouldn't drink to drown my problems. Those times I told you about when I didn't drink, that's because things seemed to be going all right in my life.

Therapist: That shows you can have some control over your drinking. It's not all biologically determined.

Client: But I still have this 'biological impulse' as you called it.

Therapist: Some people are more biologically prone or vulnerable to greater levels of anxiety, anger or depression. This means that such individuals have to struggle much harder to overcome these problems than others who don't have such vulnerabilities. Your vulnerability is towards alcoholism and therefore you've got a lot of work ahead of you, possibly lifelong, which will probably include turning back to drink and having binges at times. A susceptibility towards something certainly does not mean that this is how your life will turn out Do you follow my point?

Client: I think so. I can fight against my nature and also see that staying at home is not the wisest thing to do, if I want my life to turn out differently. I'm not happy about the lifelong hard work though. Is it worth it?

Therapist: It depends on how much you want to change. A lot of hard work will be the grim reality for you. How did your sister avoid not turning out an alcoholic given the same family conditions?

Client: I don't know. She just turned her mind against drink and left home as soon as she could. There isn't much contact with her now.

Therapist: Maybe as part of your new learning you could contact her to discover why she did not succumb to alcohol like the rest of the family. Your mother doesn't drink as much as your father you said. Do you know why this is?

Client: I think she is stronger minded than he is.

*Therapist:*Does your brother drink more or less than you do?

*Client:*Oh, much more.

Therapist: So given the same family situation and biological vulnerabilities, there is considerable individual variation among you in how you respond to these factors.

Client: Seems so. And I know what you're getting at.

Therapist: Which is...?

Client: I have some control over my life and I can to some extent choose how I want to live my life.

Therapist: Exactly. I'll be showing you how to exercise that control and choice over your life in the coming months – if you choose to stay in therapy.

Client: I do want to but I'm not sure if I'm up to it.

Therapist: Let's see.

In the above dialogue, the therapist is not promising a cure for alcoholism and suggests that the client's struggle against it could be lifelong with frequent lapses and relapses. REBT theory would argue that biological causality is not behavioural inevitability because 'all behaviour is multiply determined and, therefore, clients with strong biological predispositions to a specific problem had better work harder to maximize the influence of psychosocial factors' (Ellis et al., 1988, p.23).

'They're not my feelings'

In REBT, the concept of emotional responsibility means that individuals largely create (but not totally) their emotional reactions to life events. Clients who believe in the general principles of free will and self-determination may deny that these apply in specific contexts in which they are emotionally upset:

Client: I do believe that life is what you make it.

Therapist: So you are in control of your life then.

Client: Yes, to a large extent.

Therapist: Okay, let's examine this present problem of yours.

Client: My husband makes me so angry with his ingratitude. His business wouldn't be as successful as it is without my support over the years. But to hear him talk you'd think he'd done it all himself.

Therapist: When you say he 'makes me so angry' are you implying that you play no part whatsoever in creating your angry reaction to his ungrateful behaviour?

Client: I'm not implying it, I'm stating it! Look, I don't like feeling angry, it's an unpleasant emotion. So if I don't want anger in my life it obviously follows that I didn't put it there, someone else did – my husband.

Therapist: Are you in charge of any emotions in your life?

Client: Of course I am. When I'm happy that's down to me.

Therapist: And when you're unhappy?

Client: I'm in charge of that too. When my mother died a few years ago I was naturally depressed and when I forgot to send my son a birthday card I obviously felt guilty.

Therapist: So those emotions were not anyone else's responsibility.

Client: No, all mine...except in this case.

Therapist: In REBT, we would argue that other people or events can significantly contribute to our emotional reactions but not directly cause them – this we do ourselves. So the idea of self-created disturbance is not something to be wheeled in and out of the closet when it suits us – it's always there. Now your husband's ingratitude acts as a trigger which sets off some thoughts in your head which then causes you to be angry. What thoughts might they be?

Client: I can hear them in my head...'that selfish bastard...after all those years of loyal support...he should be honest and admit how I've helped him...I could swing for him sometimes.'

Therapist: What things would you need to say to yourself to get rid of your anger?

Client: I suppose something like 'He's more to be pitied really that he has to impress his friends that he built up the business alone. [sighs] Men and their delicate egos.' But I don't think like that.

Therapist: No, because you choose to think something different. When people are emotionally disturbed it can appear to them that there is no other way of seeing a particular situation – choice doesn't come into it. The choice becomes clearer when we're emotionally calmer.

Client: That doesn't make sense. If I'm emotionally disturbed and don't see that I have a choice, how then can I have a choice?

Therapist: Just because you don't see the choice it doesn't mean that it has stopped existing. As I've said, when you're emotionally calmer you're more likely to see that the choice exists. Therefore you don't have to keep on responding to your husband's ingratitude in a angry manner.

Client: How should I respond?

Therapist: That's for you to decide.

Client: Here we go again.

Therapist: I'm not trying to be deliberately argumentative. We can look at the pros and cons of each course of action and you decide which will best serve your interests.

Client: I might want to stay angry...

Therapist: If that's your choice...

Client: Is there no escape from this emotional...what's the word?

Therapist: Responsibility. We see it as a form of self-empowerment rather than as a curse. You did say at the beginning of this interview that you are in charge of your life to a large extent. Now you have the opportunity to increase that extent.

Client: Okay, that's a good point and I'm willing to see where that leads. But I still don't like his ingratitude!

Therapist: I'm not asking you [to?], but you don't have to disturb yourself about it either.

Teaching the principle of emotional responsibility can be one of the hardest tasks in REBT as clients may have habitually blamed others for their problems and now the therapist is pointing to the true source of their emotional problems – themselves. Free will and emotional responsibility go hand in hand. As Walen, DiGiuseppe and Dryden (1992, p. 28) observe: 'If something negative happens, you probably will feel negatively about it, but you have a choice in how bad you feel about it. You can decide to be self-defeatingly angry and miserable, or to feel constructively annoyed and motivated to do something about it.'

'You can't escape the past'

Many clients often state that past events dictate or shape their present feelings and behaviour and therefore they are prisoners of the past. Popular conceptions of therapy see present problems as rooted in the past, particularly in childhood. These childhood experiences, it is assumed, have to be explored laboriously before the individual can experience any remission in his current emotional distress. Present helplessness in the face of a irrevocable past means to some clients that therapy will be futile:

Therapist: In what way do you think therapy will be unable to help you?

Client: My parents screwed me up. My life today is screwed up. What else is there to say about it?

Therapist: Well, you might find there is quite a bit to say about it. Now in what way did your parents screw you up as you say?

Client: They always treated my older brother as if he was some god or something. I always felt as if I was an afterthought, 'Let's see what John wants first, we'll come to you later', that sort of thing.

Therapist: Did they actually use those words?

Client: Not exactly, but their actions told the whole story.

Therapist: Which was...?

Client: That I was inferior, second class, not good enough – worthless, in fact.

Therapist: And how has this view of yourself affected your life?

Client: As I grew up I didn't push myself for a proper career, good friends or relationships. I couldn't seem to enjoy life because of this nagging thought that I'm not good enough, I don't deserve these things. I told you, my parents screwed me up.

Therapist: Okay, let's look at this another way. I understand how overwhelming it must have felt to be considered second best by your parents and there was little you could do about it when you were younger. Now when did you start to think for yourself, independently of your parents?

Client: Er...when I was 18 I suppose.

Therapist: And you are 34 years old. Now you've had 16 years to reconsider their view of you as inferior, second best. Now why do you continue to agree with them?

Client: (indignantly) I don't agree with them. They made me think like this. That's the point.

Therapist: Let's say you got the idea from your parents, but you have been carrying and reinforcing it in your head ever since [tapping his forehead]. You still choose to believe it. It is your present thinking about past events rather than the past events themselves that continues to screw you up. That is the real point.

Client: But how can it be when they've made me like this.

Therapist: Are there things that you didn't agree with your parents on?

Client: Yeah, respect for the law. I've had some trouble with the police. Convictions for drinking and driving, a bit of shoplifting.

Therapist: So you can choose not to follow your parents' viewpoint.

Client: I know what you're getting at but you're wrong – it's still my parents' fault.

Therapist: How so?

Client: Well if they hadn't made me feel inferior then I would have respected the law because I would have had self-respect. The kind of life I would have led would have kept me out of trouble.

Therapist: Okay. Has there been a time in your life when you were happy?

Client: A few years ago I went out with a woman for about nine months. Nine happy months until it all ended.

Therapist: How were you able to be happy if you saw yourself as inferior?

Client: Because for the first time in my life I didn't see myself as worthless for those months with her.

Therapist: But you could have still believed it about yourself?

Client: But I didn't want to believe it, so I pushed it away.

Therapist: Instead of accepting it like you usually did. Were your parents responsible for those happy nine months?

Client: I can safely say they had nothing to do with it.

Therapist: Good. That means you can think for yourself when you choose to – but you don't do it very often. You can decide to change your view of yourself, and you've just provided some evidence of that, and I can show you how to do it on a more permanent basis. Remember, your parents are not the real problem. The way in which you still think about past events is the crux of the problem. You can choose to free yourself from your mental straitjacket and lead a different kind of life.

Client: Hmm. I'm still unconvinced about the things you say but I'm a bit more interested in your theory than I was at the beginning of the session.

In the above dialogue, the therapist has managed to establish a toehold in her attempts to orientate the client to the REBT viewpoint that how emotional problems are maintained is more important to examine than how they were acquired. However, clients understandably do not readily accept the proposition that the real 'iron grip' on their present life is their current thinking about unpleasant past events, not the events themselves. The therapist's task is to show them that the solution to their emotional problems lies in the present and not in the past. As Grieger and Boyd (1980, pp. 76 7) point out: '...the crucial thing is for him or her to give up these currently held ideas so that tomorrow's existence can be better than yesterday's. In a sense, the person each day chooses to either hold on to disturbed beliefs or to give them up.' The past has only as much significance in the person's present life as he or she attributes to it.

'Work stresses me out'

Stress appears to be the 'sickness' of the 1990s if media reports are accurate. Hundred of millions of working days are lost annually to stress-related illness and the resulting costs to industry are estimated to run into billions. Everyone is under pressure to cope with higher workloads with reduced workforces. When clients complain of being 'stressed' or 'burnt-out' this usually refers to physical and mental debilitation, i.e. the individual is emotionally spent and therefore deprived of productive energy; stress, or more accurately pressure, has turned into distress (Neenan and Palmer, 1996). As Abrams and Ellis (1994, p.39) ask: 'The key issue for the rational emotive behaviour therapist is: how does the environmental irritation become oppressive? The answer is largely found within the stressed individual, not in the events.' The following dialogue will illustrate this REBT viewpoint:

Therapist: What's going on at work?

Client: It's like working in a madhouse: too many tight deadlines, too many meetings, endless phone calls, lots of faxes from customers. It's all so relentless.

Therapist: How are you coping with this hectic workload?

Client: I'm not. I feel stressed out most of the time.

Therapist: What do you mean by stressed out?

Client: I'm angry a lot, short-tempered with my colleagues and even some customers. I'm also anxious about how I'll cope with all this pressure: will I let other people down? What will they think of me if I can't cope? Will I lose my job? These things go through my mind all the time.

Therapist: Do these things distract you from your job?

Client: They certainly do.

Therapist: Okay. I can understand the great pressures you are under at work but the REBT view of stress in that it really is emotional disturbance largely created by how you evaluate events in the workplace. In your case, anger and anxiety. Your thinking rather than the workplace is the key to change.

Client: I don't choose to react this way, I don't want to be like this.

Therapist: Are your colleagues under the same pressures but respond differently?

Client: Some of them cope very well and I wonder, why them and not me?

Therapist: Well, if the workplace was the real culprit then you would all be equally stressed out. How do you account for the individual variations to exactly the same situation?

Client: I don't know but I'm sure you're going to tell me.

Therapist: It is the attitudes and beliefs we hold in here (tapping her forehead) that really determine how well or badly we cope with pressure in our lives.

Client: You mean it's all in my head?

Therapist: A lot of it is. Therefore you can choose how you want to respond to pressure.

Client: I don't believe this.

Therapist: Well let's look at what you tell yourself about these endless phone calls for example. I presume you have to answer the calls.

Client: Every one.

Therapist: So what do you tell yourself then?

Client: 'The phone should bloody well stop ringing.' 'Don't they know, the customers that is, that I'm bloody busy'. 'If that bloody phone rings one more time I'm going to throw it out of the bloody window.'

Therapist: How do those thoughts help you cope?

Client: They don't. I sit there stewing about the unfairness of it all and I fall behind with my work.

Therapist: Does the workplace make you have those thoughts or are they your own invention?

Client: (sighing deeply) Well, before this conversation I would have said my work does it to me. Now I'm not so sure.

Therapist: If we examined other examples, what would we find going on in your head?

Client: The same sort of ranting and raving.

Therapist: Now imagine all that 'ranting and raving' had gone but the workplace pressures are the same. What would happen now?

Client: I'd be able to cope much better like some of my colleagues do.

Therapist: And what sort of attitudes would you need to adopt in order to change your behaviour?

Client: I want to keep the job so I'd better improve my performance and learn to accept the way things are at work.

Therapist: Such as...?

Client: Well, customers don't know or couldn't care less how busy I am but they want their calls answered promptly and their problems dealt with efficiently. If I did that in the first place I would have less problems to deal with. So both the customer and myself would benefit.

Therapist: So let's recap: you said you were working in a madhouse. Now you don't have control over your physical environment, but what or who do you have control over?

Client: Myself. If I start thinking sensibly, not crazily, I'll be much calmer, more in control and more focused on getting the job done efficiently rather than exploding over it.

Therapist: Can you see that you have a clear choice regarding your behaviour at work?

Client: It's becoming clearer. It's a strange feeling to know that when I go into work next week that I can actually decide how I want to behave.

Therapist: And no one can take that choice away from you unless you surrender it.

Bernard (1994, section 3, p. 1) argues: 'In order to think clearly and thus effectively handle stressful situations and solve practical problems, you first have to develop emotional control. Emotional self-management is a vital key to stress management.' Lack of emotional control (e.g. anger, depression) blinds people to or impairs their judgement about the various options they have in any given situation. Emotional control is brought about by attitudinal change. Once this is achieved, individuals may be better able to see that 'severe stressors are often inevitable; undue stress about them is not' (Abrams and Ellis, 1994, p.48).

'What's so good about having free will?'

REBTers attempt to show clients that their lives might be constrained more by their thinking, specifically their irrational beliefs, than by deterministic features such as biology, family or environment (although these considerations are not minimised). However, not all clients are pleased with or grateful for this insight and the greater liberation it might supposedly bring:

Client: Having free will is not going to sort my problems out.

Therapist: Not in and of itself; it depends on how you use it. You could end up with more problems. It's not that you don't have some free will already but REBT believes that if you think more rationally this will probably create greater opportunities and less problems in your life; you will have more choices before you. These choices don't seem so apparent when you're emotionally disturbed.

Client: Then everything is down to me all the time. If anything goes wrong, then it's all my fault.

Therapist: Whose 'fault' was it before then?

Client: Well, my father left home when I was 12, my teachers at school didn't really care about me, then there are no jobs about so I'm depressed most of the time and I haven't got a girlfriend. There's not much there to be happy about.

Therapist: So does that mean that your father, teachers, society and women are to blame for your current problems?

Client: I'm not exactly saying that but they don't help either, do they?

Therapist: If things go right in your life, whose 'fault' is that?

Client: That's down to me, isn't it. Not much goes right anyway.

Therapist: So when things go right in your life that's because of your efforts and when things go wrong it's the fault of others. Is that what you mean?

Client: Yeah, sort of, I suppose.

Therapist: Is there anything scary about taking responsibility for the bad things in your life?

Client: I suppose there's no one else to blame.

Therapist: Does blaming others provide you with some comfort or protection in your life?

Client: I suppose if I can blame others I don't have to look at myself too closely.

Therapist: And how has blaming your father, teachers, society and women helped you to tackle your problems or bring happiness into your life?

Client: (sheepishly) It hasn't.

Therapist: Do you want to stay with the comfort of blaming others yet remaining miserable or start taking responsibility for the decisions needed for a different kind of life?

Client: I do want to change but I'm afraid of blaming myself for everything that goes wrong.

Therapist: In REBT, we make a clear distinction between responsibility which means that you are largely in control of your reactions to unpleasant life events or when things go wrong, and blame which means putting yourself down when things go wrong. We teach personal responsibility but not self-blame. Free will is a lot less scary if you don't include self-blame as part of the package, so to speak.

Client: Okay, that's reassured me a little.

Therapist: Now a choice: do you want to try out a few more sessions of REBT or call it a day?

Client: I'm willing to try it out.

Therapist: Do you think you have a little more freedom of choice at the end of the session as opposed to at the beginning of it?

Client: A little. I suppose that's a start.

In the above dialogue, the client is obviously not intoxicated by the concept of free will. He sees it in more fearful terms: greater failure, blame and uncomfortable self-examination. In a sense, as the client indicated, there is no hiding place from it – whatever happens in your life, you are responsible for your reaction to these events. This can seem both liberating and frightening, and REBTers will need to deal with both aspects of this issue if it arises.

Conclusion

Although the determinist argument appears to be gaining ground particularly with discoveries in science, e.g. '...modern genetics feeds the view that behaviour is determined by DNA, while neurology is uncovering the brain chemicals that govern various emotions' (*The Economist*, 1997, p.66), de Botton (1997) in *The Daily Telegraph* states: 'There are significant reasons why determinism can't be the whole story. The most persuasive argument, and also one grounded in common sense, is that, however determined we may be, we don't actually *feel* ourselves to be so. Most of the time we feel (often agonisingly) free.' Painful feelings like guilt remind us of the freedom we had previously in choosing a different course of action to the one we had actually pursued. If we were wholly determined, would we experience such intense feelings?

Berlin (1982, p.6) makes a similar point when he says: 'In the end, of course, a man has to accept personal responsibility, and to do what he thinks is right: his choice will be rational if he realises the principles on which it is made, and free if he could have chosen otherwise. Such choices can be very agonising.'

REBT encourages clients to examine the principles underpinning both their irrational and rational beliefs in order to help them decide which set of beliefs are disturbance-reducing, goal-orientated and carry the potential for self-actualisation. Choosing between stasis and change can be a painful decision for clients to make yet it reminds them (whether they like it or not) that they have the ultimate choice for the kind of life they wish to lead.

References

Abrams, M. and Ellis, A. (1994). Rational emotive behaviour therapy in the treatment of stress. British Journal of Guidance and Counselling, 22(1), 39–50.

Berlin, I. (1982). (discussion) An introduction to philosophy. In B. Magee, Men of Ideas. Oxford: Oxford University Press.

Bernard, M.E. (1993). Are your emotions and behaviours helping you or hurting you? In M.E. Bernard and J.L. Wolfe (Eds), The RET Resource Book for Practitioners. New York: Institute for Rational-Emotive Therapy.

de Botton, A. (1997). Is freedom a fantasy? The Daily Telegraph, 24th May.

Dryden, W. and Neenan, M. (1995). Dictionary of Rational Emotive Behaviour Therapy. London: Whurr.

Dryden, W. and Yankura, J. (1995). Developing Rational Emotive Behavioural Counselling. London: Sage.

Ellis, A. (1980). Overview of the clinical theory of rational-emotive therapy. In R. Grieger and J. Boyd (Eds), Rational-Emotive Therapy: A Skills-Based Approach. New York: Van Nostrand Reinhold.

Ellis, A. (1990). Toward a theory of personality. In W. Dryden (Ed), The Essential Albert Ellis. New York: Springer.

Ellis, A. and Bernard, M.E. (1985). Clinical Applications of Rational-Emotive Therapy. New York: Plenum.

Ellis, A., McInerney, J.F., DiGiuseppe, R. and Yeager, R.J. (1988). Rational-Emotive Therapy with Alcoholics and Substance Abusers. New York: Pergamon Press.

Grieger, R. and Boyd, J. (1980). Rational-Emotive Therapy: A Skills-Based Approach. New York: Van Nostrand Reinhold.

Neenan, M. and Palmer, S. (1996). Stress counselling: a cognitive-behavioural perspective. Stress News, the Journal of the International Stress Management Association (UK Branch), 8(4), 5–8.

The Economist (1997). The passing of a hero. The Economist June 28th.

Thomas, A. and Chess, S. (1980). The Dynamics of Psychological Development. New York: Brunner/Mazel.

Vesey, G. and Foulkes, P. (1990). Dictionary of Philosophy. London: Harper Collins.

Walen, S.R., DiGiuseppe, R. and Dryden, W. (1992). A Practitioner's Guide to Rational-Emotive Therapy, 2nd edition. New York: Oxford University Press.

Chapter Four
An Elaboration of the REBT Concept of Ego Disturbance

Introduction

In this chapter we present a detailed account of ego disturbance and the countless ways in which individuals denigrate themselves. We believe that sophisticated analyses of this important subject have been few in REBT scholarship; moreover, the impression is often given that ego disturbance is synonymous with the concept of shithood and thereby militates against the complexity of ego conflicts. Our view of ego disturbance encompasses inferential themes associated with particular unhealthy negative emotions; how these themes are reflected in the cognitive content of the disturbance-producing beliefs; and how negative interpersonal experiences activate these beliefs leading to compensatory strategies to restore a positive self-image. Finally, we emphasise that this chapter on ego disturbance is not definitive but, through it, we hope to promote further discussion on this issue among REBTers.

Ego disturbance involves individuals making demands upon themselves, others and the world, and when these demands are not met to engage in some form of self-depreciation, e.g. 'As I didn't pass this exam, which I absolutely should have done, this means I'm a total failure.' Such beliefs can lead to depression, anger, anxiety, shame, and guilt. Ego disturbance represents one of the 'two main sources of just about all neurosis [the other source is low frustration tolerance or discomfort disturbance]' (Ellis, quoted in Dryden, 1991, p.28; Ellis, 1994). Given the centrality of ego disturbance in clients' presenting problems, it is surprising that in over 40 years of REBT's existence few detailed analyses of the various belief structures underpinning this form of disturbance have been carried out.

Sometimes it can appear in REBT that ego disturbance has been bundled into one scatological category: 'self-esteem...depends on your doing the right thing, and when you do the wrong thing, back to shithood you go...shouldhood equals shithood' (Ellis, quoted in Bernard, 1986, pp. 52–3). As Neenan and Dryden (1996) point out, clients' self-denigratory epithets (e.g. worthless, useless) are not necessarily synonymous in their minds with shithood and therefore therapists need to be wary about introducing the term as a matter of course. Much better to use the client's form of self-denigration as this will keep REBTers alert to the manifold ways ego disturbance is expressed (and the subject of this chapter).

An earlier attempt to categorise the varieties of ego conflicts was Young's (1988) diagnostic framework for dealing with TC's (tough customers) by discriminating between their different thinking styles: bad me (e.g. 'If I fail at my exams then I'm a failure'); less me (e.g. 'If my girlfriend doesn't have an orgasm when we make love then I'm not much of a man'); damn me (e.g. 'I'm a rotten, wicked parent for letting my son waste his life on drink and drugs'). This chapter follows on from Young's work and others (Beck, 1976; Crawford and Ellis, 1989; Dryden, 1995; Dryden and Yankura, 1993; Gilbert, 1992) by presenting a detailed account of the many manifestations of ego-disturbance-producing beliefs.

Beliefs, themes and emotions

Separating a client's compacted presenting problems into their ABC components can be an exceedingly difficult task. Especially important for the REBTer is to locate the client's irrational or disturbance-creating beliefs (often expressed in a derivative form such as 'I am useless'). As Grieger and Boyd (1980, p.37) ask: 'How do these basic [or multifarious] irrational ideas manifest themselves, for instance, in anxiety problems or anger problems [we are specifically concerned in this chapter with the ego aspects of these and other problems]?' These manifestations can be legion, so the REBT therapist needs to bear in mind that applying catch-all categories of, for example, worthlessness or inadequacy to whatever emotion is experienced by the client obviously lacks subtlety, empathy and clinical acuity.

To illustrate this point, when we listen to supervisees' counselling tapes there is often a tendency on the part of the supervisee to jump to the conclusion that the client believes he is a failure simply because he is talking about failures in his life. I (MN) recently did something similar when I 'press-ganged' a client's problems into the category of inadequacy because the theme of his current difficulties was falling behind his work colleagues. The client was indignant and retorted that he had never in his life seen himself as inadequate but probably incompetent was nearer the mark. The client's reply may seem like mere quibbling or much of a muchness to some REBTers but was vitally relevant to him because it carried an important distinction in his mind.

Eliciting the diverse personal meanings that individuals attach to events is a vital part of the assessment process. Therefore REBTers who do not carefully differentiate between general and specific ego disturbance-producing ideas (e.g. 'I've lost face' vs. 'I am utterly weak') run the considerable risk of penetrating only the outer layers of a client's belief system instead of finding its centre and thereby falling short of a thorough cognitive and behavioural analysis of her emotional distress.

To try and avoid some of these pitfalls, this chapter lays out a detailed account of ego problems and the various factors that interlock to produce them. Emotional disorders have particular themes associated with them which reflect the cognitive content of the specific disturbance-creating beliefs. These beliefs, which are developed through our experiences with others, are activated in interpersonal contexts when we negatively appraise ourselves in some way. In order to retrieve our premorbid personality or rescue our present damaged self, we engage in some compensatory strategy. For example, the theme in guilt is moral violation, so a father who has thoughts of harming his daughter believes he is a wicked person ('bad' would not be condemnation enough) and in order to try and dispel this self-image he showers her with love and presents.

A framework of Ego disturbance

Emotion: Anger.
Inferential theme related to ego disturbance: Transgressed against.
Specific belief(s) which lead to self-created disturbed emotions:

> I have been revealed as/made to look stupid and this proves I am stupid.
> I have been revealed as/made to look foolish and this proves I am foolish.
> I have been revealed as/made to look weak and this proves I am weak.
> I have been revealed as/made to look unimportant or insignificant and this proves I am unimportant or insignificant.
> I have been revealed as/made to look incompetent and this proves I am incompetent.

[Note that here the individual agrees with these apparent negative evaluations of himself.]

Relationship of self to others

When others are involved in ego-related anger, these others are seen to have the ability, intentionally or unintentionally expressed, to devalue the individual's perceived self-esteem or violate his personal rules of living, e.g. a lecturer who chides a student for late submission of an essay is interpreted by the student as humiliating him in front of the rest of the class. The person thus operates according to the following axioms: I am defined by what others think of me (or how I think they think if me); I am defined by how others treat me (or how I think others treat me).

Compensatory strategy

To attack the transgressor, physically, verbally or through passive-aggressiveness, in order to get one's own back by making her suffer in a similar or greater way and thus raise one's perceived self-esteem, e.g. the student spreads malicious rumours that the lecturer is an alcoholic and shouts at students 'when she has the shakes'.

Emotion: Anxiety.
Inferential theme related to ego disturbance: Threat or danger.
Specific belief(s) which lead to self-created disturbed emotions:

> I will be worthless.
> I will be a failure.
> I will be a fool.
> I will be incompetent.
> I will be a shit.
> I will be useless.
> I will be no good.
> I will be inferior.
> I will be weak.

Relationship of self to others

When other are involved in ego-related anxiety, the self is seen as a commodity whose value rises or falls depending upon others' future investment in or withdrawal from it (as if on the stock market), e.g. a woman's stock (or self-esteem) rises when she is promoted by her boss but starts to fall when he criticises her performance. The person thus operates according to the following axiom: I am defined by others' predicted investment in me.

Compensatory strategy

To reverse the decline by proving her worth to her 'stockholders', e.g. the woman strives to make herself efficient, conscientious, competent, even indispensable in order to regain and maintain her worth in the eyes of her boss.

Emotion: Depression.
Inferential theme related to ego disturbance: Loss of Value.
Specific belief(s) which lead to self-created disturbed emotions:

> I am worthless.
> I am unlovable.
> I am unlikeable.
> I am repulsive.

I am a failure.
I am incompetent.
I am a shit.
I am useless.
I am no good.

Relationship of self to others

When others are involved in ego-related depression, others are seen as possessing the attributes, elements and qualities that the individual believes he needs in his life for his happiness, sense of worth, and when these things are withdrawn or lost his self-esteem plummets, e.g. a husband who built his life around his wife falls into suicidal despair when she leaves him because he now concludes that he is worthless and can never be happy without her. The person thus operates according to the following axiom: I am defined by what others give me.

Compensatory strategy

To repair the defect(s) in himself in order to regain what he has lost, e.g. promising to be more attentive and sociable as a means of trying to get his wife back. Through this strategy he hopes to restore his happiness and self-esteem. However, when the person is convinced that he is incapable of repairing the defects (helplessness), or that his efforts will not be successful (hopelessness), his depression deepens.

Emotion: Envy.
Inferential theme related to ego disturbance: Others experience the good fortune which the person lacks and therefore covets.
Specific belief(s) which lead to self-created disturbed emotions:

I am a loser.
I am second rate.
I am unsuccessful.
I am inferior.
I am less worthy/worthless.

Relationship of self to others

When others are involved in ego-related envy, the individual sees herself as inferior, unsuccessful or disadvantaged when compared with someone who has the possessions or qualities she covets, e.g. a woman who has great difficulty in finding a boyfriend begrudges a colleague's romantic success with men. The person thus operates according to the following axiom: I am defined by what I possess.

Compensatory strategy

To denigrate her colleague's success with men as a means of getting even and also convincing herself that she is better off the way she is, e.g. 'They're not real men – just shallow and vain. If she didn't have those long legs and sunbed suntan, they wouldn't touch her with a bargepole.'

Emotion: Guilt.
Inferential theme related to ego disturbance: Moral violation.
Specific belief(s) which lead to self-created disturbed emotions:

> I am bad.
> I am wicked.
> I am depraved.
> I am immoral.
> I am evil.
> I am sinful.
> I am selfish.
> I am rotten.

Relationship of self to others

When others are involved in guilt, an individual views his acts of omission or commission as directly harming or hurting others, e.g. a father condemns himself as 'bad' when his daughter becomes distraught over not getting into university. He believes he is the cause of her unhappiness because he should have pushed her harder when she was at school and therefore he set her up to fail. The person thus acts according to the following axioms: I am defined by what I do; I am defined by what I fail to do; I am defined by my impact on others.

Compensatory strategy

In order to purge his guilt as a 'bad' father, he spends more money on personal tutors for his daughter than he can afford in an attempt to ensure that she is accepted on her second application to the university.

Emotion: Hurt.
Inferential theme related to ego disturbance: Wronged.
Specific belief(s) which lead to self-created disturbed emotions:

> I am no good.
> I am unlovable.
> I am unlikeable.
> I am insignificant.
> I am of no account.
> I am disposable.

Relationship of self to others

In ego-related hurt, the individual sees others as having, through their actions, the ability to inflict injustice or unfairness on her, e.g. a wife is very hurt when her husband fails to acknowledge, let alone celebrate, their silver wedding anniversary. Because of his apparently uncaring behaviour, she believes that all her years of loyalty and faithfulness mean nothing to him and therefore she must be of no account for being treated this way. The person thus operates according to the following axiom: I am defined by how significant others treat me (or how I think significant others treat me).

Compensatory strategy

The wife becomes withdrawn, silent and frequently tearful as a means of punishing or getting even with her husband. Through this behaviour she hopes to make him feel guilty for hurting her.

Emotion: Jealousy.
Inferential theme related to ego disturbance: Threat to present relationship posed by another person.
Specific belief(s) which lead to self-created disturbed emotions:

> I am unlovable.
> I am inferior.
> I am worthless.
> I am inadequate.
> I am nothing.
> I am unattractive.
> I am repulsive.

Relationship of self to others

In ego-related jealousy, others are viewed as potential or actual rivals for his partner's love or romantic interest, e.g. a husband who saw his wife talking to a stranger immediately assumed that she must be having an affair with the man because she had tired of him.

Because of the husband's inferiority complex, he overestimates both the attractiveness of this rival to his wife and her interest in him. The person thus operates according to the following axioms: I am defined by how I am (or think I am) viewed by my partner; I am defined by my partner's presumed or actual interest in others.

Compensatory strategy

The individual seeks to control, restrict, check, and/or monitor his partner's movements in order to reduce the occasions in which she can engage in her presumed unfaithfulness, e.g. the husband insists that he accompanies his wife when she goes on trips to the shops, hairdresser, gym, job centre, etc. to 'protect his property' and keep rivals at bay.

Emotion: Shame.
Inferential theme related to ego disturbance: Pubic revelation of weakness or defect; public humiliation.
Specific belief(s) which lead to self-created disturbed emotions:

> I am pathetic.
> I am disgusting.
> I am spineless.
> I am stupid.
> I am a fool.
> I am despicable.
> I am contemptible.
> I am insignificant.
> I am weak.
> I am defective.
> I am inferior.

Relationship of self to others

In shame, the person conducts herself in the way in which she believes others must see her and tries desperately to conceal what she perceives to be weaknesses or defects. When the person assumes that others have identified her weakness or defects, she thinks they will look down on her, ridicule her or turn away from her in disgust, e.g. a woman who believes she must be seen as cool under pressure or in a crisis, panics in a crowded lift when the doors fail to open and believes she has lost face because others present will, for example, look down on her. The person thus operates according to the following axioms: I am defined by how I present myself to others; I am defined by how I am (or how I think I am) viewed by others; I am defined by how others treat me (or how I think others treat me).

Compensatory strategy

To try and restore her public persona of unflappability and re-establish her perceived superiority over others, the woman engages in daredevil activities such as parachuting, abseiling down buildings and bungee jumping.

Conclusion

By using this elaboration of ego disturbance as a guide (certainly not a definitive one), REBTers can become more attuned to the numerous ways individuals express their irrational and self-defeating beliefs and thereby achieve greater precision in isolating the key disturbance-inducing idea(s). This is likely to convince clients that the therapist is genuinely empathic and therefore she is not seen as trying to manoeuvre them into declaring their shithood or some other preordained self-downing category. Also, this precision helps to target more effectively the therapist's disputing interventions.

While we have sought to elaborate on the concept of ego disturbance in this chapter, we wish to reiterate that our framework is far from the last word on the subject. Rather, we hope to stimulate the thinking of other REBT scholars on this issue so that the complexity of ego problems receives the scrutiny it has often lacked.

References

Beck, A.T. (1976). Cognitive Therapy and the Emotional Disorders. New York: International Universities Press.

Bernard, M.E. (1986). Staying Rational in an Irrational World: Albert Ellis and Rational-Emotive Therapy. Carlton, Australia: McCulloch.

Crawford, T. and Ellis, A. (1989). A dictionary of rational-emotive feelings and behaviours. Journal of Rational-Emotive and Cognitive-Behaviour Therapy, 7(1), 3–28.

Dryden, W. (1991). A Dialogue With Albert Ellis: Against Dogma. Buckingham: Open University Press.

Dryden, W. (1995). Preparing for Client Change in Rational Emotive Behaviour Therapy. London: Whurr.

Dryden, W. and Yankura, J. (1993). Counselling Individuals: a Rational-Emotive Handbook. London: Whurr.

Ellis, A. (1994). Reason and Emotion in Psychotherapy, 2nd edition. New York: Birch Lane Press.

Gilbert, P. (1992). Counselling for Depression. London: Sage.

Grieger, R. and Boyd, J. (1980). Rational-Emotive Therapy: A Skills-Based Approach. New York: Van Nostrand Reinhold.

Neenan, M. and Dryden, W. (1996). Dealing with Difficulties in Rational Emotive Behaviour Therapy. London: Whurr.

Young, H.S. (1988). Teaching rational self-value concepts to tough customers. In W. Dryden & P. Trower (Eds). Developments in Rational-Emotive Therapy. Milton Keynes: Open University Press.

Chapter Five
Beyond Low Frustration Tolerance and Discomfort Disturbance: The Case for the Term 'Non-ego Disturbance'

Introduction

In this chapter, a case is made for the term 'non-ego disturbance' to replace low frustration tolerance (LFT) and discomfort disturbance as the generic alternative to ego disturbance in REBT theory. The issues of valence and varying levels of non-disturbance are introduced and discussed and an initial version of a taxonomy of non-ego disturbance is presented. Finally, a plea is made for the development of a scale to measure non-ego disturbance.

In the late 1970s and early 1980s, Albert Ellis (1979; 1980) published two parts of an important paper outlining his views on what he called discomfort anxiety which he contrasted with ego anxiety. In that paper, Ellis (1979, p.3) defined discomfort anxiety as:

emotional tension that results when people feel (1) that their comfort (or life) is threatened, (2) that they should or must get what they want (and should not or must not get what they don't want), and (3) that it is awful or catastrophic (rather than merely inconvenient or disadvantageous) when they don't get what they supposedly must.

Since that time the concept of discomfort anxiety has been broadened and renamed 'discomfort disturbance' in order that it might encompass other discomfort-related disturbances such as discomfort depression. REBT therapists also commonly employ the term low frustration tolerance to indicate a person's poor ability to bear frustration. To our knowledge, there exists in the REBT literature no systematic attempt to distinguish between discomfort disturbance and low frustration tolerance with the result that the terms are frequently used synonymously by REBT practitioners. Indeed, these terms are used so broadly in the REBT literature that quite different disturbances are referred to as examples of LFT.

Furthermore, the term 'low frustration tolerance' is ambiguous. As we pointed out above, it is taken to mean a perceived inability to bear frustration, but it can also be taken to refer to an ability to bear low levels of frustration. These issues have prompted us to write this chapter, the purpose of which is to make the case for the use of the broad category, 'non-ego disturbance' (which can be readily distinguished from the equally broad category of 'ego-disturbance') and to outline the range of disturbances that might fall under the heading 'non-ego disturbance'. In doing so, we wish to point out that this chapter represents an initial attempt to develop a taxonomy of non-ego disturbance and as such it is our hope that it will stimulate further thought among REBT theorists. Before outlining a preliminary taxonomy of non-ego disturbance, we discuss a number of salient issues.

Ego disturbance vs. non-ego disturbance rather than ego disturbance vs. discomfort disturbance

As we pointed out above, Ellis (1979; 1980) has contrasted discomfort anxiety with ego anxiety and more recently (Ellis, 1994) has differentiated ego disturbance from discomfort disturbance. The difficulty with this distinction is that it does not easily allow for ego disturbance in the realm of discomfort. Thus one of our clients kept on complaining that she could not bear to be uncomfortable at work. I, (WD) initially considered this to be a clearly articulated example of discomfort disturbance, but was proved wrong when my client resisted my attempts to dispute it as such. Finally, and somewhat exasperated she said: 'You don't seem to understand. It's not that I can't bear to be uncomfortable at work because I can't bear the discomfort per se. I can't bear it because it proves that I am a failure if I'm uncomfortable. I shouldn't be uncomfortable there'. I was treating this client's problem as an example of discomfort disturbance because she said that she couldn't bear to be uncomfortable at work. My implicit and rapid reasoning was thus: My client has said that she can't stand discomfort; this means that she has LFT. Thus, her problem is not ego-related. This implicit (and incorrect!) reasoning was influenced, I believe, by the contrast that is made in REBT circles between ego-disturbance, on the one hand, and discomfort disturbance, on the other. My client happily made no such distinction and was able to point me in the right direction. In short, I incorrectly conceptualised my client's problem thus:

'I must not be uncomfortable at work. I can't bear this discomfort' (discomfort disturbance).

An accurate conceptualisation of her problem turned out to be:

'I must not be uncomfortable at work. I can't bear this discomfort because it proves that I am a failure and not because I can't bear the experience of discomfort'(ego disturbance).

As I have said above, I believe that my error was influenced by the tendency to see disturbance as either ego-related or discomfort-related. A better distinction is that between ego disturbance and non-ego disturbance. As we discuss below, non-ego disturbance encompasses a variety of psychological problems including (rather than only comprising) a perceived inability to tolerate discomfort and frustration.

If I (WD) had used this distinction, I would not have been quick to assume that my client's problem lay in the realm of discomfort disturbance just because she said that she couldn't bear to be uncomfortable at work. Rather, I would have explored further to establish whether her problem was an example of ego disturbance or non-ego disturbance. This distinction, then, helps REBT therapists to identify ego disturbance masquerading as discomfort disturbance.

The issues of varying levels of non-ego disturbance

In REBT theory, the concept of low frustration tolerance is used very loosely. Thus, a client who complained that she could not bear to sit down to work on an essay because she predicted that she would experience discomfort is said to have a philosophy of low frustration tolerance, as is another client who said that she was not able to tolerate being taken hostage by a man who locked her up for 10 days in a small box. To view these two situations as indistinguishable examples of LFT is clearly preposterous. How then can they be distinguished? They can be better differentiated if we use the terms 'tolerance' and intolerance' more carefully and apply these terms to varying levels of frustration and discomfort. Thus, we may speak of the following:

1. Low frustration intolerance (LFI). This term would cover situations where a person believes that she cannot tolerate low levels of frustration. The above example of the student who procrastinated on her essay would probably be an example of LFI.
2. Moderate frustration intolerance (MFI). This term would cover situations where a person believes that she cannot tolerate moderate levels of frustration, but where she believes that she can tolerate low levels of frustration.
3. High frustration intolerance (HFI). This term would cover situations where a person believes that she cannot tolerate high levels of frustration, but where she believes that she can tolerate low and moderate levels of frustration. The above example of the client who was taken hostage would be an example of exceedingly high frustration intolerance.

4. Low frustration tolerance (LFT). This term would cover situations where a person believes that she can tolerate low levels of frustration. As such, LFT would be used in a very different way in REBT theory and practice than is currently the case.
5. Moderate frustration tolerance (MFT). This term would cover situations where a person believes that she can tolerate low and moderate levels of frustration.
6. High frustration tolerance (HFT). This term would cover situations where a person believes that she can tolerate low, moderate and high levels of frustration.

This way of construing varying levels of disturbance can be applied to other forms of non-ego disturbance to be discussed below. For example, we can clearly distinguish between high discomfort disturbance (the perceived inability to bear a high level of discomfort) and low discomfort disturbance (the perceived inability to bear a low level of discomfort).

Non-ego disturbance: the issue of valence

The issue of valence and non-ego disturbance has long been neglected in REBT. By valence, we mean the positive or negative value of an internal state or external condition. In this section of the chapter, we consider non-ego disturbance as it relates to both positive and negative states and conditions.

Non-ego disturbance and positive states and conditions

Non-ego disturbance occurs when a person believes that he must establish, maintain or intensify a positively valued internal state and/or find, maintain, increase or intensify a positive external condition. Some examples will illustrate this point.

Establishing a positive internal state

Here, the person believes that she has to initiate a positive internal state. For example, Lucy was in a neutral frame of mind when she decided that she must feel good at that moment. She therefore chose to smoke some dope which quickly achieved for her the desired state.

Maintaining a positive internal state

Here, the person believes that once he has begun to experience a positive internal state then he has to maintain this state. Thus, Luke, a 'recovering' alcoholic was chilling out with his friends and was beginning to lose that desired internal state which he believed he must maintain. He, thus, began to drink beer even though he had successfully abstained from alcohol for three months.

Intensifying a positive internal state

Here, the person believes that having established a positive internal state, then at some point he has to intensify it. For instance, Sam was having a great time at his son's bar mitzvah party where he was the life and soul of the party. Because it was such a special occasion for Sam, he believed that it had to be an even more special time for him. He thus engaged in a lively Russian dance even though his physician strongly advised him to forego vigorous physical activity due to his high blood pressure. Tragically, Sam's need to increase his positive emotional state resulted in a coronary which left him paralysed down one side.

Finding a positive external condition

Here, the person believes that she has to find a positive external condition. This may be any condition as in the case of Sarah or a specific condition as in the case of Beatrice. Thus, Sarah who was financially unable to leave her boring job in the accounts office of a large firm of lawyers believed that because her job was so boring she had to find something enjoyable to do in the evening. Whenever she failed to do so, she became depressed.

Beatrice, a collector of rare coins, on the other hand, believed that she had to find a specific rare coin that would complete her collection. This belief led her to tour the country desperately looking for the coin to the detriment of her work and relationships.

Maintaining a positive external condition

Here, the person believes that once he has obtained something then he has to keep hold of it. Thus, Lawrence believed that once he had found a valuable antique, he had to hang on to it at all cost. This led him to become very suspicious that others were out to cheat him of his prized possession.

Increasing or intensifying a positive external condition

People, like George, who believe that once you get something good, you have to have more of it or, like Marion, who believe that once you get something good, you have to get something better are very rarely, if ever, satisfied with what they have. This type of non-ego disturbance is the basis of greed. Thus, George was never happy for long with his collection of soccer programmes. He believed that he had to keep increasing it with the result that he got himself into severe debt. Marion, on the other hand, believed that she had to experience bigger and better orgasms. This led her into some potentially dangerous situations with men with whom she thought she might have such experiences.

You will no doubt have noted that there can be a great deal of overlap between initiating, maintaining and increasing internal positive states and finding, maintaining and intensifying external positive conditions. However, the two are by no means synonymous. Thus, a person may believe that he must intensify a positive external condition when he is experiencing a negative internal state. Thus, conceptually it is important to distinguish between positive internal states and positive external conditions in deepening our understanding of the development and maintenance of non-ego disturbance.

Non-ego disturbance states and conditions

Non-ego disturbance also occurs when a person believes that he must eliminate, maintain or reduce the intensity of a negatively valued internal state and/or external condition. Some examples will again illustrate this point.

Eliminating a negative internal state

Here, the person believes that he must get rid of, usually quickly, a negative internal state. Thus, Peter believed that he could not stand boredom. This led him to procrastinate on his studies because he demanded that he must not be bored. It is interesting to note that some people, as was the case with Peter, swap one negative state for another. Thus, Peter would tidy up his desk or go to the launderette – activities which he found unpleasant – rather than sit at his desk. The important point to bear in mind here is that the person may hold this belief about specific internal states at specific times, rather than about all negative states at all times.

Maintaining a negative internal state

Here, the person believes that the negative internal state that she is experiencing must not get any worse. She would, of course, like to eliminate the state or ameliorate it, but failing that she believes that she can cope as long as the state remains as bad as it currently is. Paula suffered from chronic arthritic pain which she could cope with, but she was constantly anxious lest her pain should increase. She believed that she could not bear it if that happened.

Reducing a negative internal state

Here, the person does not believe that he must eliminate the negative internal state that he is experiencing, rather that he must reduce its intensity. In contrast to the person who can tolerate a currently experienced negative state as in the above category, the person here believes that he cannot put up with what he is currently experiencing. Whenever Stephen experienced moderate levels of depression (according to his objective score on the Beck Depression Inventory) he believed that this level of depression was intolerable to him. He did not demand that he must get rid of his depression entirely; rather that he must reduce it to a level that he found tolerable. Paradoxically, Stephen's belief only served to increase his depression because he began to make himself secondarily depressed about his primary depression.

Eliminating a negative external condition

Here, the person believes that she must get rid of a negative external condition, again usually quickly. Most commonly, this belief is held about specific external conditions. Thus, Cynthia believed that she must quickly get rid of the mould that had started to grow around the doorframe of her bathroom. She thus engaged a builder on an emergency call out basis and ended up paying a lot of money for an inferior job.

There are some individuals, however, for whom this is a core belief – in that they hold this belief frequently about a large number of negative external conditions. For example, John believed that he must rid himself of all hassles in his relationships with women. Since for John a hassle occurred whenever a woman asked him to do something that he did not want to do, he ended up having very short relationships.

Maintaining a negative external condition

Here, the person believes that the negative external condition that he is facing must not get any worse. For example, Harry disliked his job, but believed that he was able to put up with it as long as it didn't get any worse. When it did, he disturbed himself and became depressed.

Additionally, a person may believe that she must not encounter any further negative events in her life as long as the current negative condition exists. For example, when her mother died, Jenny grieved appropriately. Just before she had fully adjusted to this loss, however, Jenny's cat was run over by a train. Jenny made herself very depressed about this primarily because she believed that one loss was enough for her and therefore she should not have to face a second loss until she had fully adjusted to the first.

Ameliorating a negative external condition

Here, the person does not believe that he must eliminate the negative external condition he is facing, rather that he must ameliorate it. In contrast to the person who can tolerate a currently existing negative event as in the above category, the person here believes that he cannot bear the situation that he is in. Gerald had been dating Brenda for two years and recently their relationship had deteriorated. Gerald made himself anxious because he believed that he had to find a way to ameliorate the situation. This belief resulted in Gerald trying desperately to improve matters between him and Brenda. Unfortunately, Gerald's desperation was a real turn-off for Brenda who eventually ended their relationship.

Towards a taxonomy of non-ego disturbance

In this section, we will provide and briefly comment on a list of the different forms that non-ego disturbance can take. This list should not, in any sense, be regarded as definitive. Rather, it should be seen as an initial attempt to provide the foundations for a taxonomy of non-ego disturbance. It is our hope that this list will stimulate others to contribute to the debate concerning the nature and extent of non-ego disturbance.

Emotion intolerance

As the name suggests, emotion intolerance refers to instances when an individual believes that he cannot tolerate the experience of an emotional state. There are several consequences of holding this belief. First, the person may deny to himself that he is experiencing the emotion in question and may mislabel his experience in ways that are psychologically safer for him. Thus, Sam mislabelled his anger as stress pain because he believed that he could not bear to be angry.

Second, the person may avoid situations where he previously experienced the 'intolerable' emotion. Thus, Benny avoided all crowds because he once became claustrophobically anxious in a large crowd. The effect of such avoidance is well known. It limits the life of the individual and serves to perpetrate his psychological problem.

Third, the person may increase the intolerable emotion. This is what occurs when, in REBT, we talk of anxiety about anxiety. By believing that she could not bear to be anxious, Penny became anxious about the prospect of being anxious. She thus became hypervigilant about situations which she believed triggered her anxiety and intensified the experience of anxiety because she evaluated this experience as too hard to bear.

Fourth, the person may construct negative cognitive distortions (Bond and Dryden, 1996). Thus, Brian believed that he could not bear to be anxious. Consequently, he overestimated the number of situations in which he would feel anxious and greatly exaggerated the consequences of so doing.

In this section, we are only referring to emotion intolerance as an example of non-ego disturbance, although we do appreciate that it can also serve as an example of ego disturbance as when a person believes that he cannot bear to feel depressed because experiencing this emotion means to her that he is a wimp, for instance.

Sensation intolerance

Sensation intolerance refers to instances when an individual believes that he cannot tolerate a sensory-based experience (e.g. auditory, visual, gustatory, touch and olfactory). It is important to distinguish between sensation intolerance, which is defined here as a belief with an individual's biologically-based reactivity to sensory information which is non-cognitive. However, it is likely that if a person naturally finds a sensory experience highly aversive then she is more likely to bring to this experience a sensation intolerant belief than another who finds the same experience less aversive. Thus, Sue has a natural aversion to the taste of olives and believes that she cannot bear to eat them, whereas Linda who finds the taste of olives moderately unpleasant has no such sensation intolerant belief. However, people can bring a sensation intolerant attitude to sensations which they subjectively find only moderately or mildly aversive. The effect of this attitude is, as one might expect, to augment the aversiveness of the experience. This increase in the experience of aversiveness is one of the three main consequences of sensation intolerance.

The second major consequence of holding a sensation intolerant belief is avoidance of situations where one might experience the dreaded sensation. Thus Bill curtailed his life drastically when he was diagnosed as having tinnitus because he believed that he could not bear to experience even moderately loud noises. Because of his sensation intolerant belief, Bill continued to avoid such noises despite medical advice to the contrary.

The third major effect of sensation intolerance is the construction of negative cognitive distortions (Bond and Dryden, 1996). Thus, because Bill believed that he could not bear to hear even moderately loud noises, he thought that doing so would significantly damage his hearing. He would be less likely to make such an overly negative conclusion if his attitude reflected a tolerance for such auditory sensations.

As Bill's example shows, it is difficult to differentiate clearly between sensation intolerance and intolerance of actual activating events which directly impinge on one's senses and this difficulty holds true of many other cases discussed in this chapter. Thus, Bill believes that he cannot bear to hear certain noises. These noises actually exist in the environment, but they are intolerable to Bill because he is intolerant of his sensory experiences of the noises.

A purer example of sensation intolerance occurs when a person is intolerant of a sensory experience which exists in the absence of an external stimulus. This is quite common in the field of tinnitus. Thus, Mary had to be hospitalised because she believed that the ringing in her ears absolutely should not be as loud as it was. This belief led her to become acutely depressed. Unlike Bill, Mary's sensation intolerance belief came more to the fore in the absence of external stimuli.

Pain intolerance

Pain intolerance is a focused form of sensation intolerance. As such, it merits its own category, particularly as the management of pain has a central place in the specialism of behavioural medicine. It is well known that the perception of pain varies enormously among individuals from those who are ultra-sensitive to any form of pain to those who do not experience pain. This latter group has its particular problems because they do not experience the helpful warning signs that pain provides – namely that there is something wrong with us that requires attention. While it is again probably true that those who are very sensitive to pain are those with the greater pain intolerance, some people who do not feel pain intensely still believe that they cannot tolerate the experience of pain.

REBT has recently been applied to the management of chronic pain (Rothschild, 1993). Rothschild argued that the effects of disputing and changing irrational pain intolerant beliefs reduced levels of subjectively experienced pain and increased participation in leisure and social activities.

Disgust

Disgust is a rather vague term normally used by clients to denote a very unpleasant, often intolerable feeling/sensation state. Because it involves emotive and sensation features, it can be properly categorised as separate from emotion intolerance and sensation intolerance. Disgust is frequently experienced viscerally, particularly in relation to situations involving dirt, unpleasant tastes and odours, faeces, vomit and blood and with ugly-looking insects, particularly when the person infers close contact with them. As such, disgust is a common feature of spider phobia, for example. Disgust is frequently based on non-ego irrational beliefs, e.g. 'I must not come into contact with people vomiting. If I do, I couldn't stomach (bear) it.'

As with emotion and sensation intolerance, the effects of disgust include avoidance of situations in which the possibility of disgust might be experienced, an increase in the aversive nature of disgust when it is experienced and the construction of negative cognitive distortions.

Physical illness-related disturbances

There are a variety of illness-related disturbances, some which concern one's physical well-being and others which relate to one's mental well-being. In this section, we concentrate on the former and in the following section we consider the latter. One major type of disturbance related to physical illness rests on the demand that one must be in perfect health and it is unbearable if one is not. Another major type which is at the core of hypochondria stems from the demand that one must know that there is nothing wrong with oneself. This demand leads the person to overesti-mate the threat of presently unexplained physical symptoms. Believing that he must know that he is not ill and faced with the presence of an unexplained symptom, Robert both predicted that he was seriously ill and sought reassurance from his doctor and his family that his symptom was benign. This pattern of believing that one is ill and simultaneously seeking reassurance that one is not is a core dynamic in hypochondria. Another key feature of hypochondria is the belief that one needs to know immediately that one is not ill. While most people are prepared to wait for a short period to see how their unexplained symptoms develop, those suffering from hypochondria find any period of waiting intolerable. Consequently, they rush around seeking reassurance wherever they may get it. However, the effects of such reassurance are inevitably short-lived because the person does not have and cannot have a guarantee that the one giving assurance is absolutely correct in his or her opinion. This is why people with hypochondria are not reassurable.

Another form of disturbance in the physical illness domain is defined by denial and avoidance. Those who use denial as a major defence against illness are initially aware of some problem in their bodily functioning. They also believe that they must not be ill and it would be unbearable if they were. However, unlike those with hypochondria, people in this group are able to convince themselves that there is nothing wrong with them even in the presence of symptoms that clearly indicate illness. This group of people are extremely reluctant to consult a medical practitioner not only because on the surface they believe they are not ill, but also because they believe that it would be terrible if they were. Such people are also prone to magical ideas. For example, Hilda refused to go to hospital for a routine scan because she believed that the act of going to hospital would cause serious illness.

In summary, and using the language of experimental methodology, we might say that those who use denial as a defence against the 'horror' of illness commit the error of failing to detect the presence of an illness that is there. Whereas those with hypochondria commit the error of detecting the presence of an illness that is not there. While those who deny the possibility of illness experience less psychological disturbance than those with hypochondria, they are probably more likely to die from undiagnosed serious illnesses or from such conditions that are diagnosed too late.

Finally, disturbances related to physical illness can also be linked to death-related disturbances discussed later. This can be a reciprocal relationship. Thus people who have a horror of death often overestimate the seriousness of their actual or presumed illnesses and those with a horror of illness often predict that they will die from their actual or inferred physical complaints.

Disturbances related to psychological problems and mental illness

Perhaps the most common form of non-ego disturbance related to psychological problems and mental illness is that known as phrenophobia – a term first made popular in the cognitive psychotherapy literature by Victor Raimy (1975) and developed by Sue Walen (1982). Phrenophobia is literally a dread of disorders related to the mind and often is articulated by clients as a fear of going mad. Raimy (1975) noted that most clients who are fearful that their concerns mean that they are mentally ill or that they will go mad can be reassured by their therapists that this is not the case. This involves therapists carefully explaining to clients that their concerns are examples of psychological problems and not of mental illness (assuming that this is indeed the case) and are amenable to therapeutic interventions. However, a small number of clients will not be so reassured and this group can be said to suffer from phrenophobia. Mary had a morbid dread of mental illness even though there was no evidence that she was or had ever been mentally ill. This dread led her to be intolerant of anxiety and depression since she assumed that these emotions were the first sign of mental illness. This intolerance then increased her feeling of anxiety and depression which she interpreted within her meaning system as stronger evidence that she was losing her mind. Halfway through therapy, Mary was diagnosed as having cancer of the bowel which she accepted stoically. Her repeated lament during this period was: 'I'd much rather have cancer than lose my mind.'

Some manifestations of phrenophobia can be seen as a specific sub-type of control-related disturbances discussed later. Here such clients are scared that they may lose control and act out their madness. Other manifestations of phrenophobia are centred more on the fear that one will live an isolated existence locked away somewhere in some inaccessible Victorian madhouse. Needless to say, the very fact of consulting a therapist is, in the mind of the true phrenophobiac, evidence that one is going mad. Hence, such individuals stubbornly refuse to consult mental health practitioners and will not go near psychiatric clinics.

Other clients do not suffer from phrenophobia, but are very fearful of experiencing psychological problems because of the stigma of so doing. Here, we are not speaking of clear-cut cases of ego disturbance where clients feel ashamed of having such problems because it proves to them that they are weak, inadequate individuals. Rather, we are concerned with those cases where clients are fearful of what they will lose once others discover that they have experienced a psychological problem. Such clients believe that it is unbearable to lose out because of the stigma associated with psychological problems. While it is undoubtedly true that some people will stigmatise a person once they learn that that person has experienced a psychological problem (and this group of clients have a wealth of such anecdotes gleaned from the press and what they have learned from 'friends of friends'), these clients tend to see this as a mechanism that is ubiquitous, existing in both work and non-work settings. They also exaggerate wildly the extent of the losses that they (and others) will encounter as a consequence of having had a psychological problem. Furthermore, they edit out or distort the many exceptions to what is to them the omnipresent stigma associated with psychological problems.

Death-related disturbances

There are a variety of non-ego disturbances related to death and a careful assessment is needed to distinguish one from another. In this section we discuss briefly the main ones. First, there are disturbances related to the state of being dead. Here, it is as if the person exists after dying holding the belief: 'Oh, my God, I'm dead. How horrible.' Many people fear death because they predict that once dead they will be very lonely. Note again the predicted state of consciousness after death. These people are not so scared of the state of being dead; rather, they disturb themselves about the prospect of being alone, a state which for them accompanies death. Then there are a variety of 'hell' disturbances. For example, Diana was scared to die because she was convinced that she would go to hell, a place where she would be given an endless series of unendurable punishments. This type of problem often stems from an earth-bound guilt-related, ego disturbance which needs initially to be targeted for change.

A second type of disturbance relates to the process of dying. Here people disturb themselves about various aspects of dying such as pain, loss of autonomy and seeing the distress of loved ones, to name but three.

The final death-related disturbance mentioned here centres on knowing that one is dying. It is a truism to say that we all know that we are going to die, but there is an important difference between knowing this theoretically and knowing experientially that this will definitely happen. Some people are so scared about knowing that they are dying that their relatives insist that doctors keep this knowledge from them. There was recently a tragic case reported in the press of a man who killed himself when he was told that he was suffering from terminal cancer. Soon after it was discovered that a mistake had been made by the hospital and that he was perfectly healthy. He would be alive today if he had not severely disturbed himself about the knowledge that his death was imminent.

Cognition intolerance

As the name suggests, cognition intolerance refers to situations where a person believes that he cannot tolerate thinking in a certain way. As with emotion intolerance, there are several consequences of holding this belief. First, the person may deny to himself that he is having the forbidden thought. If the person cannot edit out such thoughts, he may well report that the thoughts are being put into his brain by an outside force. One example of this process is where people claim that they experience alien thoughts spoken to them by voices in their head. Thus, Frank reported hearing a voice in his head uttering obscenities. These were thoughts that

Frank would not be able to tolerate if he took responsibly for thinking them himself.

Second, the person may avoid situations in which she had experienced the 'intolerable' thoughts. Thus, Betty, a committed Christian, avoided going to church because she began to think of having sex with Jesus Christ. The effect of such avoidance is well known. It limits the life of the individual and serves to perpetuate his psychological problem.

Third, the person may increase the likelihood of thinking the forbidden thoughts. Albert Ellis often tells his clients of how a king prevented his daughter from marrying someone of whom he disapproved. Having set the young man various tests of physical endurance which he passed, the king ordered his advisors to set the man a test that he could not pass. One advisor suggested that the young man not think of a pink elephant, a test which he failed, to the delight of the king. This story shows that when one tries not to think certain thoughts one increases the chances of thinking them.

Fourth, the person may construct negative cognitive distortions (Bond and Dryden, 1996). For example, Jean believed that she could not bear to think about her dead husband. Consequently she overestimated the number of situations in which she would think of him and greatly exaggerated the consequences of so doing.

Behaviour intolerance

Here the person believes that he cannot bear to act in a certain way, but not for ego reasons. Henry had developed a habit of biting his nails when he felt anxious. While he did not condemn himself for doing so, he did find the habit 'unbearable' and believed that he must not do it. This belief increased Henry's anxiety which he tried to relieve by biting his nails. As with emotion intolerance and cognition intolerance, behaviour intolerance leads to 1 denial – a refusal of the person to take responsibility for his behaviour; 2 avoidance of situations in which one may perform the 'intolerable' act; 3 an increase in the likelihood that one will act in the 'dreaded' manner (as in the example of Henry above); and 4 the construction of cognitive distortions (e.g. one may predict dire consequences if one acts in the way one evaluates as 'intolerable').

Inaction intolerance

Inaction intolerance describes an attitude based on the person's dire need to take action and the related idea that not being able to take action is unbearable. This belief can underpin impulsive action where the person acts before adequately evaluating the pros and cons of a particular course of action. Such a person considers this type of evaluation as doing nothing, which she abhors.

Inaction intolerance can sometimes underpin worry. Melvin, for example, was prone to worry, but did not worry as long as he could take effective action while he was at work. However, at night he worried considerably about work due to the fact that he could not do anything. 'I can't stand the fact that I can't do anything at night. If only I could do something, I wouldn't worry', he said.

Intolerance of unfairness and injustice

We have placed these two non-ego disturbances together because while there are differences between unfairness and injustice, these differences are often very subtle. As Paul Hauck (1979) has noted there is a difference between self-pity and other-pity. In self-pity, one demands that one must not be treated in an unfair or unjust manner, while in other-pity one demands that other people must not be treated unfairly or unjustly. When you ask such a person why he thinks that he (or other people) must not be treated unfairly or unjustly, he frequently replies that he (or the others in question) does not deserve such treatment. Hence, at the root of intolerance of unfairness and injustice is the philosophy of deservingness.

The philosophy of undeservingness states that because a person does not deserve to be treated unfairly or unjustly, therefore he must not be so treated. Social psychologists have called this the 'just world' hypothesis (Lerner, 1980). Interestingly, religious people often give up their faith when they or people close to them experience gross unfairness or injustice. 'How could God allow this to happen?' is the oft-heard cry on such occasions. Rabbi Harold Kushner (1982) has attempted to address this issue in an interesting book called *Why Bad Things Happen to Good People*.

People who are intolerant of unfairness and/or injustice are often hypersensitive to their presence. When they are accurate in their inferences such people often engage in attempts to gain justice or receive fair treatment on behalf of themselves and/or others, but do so in a dogmatic manner and frequently devote inordinate amounts of time to their crusades. They are often proud of their refusal to admit defeat. However, given their intolerance of unfairness and injustice they are frequently inaccurate in their inferences that unfairness/injustice exists. Because they are dogmatic in their beliefs about unfairness/injustice they are rarely open-minded enough to consider the views of those that they see as the perpetrators of the unfairness or injustice. They thus tend not to question the accuracy of their inferences and do not listen to evidence that may disconfirm their views.

The dire need to be right

At the end of the above section, we pointed out that people who have a dogmatic belief about unfairness/injustice are frequently closed-minded. This is an example of the dire need to be right in one's views. While the dire need to be right is often an ego-based problem, here we are only referring to the non-ego form of this disturbance. It is as if the person who needs to be right believes: 'I must be right and it's terrible if I'm not. I couldn't stand being wrong, not because it would prove that I am less of a person, but because it would go against the world as I see it. The world must be as I see it.'

Those who believe that they must be right hold the corresponding view that others who hold a different opinion must be wrong. Such people do not see that opinions are subjective and truth is a relative construct. Rather, they hold that truth is absolute and opinions are either objectively right (the position held by themselves) or wrong (the position held by others).

Frequently, people who have a dire need to be right also believe that those who start off by holding an opposing (i.e. wrong) position eventually have to admit the error of their own ways and acknowledge the correctness of the objectively right position. As may be expected, people who need to be right (and be shown to be right) do not attempt to show understanding of any differing opinions and are very difficult to reason with. Discussions with such individuals often degenerate into slanging matches with those who need to be right denigrating those who have the temerity to disagree with their 'correct' opinions.

Frustration intolerance

Frustration may be defined as a state that exists when what we want to exist does not exist. In itself frustration is not a problem for people, particularly if they believe that they are able to tolerate it. Tolerating frustration often motivates people to find creative ways to overcome obstacles to gaining what they want or to adjust healthily if they are unable to get what they want. However, a frustration intolerant philosophy does often cause people problems. This philosophy is characterised by the belief: 'I must get what I want and must not be blocked in my efforts to get what I want. I can't bear to be frustrated.'

Frustration on its own does not lead to aggression as held many years ago by proponents of the frustration-aggression hypothesis. Rather, aggression often occurs when a person brings his frustration intolerant attitude to the particular frustrating event. When this occurs the person concerned frequently personalises the frustration and believes, for example, that others are out to deliberately frustrate him. He will also magnify the extent of the frustration and exaggerate the number of past frustrations experienced. Correspondingly, he will edit out the number of occasions when he has achieved what he wanted.

While frustration intolerance has been the cornerstone of what we have chosen to call here 'non-ego disturbance', in the present analysis it is only one of a large number of such disturbances.

Deprivation intolerance

Deprivation intolerance is the attitude where a person believes that she cannot bear some actual or inferred deprivation. This deprivation can refer to something that the person believes she missed out on in the past or in the present. Mary, for example, considered that she was deprived of maternal love in her childhood. She believed that because her friends were loved by their mothers therefore her mother absolutely should have loved her and it is unbearable that she was deprived of that love. As a result of this belief, Mary disturbed herself whenever she saw mothers show affection to their daughters in public and she herself tried to get affection from older women with whom she became friendly and saw as mother substitutes.

This latter strategy is common in deprivation intolerance. People with this belief frequently try to get what they believe they were deprived of in the past. This strategy is frequently counter-productive for several reasons. First, others rarely can make up in the present for past deprivations. Thus, even if Mary does succeed in getting maternal love from one of her older women friends, this does not eradicate the actual or inferred past deprivation. Second, other people are rarely in a position to give the person what she believes she needs now. Mary eventually had to admit that none of her older women friends were interested in becoming a substitute for her mother. Consequently, one by one they stopped being friends with Mary. This only served to strengthen her attitude of deprivation intolerance. Third, this strategy keeps the deprivation to the forefront of the person's mind and this also serves to strengthen her deprivation intolerance. Thus, every time Mary tried to get maternal love from one of her older female friends, she reinforced her idea that getting such love was a number one priority in her relationships with her female friends.

Discomfort intolerance

As we have already discussed, one of the ways in which REBT theorists have traditionally referred to non-ego disturbance is as discomfort disturbance. We argued earlier in this chapter that discomfort disturbance was an insufficient term to account for all the psychological problems that people have in the non-ego domain. Indeed, in the present taxonomy, discomfort intolerance is but one of over 40 such problems. Here, discomfort is viewed as a non-specific sensory-based feeling where one's sense of comfort has been disrupted.

As the term implies, people who hold an attitude of discomfort intolerance actively seek to avoid discomfort. In doing so they frequently exaggerate the intensity of the discomfort they think they will experience and overestimate how long they will experience it. They also predict that they will experience more uncomfortable experiences than people who hold a discomfort tolerant attitude. Because they are so keen to avoid discomfort, people with a discomfort intolerant attitude often live unfulfilling lives because they refuse to experience the short-term discomfort that usually precedes long-term fulfilment.

Boredom intolerance

Boredom occurs for some people when they are not engaged in meaningful activity while others are bored when they are not doing anything active at all. Whatever leads people to be bored when they believe that they cannot tolerate boredom, they will do anything to avoid it. If they cannot involve themselves in meaningful activity, then throw themselves into any activity as long as it distracts them from boredom. As with the other problems discussed in this chapter, boredom intolerance leads to self-defeating consequences. These include: overestimating the extent and the duration of one's boredom; predicting that one will go mad if one is bored for any length of time; and taking mood-altering substances to prevent the onset of boredom.

The dire need for excitement

People who have a dire need for excitement easily become bored when they do not experience excitement in their lives. Since they frequently believe that they cannot tolerate boredom, they constantly seek new thrills and adventures. However, in striving for these new thrills and adventures they experience the law of diminishing returns. In their words, new thrills and adventures are only exciting to them for shorter and shorter periods. As new thrills quickly lose their excitement, these people turn to bigger and bigger thrills. In doing so, the often seek out experiences which are unlawful. Since they have very little regard for the consequences of their actions at the time when they believe that they need excitement, these people often get into trouble with the law. Needless to say, they frequently turn to illegal drugs in their search for excitement.

The dire need for novelty

People with a dire need for novelty believe they cannot tolerate sameness. They abhor routine and actively look for novel experiences. They differ from those who have a dire need for excitement in that the new experiences that they seek out do not have to be exciting. They just have to be novel. David was constantly on the lookout for new computer software to play around with. However, before he learned how to use any of these new systems properly, he had bought and tinkered around with an even newer software system. Because such people are addicted to the novel they do not persist with anything for very long.

The dire need for familiarity

As can be appreciated, a person who has a dire need for familiarity is very different from someone who has a dire need for novelty. While the latter abhors familiarity, the former craves it. Believing that they need familiarity, such people often construct routines and rituals to maintain a familiar environment. Consequently, they experience much agitation if their routine and thus their familiarity is disrupted. Not surprisingly, such people are very loathe to move job or home. If they do have to move home, for example, they disturb themselves greatly about this and take a very long time to adjust to their new environment, often visiting their old environment to gain that craved for sense of familiarity. However, once they have adjusted to their new surroundings, they then disturb themselves about any disruptions to this now familiar environment.

Change intolerance

In the previous section, we wrote about the dire need for familiarity. More accurately, this really refers to the dire need for external familiarity where people seek out familiar environments. In this section, what we call change intolerance is based on the dire need for internal familiarity. Internal psychological change means that the person changing will experience unfamiliarity as she, for example, reacts to an activating event with remorse rather than guilt. If the person has a change intolerance belief she will tend to return to the guilt-inducing philosophy so that she experiences the familiar feeling of guilt. Maultsby (1975) called this change-intolerance belief 'the neurotic fear of feeling a phony'.

In a previous section (see pp. 70–1), we discussed hypochondria. In the present context, people with hypochondria are intolerant of internal physical change from a state of well-being. Because they believe that they must know that they are well, they view any physical change from well-being that they cannot account for as evidence that they are seriously ill.

Repetition intolerance

People who have an attitude of repetition intolerance believe that they cannot bear to do the same thing over and over again. They differ from those with a dire need for novelty in one important sense. While the latter are oriented towards novelty, people with repetition intolerance are oriented away from repetition. The former group would not be able to tolerate working on an assembly line at all while the latter group could put up with this experience as long as they could introduce different (i.e. novel) ways of making the same product.

Persistence intolerance

One of our colleagues once referred a female client to me (WD) whom he had been seeing and who had not made very much progress. He asked me if I would tape-record the sessions so that he might, with the client's permission, listen and learn from the work that I had done with her. After therapy ended with a good outcome, I asked my colleague for his reaction to the tapes and what he said to me has stayed with me ever since. He said,

'What you did with her was basically what I did with her, but you persisted for much longer than I did.' Since persistence is often the key to success in many areas, persistence intolerance is a major obstacle to the achievement of one's goals.

Persistence intolerance occurs when one believes that one must achieve whatever one is doing quickly and that persisting with an activity is too hard to bear. As the name implies, people with an attitude of persistence intolerance tend to give up on tasks very quickly and when they are successful at work, for example, they are so because they have managed to find a job which either does not require much persistence or for which they have a natural talent so that they do not have to persist at it. However, since these two situations are fairly rare, people with an intolerant philosophy towards persistence are frequently unfulfilled and often flit from college course to college course or from job to job hoping to find an occupation at which they can succeed and enjoy without persistence.

Effort intolerance

The major difference between effort intolerance and persistence intolerance is that people with the former attitude are prepared to persist at a task as long as it does not take much effort while those with the latter attitude are prepared to exert effort, even great effort, as long as they do not have to do so persistently. People with a philosophy of effort intolerance frequently exaggerate in their minds the amount of effort a task requires and thereby react against a task that they have largely constructed.

In the first part of this chapter we discussed the issue of varying levels of non-ego disturbance. This is relevant to effort intolerance in the following way. Some people may be prepared to exert an effort as long as the effort is not great. These people may be said to have a philosophy of great-effort intolerance (a perceived intolerance of making a great effort). While such people will be hampered by holding such an attitude, they will not be as handicapped as those who have a philosophy of slight-effort intolerance (a perceived intolerance of making even a slight effort).

I (WD) once sat in on a supervision session where the therapist was discussing a client who had such a philosophy. This client refused to make even the slightest effort, staying in bed all day, not washing or cleaning himself. It should be noted that this client was depressed (an attitude of slight-effort intolerance is characteristic of very severe depression) and that he was rich enough to hire a host of people to do menial jobs for him including cleaning his teeth! How did he get to the therapist's office? As you may have already guessed, the therapist was paid handsomely to make house calls!

Intolerance of task difficulty

Intolerance of task difficulty is based on the belief that a task must be relatively easy if one is to attempt it and that if this task is seen to be difficult it is too difficult. This belief leads the person to overestimate consistently the difficulty of tasks and to recruit others to undertake these tasks on his behalf. Every time someone does such a task for the person concerned this strengthens his intolerance of task difficulty belief.

The dire need for control

The dire need for control occurs in basically four areas. First, a person can believe that he needs to be in control over his psychological processes. This issue has been discussed on pp. 71–2. Basically, as long as a person believes that she must control one of her own psychological processes and she infers that she is not in total control of this process then she tends to think that she is out of control. In other words, believing that she must be in control of her feelings, for example, leads the person to think in black and white terms: either she is totally in control of her feelings or she is totally out of control of them.

Second, a person can believe that she must be totally in control of her physiological processes. Thus, a person may think that she has to be in control of her breathing. Once she becomes anxious, for example, and loses control of her breathing, her dire need to be in control increases her anxiety and leads to further loss of control of the way that she breathes. This leads the person to redouble her efforts to control her breathing, which only serves to increase further her anxiety and further lose control of her breathing. This spiralling anxiety is a major feature of panic disorder.

Third, a person may believe that he must be in control of another person. For example, in jealousy, a man may believe that he must ensure that his wife does not find another man attractive. This may lead him to restrict his wife from going anywhere she may come into contact with other men. This strategy invariably fails because the woman will eventually resent such restrictions and may well become interested in a man who will not try to place unhealthy demands on her.

Finally, a person may believe that he must control certain aspects of his environment. Harry, for example, believed that he must ensure that his garden was free of birds. This led him to spend large amounts of money on various gadgets to scare off the birds. Unfortunately, this proved unsuccessful and Harry became depressed by his failure to achieve absolute control over his garden. This example shows that it is often impossible for a person to gain absolute control over his environment. The only alternative is for that person to give up his dire need for such control.

The dire need for certainty

The dire need for certainty occurs in two ways in people's thinking. First, a person may believe that she must know that bad things will not happen to her. This is at the core of hypochondria discussed on pp. 70–1. Believing that she must know that bad things must not happen to her and faced with uncertainty over this issue, the person convinces herself that bad things definitely will occur. Again, the dire need for certainty lead to black and white thinking: either I must be sure that bad things will not happen or they definitely will happen. This leads the person constantly to seek reassurance from others that bad things will not happen to her. Every time she obtains such a reassurance this only serves to strengthen her dire need for certainty that bad things will not happen.

The dire need for certainty may also occur in the following way. A person may believe that he must know what will happen whether it is bad or good. In their book, Wessler and Wessler (1980) presented a transcript of an REBT session with a man who had this type of certainty need. He was drinking in a bar and encountered a man who looked as if he might pick a fight with him. Since the client believed that he had to know what would happen he provoked a fight with the man rather than put up with the uncertainty of the situation.

The dire need for understanding

A person who believes that she must understand what is happening or what has happened frequently disturbs herself when she does not have such understanding. A good example of this dire need for understanding can be seen in the case of Georgina, whose boyfriend suddenly ended their two-year relationship. While Georgina was sad about the loss of her relationship she disturbed herself about the fact that she did not understand why he ended it.

The ability to tolerate not understanding a phenomenon is the hallmark of effective psychotherapists. Psychotherapists who have a dire need to understand their clients and what is going on in the therapeutic process frequently end up by misunderstanding the complexity of therapeutic phenomena. This is because they place such phenomena in oversimplified categories which enable them to gain a false understanding of what is going on.

Ambiguity intolerance

Ambiguity intolerance refers to the belief that one cannot bear ambiguous situations. This stems from the idea that one must only be faced with clear-cut unambiguous situations. Holding this belief leads the person to oversimplify the complexity of ambiguous situations and leads to black and white thinking. Consequently, the person holding this belief will often miss the subtlety of ambiguous life events. More dangerously, the person will assume that danger does not exist in a situation where at first sight the situation seems safe. Thus, people with an attitude of ambiguity intolerance often make surface judgements and take things at face value.

The dire need to be looked after

When a person believes that he must be looked after, usually by another person, he tends to minimise his ability to cope independently and to exaggerate the capability of others. Believing that he is dependent on the help and support of others, the person may develop overt and subtle ways of eliciting such help and support. These attempts are often successful because the person provides other people with an activating event to which they tend to respond either with feelings of pity which encourages them to help and/or support the other person or with guilt if they refuse to offer such help and/or support.

Every time the person succeeds in eliciting help and/or support from other people he tends to strengthen the idea that he needs to be looked after and that he does not have the resources to stand on his own two feet. Every time the person reconfirms that he needs to be looked after he also strengthens the idea that he is helpless and/or weak. On its own, this is not an evaluative ego belief (although the person may well condemn himself for being helpless/weak). Rather it is a trait statement that is an overgeneralised description of the self. This process also occurs in many of the other non-ego disturbances discussed in this chapter.

The dire need for autonomy and freedom

The dire need for autonomy and freedom is the philosophy underpinning reactance (Brehm and Brehm, 1981). Reactance is an oversensitivity to the curtailment of one's perceived freedom. Clients who are highly reactant frequently infer that their REBT therapists are telling them what (or how) to think. They then react against being told what (or how) to think and may hold on to their irrational beliefs in a misguided attempt to retain their autonomy. In working with such clients it is important to emphasise that they have the freedom to think in whatever way they choose and to help them, through Socratic methods, to see the consequences of both irrational and rational beliefs. As may be apparent, didactic methods should be used sparingly with such clients.

People with a dire need for freedom often exaggerate threats to their autonomy and perceive others as attempting to constrain them. Consequently, they frequently rebuke others for telling them, as they see it, what to do/say/think/feel. Interestingly and ironically, because of their oversensitivity to constraints on their autonomy, they can easily be manipulated. If you want such a person to do something just tell him to do the opposite!

Conflict intolerance

As the name suggests, conflict intolerance is the perceived inability to tolerate conflict. This is most frequently manifest in the person's relationships with others. As such, the person will do anything to avoid conflict. Since this often means capitulating to the actual or perceived desires or demands of others, the person often finds himself in relationships where he does what the other person wants rather than what he wants. As such, conflict intolerance stems from the demand that one must at all times have harmony with others.

Conflict intolerance also occurs when the person holding this belief is not directly involved in the conflict. Jonathan was in a constant state of anxiety at work about the likelihood that there would be conflict expressed by people in his team before an audit. Jonathan was more anxious about conflict between others than he was about conflict between himself and others. 'I can't stand seeing conflict between people', was Jonathan's repeated claim.

As occurs with other disturbances in the non-ego domain, when a person holds an attitude of conflict intolerance, she will tend to overestimate the frequency, intensity and duration of conflict between herself and others and between others when she is not involved. Also, this belief leads the person to think that if such conflict occurs, then it is irreparable and will lead to relationship breakdown.

Transition intolerance

By transition intolerance we mean the perceived inability to tolerate movement from one state to another or from one place to another. This may involve a major transition when a person, for example, moves from one country to another or it may involve a much more minor transition. Lesley, for example, experienced a lassitude which lasted for most of the day. As part of her treatment programme, she agreed to go to bed at 10.30 p.m., a task which she found enormously difficult to accomplish. This resulted in her falling asleep on the sofa while she watched television. On exploration, it transpired that Lesley believed that she could not stand moving from a comfortable state (sitting on the sofa) to an uncomfortable state (getting up and preparing to go to bed), despite the fact that this latter state was a very temporary one since she knew that she would soon be comfortable again once she was in bed. As with others who hold a attitude of transition intolerance, Lesley exaggerated in her mind the amount of discomfort she would experience once she got up from the sofa. As this example shows transition intolerance is often related to discomfort intolerance (see p.77).

Intolerance of code violations by others

As humans, we frequently develop codes of conduct to which we anticipate other will adhere. Thus, in certain countries, we anticipate that others will line up in an orderly queue when waiting for a bus, and that when we are watching an opera we anticipate that others will remain silent. Intolerance of code violations by others occurs when we believe that we cannot put up with violations of these codes. This stems from our demand that others must adhere to our codes. When they do not do what we demand we tend to condemn them. As such, intolerance of code violations by others is an important feature of unhealthy anger (Dryden, 1996).

Intolerance of code violations by ourselves is a feature of guilt (when the code is in the moral domain) and of self-anger (when the code is in the non-moral domain) as such this intolerant attitude is best regarded as a type of ego disturbance since it leads to a global negative evaluation of the self.

Disturbances related to time

People often disturb themselves about issues related to time. The most frequent time-related disturbance concerns lateness. A person may disturb himself because he may be late for something. This may be a ego disturbance, but when it is a non-ego disturbance it is based on the belief that one must be on time for things and it is unbearable when one is late; however, the person does not put himself down for being late. Lateness disturbance can also relate to others being late or things like trains being late. Here, the person believes that they must not be kept waiting and it is unbearable if this happens.

When one has a lateness disturbance related to one's self, one can get around this by setting out very early for an appointment. However, most people do not do this and set out thinking that nothing will disrupt their schedule. Therefore, such people are vulnerable to disturbance since numerous events may occur to disrupt their tightly organised schedules. When the person has a lateness disturbance related to others, for example, she can again minimise such disturbance by planning activities in which she can become involved should these others be late. When the person does not make such contingency plans, she may enhance her disturbance by engaging in activities such as pacing up and down. These activities usually keep the activating event clearly in mind and serve as an ever-present trigger to the person's lateness disturbance belief.

Another, time-related non-ego disturbance concerns the belief that one must use one's time profitably. A person who believes this finds it difficult to relax because she considers relaxation a waste of time. When it relates to others, the person believes that others must not waste one's time. As a result, the person finds it difficult to appreciate others' interests because she is preoccupied with her own.

Disturbances related to geography

People also disturb themselves with respect to issues of geography. Perhaps the most common of such disturbances occurs in agoraphobia.

Agoraphobics frequently will not move out of an area which they define as safe (see also the section on the dire need for safety, pp. 89). Once such individuals define an area as safe, they believe that they must not venture forth out of this area and if they do terrible things will happen to them which they would not be able to tolerate. Believing this, the overestimate the danger that they will be exposed to in the 'unsafe' area and underestimate their ability to cope with it. Every time they avoid 'unsafe' areas they strengthen their irrational beliefs with respect to geography and perpetuate their agoraphobia.

A very different disturbance that relates to geography occurs in people who may be said to have compulsive wanderlust. Such individuals demand that they must keep moving on and it would be unbearable if one was confined to one geographical area. Individuals with this kind of belief frequently complain of 'feeling' trapped if they are in one geographical area for (what for them would be) a long period of time. This disturbance could also be seen as a variant of the dire need for freedom (discussed on p. 83).

A cognitively similar problem to compulsive wanderlust, but one which has very different effects is claustrophobia. People with claustrophobia also believe that they must not be confined to a geographical space and that it would be unbearable if they were so confined, but this space would be much smaller than the space experienced as 'suffocating' by those with compulsive wanderlust. People with claustrophobia are scared of being in the midst of a crowd, whereas those with compulsive wanderlust would welcome being in the midst of a crowd if it was in a new geographical location.

The dire need for immediate gratification

The dire need for immediate gratification is often expressed by those with such a philosophy as 'I must have what I want when I want it and I must have it NOW!' As such it is a particularly virulent form of non-ego disturbance.

While this type of disturbance may appear identical to other forms of non-ego disturbance such as frustration intolerance, its unique feature is in the demand to be gratified *immediately*. We call this philosophy 'nowism' to emphasise its distinctive character.

The dire need for immediate gratification is found in a variety of situations. For example, it is often present in clients who overeat. Such clients will eat chocolate, for example, because they believe that they must eat what they want when they want it. This belief is also found in a variety of other impulsive disorders. Helping such persons to delay their impulsive behaviour while they challenge their dire need to be gratified immediately is a central therapeutic task when working with them.

The dire need to do things quickly

People who have a dire need to do things quickly are basically intolerant of spending an extended period on any task. Consequently they rush through tasks, cut corners and are not prepared to spend the time to stop and think through any problems that they might encounter during the task. One thing that they are loathe to do is to check their work with the result that they may make avoidable errors. Consequently, such people should ideally not be given tasks which involve their or other people's safety.

The problem for people with a dire need to do things quickly is exacerbated when they assume or are given too many tasks to accomplish in a given time period. When this happens such people tend to believe that they have to finish their task load as quickly as possible. Given this, they rush from task to task and often fail to finish a particular job before moving on to another.

Loss intolerance

People who have an intolerance of loss cannot accept that such losses are part of life. They tend to believe that things must always stay the same in the sense that they must not lose anything of importance to them. Because they believe that they must not experience loss, they tend to conclude that they will never recover from the loss and tend to feel hopeless about the future. This idea is a core feature of some forms of depression and can lead to the development of suicidal ideation (Beck, 1976).

When the loss has not yet occurred, an attitude of loss intolerance leads the person to become hypervigilant to the possibility of such loss. This may lead to frequent checking that the valued person or object is safe and often leads to overprotection. When the person is scared of losing a child, for example, this overprotection can lead the child to form the idea that the world is a dangerous place from which they need constant protection. Consequently, the child may become anxious and not develop adequate resources to deal with adversity. This occurs because the child is not exposed to negative activating events and as a result he or she does not have the opportunity to deal with such events.

The dire need for completion

People who believe that they must complete a task once they have started it, find it almost impossible to leave a task undone. For example, they often stay up far into the night completing a task and they are frequently late for appointments because they will not leave for their next appointment until they have finished what they are currently working on.

Gestalt therapists, in particular, hold that it is important for people to complete unfinished business and often target their therapeutic interventions to this end (Clarkson, 1989). REBT therapists would concur that it is often important for people to complete such unfinished business, but hold that when people believe that they absolutely must complete such unfinished business, they will disturb themselves when they are not able to do so. When such people are indeed not able to finish their unfinished business, REBT therapists will help them come to a healthy resolution about this by encouraging them to challenge and change their dire need for completion.

Aloneness intolerance

Aloneness intolerance occurs when the person is alone either physically or psychologically (where the person experiences little or no emotional connection with others around him) and when the person believes that he must have the company of or some kind of emotional connection with others. Aloneness intolerance can, of course, be an ego disturbance and here the person believes that she is in some way less worthy for being alone. However, our main preoccupation here is with non-ego disturbance and when this is the main feature of aloneness intolerance, the person believes that the state of physical or emotional aloneness is intolerable. When this occurs, the person is likely to take great pains to avoid the state of aloneness ensuring, for example, that he is always in the presence of others or that others are near to hand. Such individuals, when they are physically alone, take steps to distract themselves from the awareness that they are alone. They may, for example, make frequent use of the telephone or they ensure that their television or radio sets are constantly on. This gives them a sense that they are not alone.

Of course, the more a person believes that he cannot bear to be alone the less time he will spend on his own and the more he will feel emotionally disconnected and withdrawn from others when he is in their presence. These avoided and withdrawn states only serve to strengthen the person's attitude of aloneness intolerance. Our clinical experience suggests that people who do not have a rich inner life and who have never developed the skills of what might be called self-interaction or of self-nurturing are more liable to develop and sustain the philosophy of aloneness intolerance. This clinically derived suggestion, of course, awaits empirical enquiry.

The dire need for solitude

Some people with a dire need for solitude may crave this state because they find being with others difficult for ego reasons. However, others believe that they need to be by themselves for non-ego reasons. When this is the case, such people find being with others intolerable because they cannot think clearly in the presence of other people or because they cannot bear not being themselves. Here, they find that they can only be themselves when they are on their own. People with an avoidance personality disorder or with a schizoid personality disorder frequently have a dire need for solitude. So do people who believe that they cannot be creative if they are in the actual or near presence of others. People who are introverted are more likely than extroverts to have a dire need for solitude while extroverts are more likely than introverts to have a philosophy of aloneness intolerance. The reason for this has been noted by Phares (1984, p. 259): '...introverts and extroverts differ in their arousal level, as shown by electroencephalographic measures. Introverts seem to avoid stimulation from external sources while extroverts constantly seek it. This effect is traceable to a differential capacity for cortical arousal.' It is possible that these biologically-based preferences (which are in accord with REBT theory – see Ellis, 1976) are then cognitively transferred into dire needs, particularly when such preferences are strong.

The dire need for safety

The dire need for safety in the non-ego domain is the belief that people have who think that the locus of safety is exclusively external to them and that they need external safety to have an inner feeling of safety. Needless to say, this belief is a main feature of much anxiety. The more a person believes that he needs to feel safe and when he locates safety in the presence of particular people or the existence of a particular set of environmental conditions, the more that person will experience anxiety. The more the person experiences anxiety the more desperate he becomes to have the presence of these other people or conditions. In this way a tightly closed vicious circle is established.

Indeed, the more the person gains the presence of these people or conditions – and such individuals often become quite adept at gaining this – the worse the person becomes in the long term even though in the short term his feelings of anxiety are relieved (because he has gained that which he believes he absolutely needs). The person gets worse under these conditions for two reasons. First, the attainment of the needed person or set of conditions and the reduction of anxiety that is temporarily achieved only serve to strengthen the person's dire need for external safety. Also, the more the person believes that he needs to rely on external resources to feel safe, the less he will try to develop and rely on his inner resources to gain a sense of inner-derived safety. Consequently, the person increasingly experiences himself as vulnerable and lacking the inner resourcefulness to do anything about this vulnerability, this 'I'm vulnerable' self-image becomes more fixed with every revolution around the vicious circle.

Disorder intolerance

Disorder intolerance is an attitude which stems from a dire need for order. It is important to note that the concept of order here is very subjective and in working with clients who have an attitude of disorder intolerance it is important to discover what their own view of order is. Thus, for some clients 'order' may be represented by tidiness and knowing where everything is, for others it is having and following a set routine, while for yet other clients it is working or living in an environment where everyone knows, agrees to carry out and does, in fact, carry out their duties.

The important point to appreciate when working with clients with an attitude of disorder intolerance is that like those with a dire need for control, for example, they do not operate according to an 'order continuum' with perfect order at one end and chaos at the other. Rather, such clients operate according to two categories: 'perfect order' and 'chaos'. Consequently, as soon as the person's order begins to break down (or looks as if might break down) he predicts that chaos will soon follow. In addition to overestimating the speed at which chaos follows the break-down of order, the person with an attitude of disorder intolerance overestimates the frequency of chaos and the duration of the chaotic state of affairs should it ever come to pass.

A person for whom the dire need for order involves the behaviour of other people and/or the presence of a set of external conditions that is outside his direct control is more vulnerable to emotional disturbance than the person whose disorder intolerance only encompasses his own behaviour or an environment that is potentially under his control. The reason for this is that the latter is more able to achieve the order that he demands than the former who is more dependent on others and/or the external environment for a sense of order. Having said this, people in the latter group are still vulnerable to disturbance because even if they have achieved an orderly state they are constantly anxious lest they are unable to sustain it.

Intolerance of the intolerance of others

By now, it will have become apparent that people can and do disturb themselves about a large range of events in the non-ego domain. The last category illustrates that people can even have an attitude of intolerance about the intolerance of other. As one of my clients succinctly and humorously put it: 'So it seems as if I am prejudiced against other people's prejudice.' Intolerance of the intolerance of others is rooted in the belief that others must not be intolerant.

A particular form of this kind of intolerance is found in clients who, once they have accepted the point that demandingness is irrational, then demand that others must not have and demonstrate a philosophy of demandingness. This shows quite starkly that human beings can often bring their own demanding philosophy to something healthy and disturb themselves when these healthy conditions are not met by others. In a phrase, they are rigidly against the rigidity of others.

Future directions

As we explained at the outset of this chapter, the taxonomy of non-ego disturbance that we have put forward here should be seen as an initial attempt to do justice to the complexity of this major form of disturbance. What is needed now is the development of a non-ego disturbance scale which can be shown to have sound psychometric properties. Once this has been achieved, factor analyses need to be carried out to identify the factor structure of non-ego disturbance. It is our hope that this chapter will facilitate the development of a non-ego disturbance scale which will enable This work to be carried out.

References

Beck, A.T. (1976). Cognitive Therapy and the Emotional Disorders. New York: International Universities Press.

Bond, F.W. and Dryden, W. (1996). Modifying irrational control and certainty beliefs: Clinical recommendations based upon research. In W. Dryden (Ed), Research in Counselling and Psychotherapy: Practical Applications (pp. 162–83). London: Sage.

Brehm, S.S. and Brehm, J.W. (1981). Psychological Reactance: A Theory of Freedom and Control. New York: Academic Press.

Clarkson, P. (1989). Gestalt Counselling in Action. London: Sage.

Dryden, W. (1996). Overcoming Anger: When Anger Helps and When it Hurts. London: Sheldon.

Ellis, A. (1976). The biological basis of human irrationality. Journal of Individual Psychology. 32, 145–68.

Ellis, A. (1979). Discomfort anxiety: A new cognitive behavioural construct. Part 1. Rational Living, 14(2), 3–8.

Ellis, A. (1980). Discomfort anxiety: A new cognitive behavioural construct. Part 2. Rational Living, 15(1), 25–30.

Ellis, A. (1994). Reason and Emotion in Psychotherapy: A Comprehensive Method of Treating Human Disturbances. Revised and updated. New York: Birch Lane Press.

Hauck, P. (1979). Depression: Why it Happens and How to Overcome it. London: Sheldon.

Kushner, H. (1982). When Bad Things Happen to Good People. London: Pan.

Lerner, M.J. (1980). The Belief in a Just World: A Fundamental Delusion. New York: Plenum.

Maultsby, M.C. Jr. (1975). Help Yourself to Happiness: Through Rational Self-counselling. New York: Institute for Rational Living.

Phares, E.J. (1984). Introduction to Personality. Columbus, OH: Charles E. Merrill.

Raimy, V. (1975). Misunderstandings of the Self: Cognitive Psychotherapy and the Misconception Hypothesis. San Francisco, CA: Jossey-Bass.

Rothschild, B.H. (1993). RET and chronic pain. In W. Dryden and K. Hill (Eds), Innovations in Rational-Emotive Therapy (pp. 91–115). Newbury Park, CA: Sage.

Walen, S.R. (1982). Phrenophobia. Cognitive Therapy and Research, 6, 399–408.

Wessler, R.A. and Wessler, R.L. (1980). The Principles and Practice of Rational-Emotive Therapy. San Francisco, CA: Jossey-Bass.

Chapter Six
Some Reflections on
Rational Beliefs

In this chapter, a number of issues concerning the nature of rational beliefs are discussed. In particular, a distinction is made between partial and full rational beliefs, which helps to explain how people transform rational into irrational beliefs. It is also argued that while a person cannot hold a full rational belief and its irrational equivalent at the very same time, she can change from holding a full rational belief to holding its irrational equivalent and back again in very short order.

The nature, characteristics and types of rational beliefs

In REBT theory, rational beliefs are deemed to be at the core of psychological health and a primary goal of REBT is to help clients to change their irrational beliefs into rational beliefs. What are rational beliefs? Basically, rational beliefs are viewed as the opposite of irrational beliefs. Thus, irrational beliefs are considered to be rigid and extreme in nature and rational beliefs are thus considered to be flexible and non-extreme. The defining characteristics of irrational beliefs are that they are inconsistent with reality, illogical and lead to predominately unhealthy results for the individual and his relationships as well as impeding his pursuit of his personally meaningful goals (i.e. they are unempirical, illogical and dysfunctional). Correspondingly, rational beliefs are deemed to be consistent with reality, logical and lead to predominantly healthy results for the person and his relationships as well as facilitating his pursuit of his personally meaningful goals (i.e. they are empirical, logical and functional).

Finally, while REBT theory posits four basic types of irrational beliefs, i.e. demands, awfulising beliefs, low frustration tolerance (LFT) beliefs and beliefs where the self, others and/or life conditions are depreciated, it also posits four basic types of rational beliefs, i.e. preferences, anti-awfulising beliefs, high frustration tolerance beliefs and beliefs where the self, others and/or life conditions are accepted.

Escalation versus transformation

In working with clients, Ellis used to speak of the tendency of people to escalate their rational beliefs into irrational beliefs (Yankura and Dryden, 1990). However, the concept of escalation implies that a person's rational belief and her irrational belief exist on a continuum. Theoretically, this is incorrect. A rational belief is qualitatively different to its irrational alternative. Consequently, it is more accurate to say that a person transforms her rational belief into an irrational belief. The concept of transformation accurately portrays the qualitative difference between rational and irrational beliefs.

Both an irrational belief and a rational belief can be placed along its own continuum which describes varying strengths of conviction. Thus, an irrational belief can be held weakly, moderately or strongly and the same applies to a rational belief. Although there is no empirical evidence on this point it is likely that a strongly held rational belief can be transformed into an irrational belief more readily than the same rational belief held weakly.

Full versus partial rational beliefs

In order to make the process of transforming rational beliefs into irrational beliefs clear, it is important to distinguish between a partial rational belief and a full rational belief. As will be shown, when transformation occurs the person changes his *partial* rational belief into an irrational belief rather than his *full* rational belief. This is best illustrated with an example.

Full versus partial preferences

Let us assume that a person holds the following rational preference: 'I want to pass my forthcoming examination.' As expressed, this belief is really a partial preference because although the person asserts her preference, she does not negate her demand. If she were to express her full preference she would say: 'I want to pass my forthcoming examination, *but* I do not have to do so.' Here the person both asserts her preference and negates her demand. These two characteristics have to be stated explicitly for it to be clear that the person's preference is truly a rational belief.

When this person transforms her rational preference into an irrational demand, she is in reality transforming her partial preference into a demand. This transformation becomes clear when the person says: 'I want to pass my forthcoming examination and therefore I have to do so.'

Indeed, whenever a person states her partial preference, we do not know for sure that this truly represents a rational belief. Thus, the person may explicitly state: 'I want to pass my forthcoming examination', and then implicitly add ('...and therefore I have to do so').

Given a person's ability to add an implicit demand to an explicitly stated partial preference, REBT therapists are strongly advised, when assessing their clients' beliefs, to encourage them to focus on their stated partial preference and to determine whether this is really full preference or an implicit demand. This can be done by taking the partial preference, e.g. 'I want to pass my forthcoming examination' and by asking them to state which of the two additions represent their true belief: (1) 'but, I don't have to do so', or (2) 'and therefore I have to do so'. When it is clear that the person's true belief is a full preference, the person should be encouraged to use the full preference form whenever referring to this rational belief.

When we take the person's full preference, it becomes clear why she cannot transform this rational belief into an irrational belief. Thus, if she believes: 'I want to pass my forthcoming examination, but I do not have to do so' she cannot logically transform this into the following demand: 'I must pass my forthcoming examination.' However, this person can at one moment hold a full preference about her passing her examination and at the next moment demand that she must pass it. But these are best regarded as two separate belief episodes whereas were the person to transform her partial prereference into a demand this can be seen as a single belief episode.

For similar reasons, a person cannot logically hold a full preference about something and a demand about that very same thing at the same time. She can however, hold a partial preference and a demand at the same time and this is probably what Ellis is referring to when he says in his advanced workshops that a person can hold a desire and a demand at the very same time. As stated above, a person can oscillate from holding a full preference to a demand and back again several times in a short period of time, but each of these oscillations is best seen as a separate belief episode.

This point about the simultaneous and consecutive adherence to beliefs also holds for partial and full anti-awfulising beliefs, partial and full LFT beliefs and full acceptance beliefs.

Full versus partial rational derivative

As is well known in REBT circles, demands are regarded by Ellis as primary irrational beliefs (to denote their central position in accounting for psychological disturbance) and awfulising beliefs, LFT beliefs and depreciation beliefs are regarded as secondary irrational beliefs or more properly irrational derivatives from these demands (Ellis, 1994). Similarly, what I have called full preferences are regarded by Ellis as primary rational beliefs (to denote their central position in accounting for psychological health) and anti-awfulising beliefs, HFT beliefs and acceptance beliefs are regarded as secondary rational beliefs or more properly rational derivatives from these full preferences (Ellis, 1994).

Similar points can be made about partial and full rational derivatives as were made about partial and full preferences.

Full versus partial anti-awfulising beliefs

When a person holds a partial anti-awfulising belief she asserts the point that it was bad that the event in question occurred, for example. This point holds regardless of the time frame of the event. Thus, in our example the person's partial anti-awfulising belief was as follows: 'It would be bad if I were to fail my forthcoming examination.' Note, however, that in this belief the person does not negate the idea that it would be awful if the target event were to occur. Given this omission, we do not know whether in fact the belief is really an awfulising belief since the person could implicitly add, 'and therefore it would be awful if this were to occur'. Indeed, if the form of this belief is partial then the person could easily transform it into an irrational awfulising belief.

Thus, we only know that a anti-awfulising belief is rational when it is stated explicitly in its full form, thus: 'It would be bad, but not awful if I were to fail my forthcoming examination.' Note that in this statement the person asserts that it would be bad if the event were to occur, but negates the proposition that it would therefore be awful if it were to happen.

Full versus partial high frustration tolerance (HFT) beliefs

The distinction between partial and full HFT beliefs is not as obvious as that between partial and full preferences and partial and full anti-awfulising beliefs. This is because asserting that you can tolerate something seems to incorporate negation of the idea that you cannot tolerate it. The problem comes back into focus when the client does not use 'tolerance' words interchangeably. Thus, the following belief seems fully rational: 'If I were to fail my exams, I could tolerate it.' However, the person could add the statement either explicitly (if asked) or implicitly, 'but if I did fail the exam I would fall apart'.

In this case, it is harder to encourage the person to develop a full HFT belief since you do not know if you have exhausted all the words she uses to denote an LFT belief. What you can do in this situation is to explain the concept of LFT beliefs to the client and elicit from her the key words she uses to denote such beliefs. You can then ensure that she negates her most common LFT belief term.

In our example, 'falling apart' was for this client a common LFT belief term so that in her mind she could tolerate something, but still fall apart. Thus, the person's partial HFT belief was: 'I could tolerate it if I were to fail my forthcoming examination', but this really hid an implicit LFT belief: 'but if it were to happen I would fall apart.' Her full HFT belief would be as follows: 'I could tolerate it if I were to fail my forthcoming examination and if it happened I would not fall apart.'

Full versus partial self-acceptance beliefs.

In this section, the focus is on self-acceptance beliefs although as is well known, acceptance beliefs can also refer to one's attitude about other people and life conditions. When a person articulates a partial self-acceptance belief, she often makes a statement about who she is not. Thus, in our example the person's partial self-acceptance belief was as follows: 'If I were to fail my forthcoming examination, it would not prove that I was a failure.' This seems rational until you note that the person has not stated who she thinks she would be if she were to fail the exam. Thus, our client could go on to say: 'But if I did fail the examination, I would be less worthy than I would be if I were to pass it.' If she did this she would be revealing that what on the surface appeared to be a self-acceptance belief was nothing of the kind. Indeed, it turned out to be a subtle form of self-depreciation belief.

Thus, when a person negates a self-depreciation statement, she reveals a partial self-acceptance belief and in doing so we cannot rule out the possibility that she may hold an implicit self-depreciation belief nor can we be sure that she will later transform this partial self-acceptance belief into a self-depreciation belief.

A full self-acceptance belief, in contrast, makes clear both who the person believes she is not and who she believes herself to be. We have dealt with the case where the client negates a self-depreciation statement, but what can she say when she asserts a self-acceptance statement? To answer this question, let us briefly consider the REBT concept of self-acceptance.

In REBT theory, unconditional self-acceptance means that the person refrains from making any kind of self-rating. Here, the person accepts or acknowledges that she is a complex, unrateable, unique process who has good aspects, bad aspects and neutral aspects and is in essence fallible. REBT theory also advocates (although less enthusiastically) the concept of unconditional positive self-rating. Here, the person regards herself as worthwhile no matter what. If she wishes to assert a reason for this she can say: 'I am worthwhile because I am alive, human and unique.' Normally, however, the person asserts her worth for reasons that change, e.g., 'I am worthwhile because I passed my examination.' This is problematic because the person's worth fluctuates according to changing circumstances. This is REBT's major objection to the concept of self-esteem: it is conditional and allows for worth to vary as was revealed in the implicit statement of the person in our example: '...But if I did fail the examination, I would be less worthy than I would be if I were to pass it.'

A full self-acceptance statement, then, should assert who the person is and this statement should be whether an unconditional self-acceptance statement or an unconditional positive self-rating statement. Thus, the person in our example could say either: 'If I do not pass my forthcoming examination, it does not mean that I am a failure, it means that I am a fallible, unique, unrateable complex human being who has failed this time. Nothing can alter this fact about me' or 'If I do not pass my forthcoming examination, it does not mean that I am a failure. I am still worthwhile even though I failed, for my worth depends on my aliveness, my uniqueness and my being human.' As you can see, in the first full self-acceptance statement the person asserts an unconditional self-acceptance belief and in the second, she asserts an unconditional positive self-rating.

In summary, a full self-acceptance belief has the following features. First, it negates a self-depreciating belief. Second, it asserts an unconditional self-acceptance belief or an unconditional positive self-rating belief. It is thus unconditionality that is important and without it the person may hold an implicit self-depreciation belief and is in danger of transforming his seemingly rational self-acceptance belief into a subtle self-depreciation belief.

The strength of partial preferences and the transformation process

Partial rational beliefs are more likely to be transformed into irrational beliefs when they are strong than when they are moderate or weak. This will be illustrated with reference to partial preferences and demands. Thus, the person in our example is more likely to transform her partial preference into a demand when it is strong ('I really want to pass my forthcoming examination and therefore I have to do so') than when it is moderate ('I would like to pass my forthcoming examination and therefore I have to do so') or weak ('I suppose I do want to pass my forthcoming examination and therefore I have to do so'). The transformations outlined in the latter two situations are possible, but less likely to be made than that illustrated in the first situation.

The converse to this is that it is easier to develop a full preference from a partial preference when the latter is weak ('I suppose I do want to pass my forthcoming examination, but I don't have to do so') or moderate ('I would rather like to pass my forthcoming examination, but I don't have to do so'). While the last case is hardest to achieve, it is perhaps the very hallmark of psychological health if the person can truly believe it.

Other issues

In this section, four further issues will be discussed: (1) the importance of probing for conditions where the person would think irrationally when he (in this case) holds a rational belief; (2) the importance of distinguishing between two different types of preferences; (3) the importance of distinguishing between true preferences and introjected, false preferences, and (4) the question of whether rational beliefs exist prior to the development of irrational beliefs.

Probing for possible irrationalities when a client holds a rational belief

When you have helped a client to construct a rational belief, it is still important to check whether or not the person holds a further irrational belief which may mean that the stated rational belief is dependent upon the existence of certain conditions. Consider this statement: 'I am not a failure for failing my examination. I am a fallible human being who has failed this time'. This seems to be a rational belief, but the client who made it went on to say: 'I can accept myself if I fail the examination, but I must not fail it really badly. If I did I would be a failure.' Another example of this was the client who, in response to questioning, admitted that while she could accept herself if she made mistakes, this would only be true if those mistakes were relatively small. 'I must not make really big mistakes and if I did I would be a failure.' In both these examples it transpired that the client's rational belief was conditional.

If a client puts forward a rational belief such as: 'I am not a failure for failing my examination. I am a fallible human being who has failed this time', ask her the following questions: (1) 'Are there any circumstances relevant to this situation where you would consider yourself a failure?' and (2) 'You are not demanding that you must pass your examination, but can you think of any circumstance relevant to failing where you would make a demand on yourself?' If these questions reveal the conditionality of the stated rational beliefs, help the person to make these beliefs unconditional by disputing the implicit irrational beliefs.

Distinguishing between two different types of preference

The statement: 'I would prefer to pass my forthcoming examination, but I do not have to do so' is clearly a rational preference, since it asserts what the person wants and negates the idea that she must achieve what she wants. Now consider the following statement: 'It would be better if I revised for my examination since it would increase my chances of passing it, but I do not have to do so.' This is also a rational preference in that it negates the demand, but in this case the person does not want to do the activity in question, i.e. revise for her examination.

Thus, one type of preference points to something that the person wants and a different type of preference points to what the person does not want to do, but is in her interests to do. In other words, in this latter type of preference the person acknowledges that she has to do something undesirable (i.e. revise for her examiination in order to get what she does want (passing it). Both are rational preferences, but they can be properly regarded as different types of preference. This becomes important when challenging the irrational version of these beliefs, which are (1) 'I must pass my forthcoming examination' and (2) 'I must revise for my examination'.

In the first example, it makes sense to ask the person: 'Why do you have to achieve what you want, i.e. passing your examination?' However, this type of question would not make sense in the second example because the person does not want to revise. In this case, it is better to ask: 'Why do you have to do what you don't want to do, i.e. revise for your examination?' The answer to the first question is: 'I don't have to pass the examination, but I do want to pass it.' The answer to the second question is: 'I don't have to revise for my examination, but it is in my interests to do what I don't want to do to get the outcome that I do want.'

Thus, it is important to distinguish between these two different types of preference and the different types of alternative demands that the person may make when he transforms his preferences into demands.

Distinguishing between true preferences and introjected, false preferences

It sometimes happens that a client's preference may not represent what the person truly believes, but what he has introjected (i.e. taken from others or from other sources without consideration) from others. An example of an introjected, false preference occurred with a client who stated that he wanted to become an accountant. When asked why he wanted to pursue this career, he found it difficult to come up with plausible reasons. He was then asked who else apart from himself wanted him to become an accountant. He replied that his father wanted this. He was then asked how he would respond if his father changed his mind and did not want him to pursue this occupation, he replied that in this case he would study to be a musician which was a career that he truly wanted.

Although Ellis has stated that REBT therapists do not challenge a client's preferences, it is useful to do so if you have a hunch that the person's preference may be introjected and false. The clues to the existence of such a preference are: (1) the person finds it difficult to provide persuasive reasons for his preference; (2) other people think that he 'should' have such a preference and (3) if presented with a scenario where these people no longer want him to have this preference, the person is prepared to relinquish it.

When a person has an introjected false preference, this is often a sign that he holds an irrational belief with respect to the people who have an interest in him having the preference. This irrational belief relates to the person believing that he must have the approval of these others. If this is the case, this belief should become the focus for therapeutic intervention.

Do rational beliefs exist prior to the development of irrational beliefs?

Ellis (1976) has argued that humans have two inherent capacities: the capacity to think rationally and be self-enhancing and the capacity to think irrationally and be self-defeating. If we take preferences and demands as representatives of the two capacities, the following question arises: Which comes first, the demand or the preference? While this might remind you of the famous chicken and egg conundrum (and as having equal practical relevance!), it is an important point to consider from the perspective of REBT theory.

The proposition put forward here is that a partial preference exists both before the full preference and before the demand. In other words, a person has a partial preference (e.g. a desire for approval) which he can either nurture into a full preference (by believing that he does not have to get his desire met) or transform into a demand (by believing that he has to get his desire met). A partial preference is then like a freshly planted seed which can either be nurtured into a plant or strangled into a weed. However, the seed precedes both the plant and the weed. It should be borne in mind that this viewpoint is conjectural and the views of other REBT therapists would be welcomed on this point and on any of the others that have been put forward in this chapter.

References

Ellis, A. (1976). The biological basis of human irrationality. Journal of Individual Psychology, 32, 145–68.

Ellis, A. (1994). Reason and Emotion in Psychotherapy 2nd edition. New York: Birch Lane Press.

Yankura, J. and Dryden, W. (1990). Doing RET: Albert Ellis in Action. New York: Springer.

Chapter Seven
The Use of Chaining in REBT

One of the drawbacks of the ABC* model of REBT is that its simplicity obscures the fact that assessing and intervening in client's problems can be quite difficult. For example, inferences are often chained together, inference and evaluative beliefs are connected in spiralling chains and these two types of cognitions interact with emotions and behaviours. In this chapter we shall outline and illustrate four types of chains that should preferably, when appropriate, become the focus for assessment and intervention during the course of REBT.

Inference chains

As noted above, inferences are often chained together. The purpose of assessing these chains is to identify the major inference in clients' emotional episodes, i.e. the one that triggers the irrational belief that creates their targeted emotional or behavioural problems at C. Moore (1983) advises that in inference chaining therapists initiate an enquiry based on 'then what?' and 'why?' questions in search of the client's most relevant inference. When clients report inferences,† 'then what?' questions are employed to uncover further inferences in the chain. However, when clients report emotional and/or behavioural consequences and these hold up the search for relevant inferences, 'why?' questions are used to help clients to continue their elaboration of inferential As. This process is exemplified in the following dialogue.

Client: So I get very scared when I think about going into the coffee bar.

Therapist: What do you think you are scared of?

---

* In this chapter, 'A' refers to activating events and to inferences (i.e. interpretations that go beyond available data) about these events. 'B' is therefore reserved for evaluative beliefs.
† It should be noted that 'Cs' can be treated as inferences and, when they are, 'then what?' questions are then employed to further the inference-based enquiry.

Client: I'm scared of my hands shaking when I go to buy a cup of coffee.

Therapist: Because if it happens, then what?

Client: People will notice.

Therapist: And if they do notice, then what?

Client: Well, they'll bring it to each other's attention.

Therapist: And if they do, then what?

Client: I'd panic.

Therapist: Why? [the client's previous response is treated as a C, hence the 'why?' question.]

Client: Because I'm sure I'd drop the cup.

Therapist: And if you do drop the cup, what then?

Client: They'd all start laughing.

Therapist: And if they did?

Client: Oh God! I couldn't stand that.

Inferences that trigger clients' irrational beliefs which, in turn, account for their targeted Cs are often expressed in close proximity to reports of these irrational beliefs (as in the above example). However, this does not always happen, in which case it is helpful to review the entire chain with clients and to ask them which inference in the chain is the most relevant to the problem at hand.

It also happens that clients may report inferences that theoretically follow from 'then what?' questions, but which may not be implicated in their problems. Thus, the client in the above example might have reported the following inferences in the chain after 'they'd start laughing'. 'I'd leave town and never come back'[arrow]'I'd become a hermit'. To assess the relevance of such inferences to the client's problem, the therapist is advised to (1) review the entire chain with the client at the end of the sequence and (2) note the degree of affect expressed by the client when these inferences are reported. Clients often report theoretically possible, but clinically irrelevant, inferences with flat affect or halting puzzlement. Thus, it is important for therapists to realise that the most relevant inference is not necessarily the final inference in the chain, although it frequently is.

Finally, when clients find it difficult to respond to 'then what?' questions with further inferences, it is helpful to include some variant of the target emotion (C) as part of the assessment question. For example:

Client: People will notice.

Therapist: And if they do, then what?

Client: Er, I'm not sure.

Therapist: Well, what would be anxiety-provoking in your mind about them noticing?

Client: Oh. They'll bring it to each other's attention.

Inference-evaluative belief chains

In inference chaining, as has been shown, the therapist assesses the way one inference leads to another. However, in reality, clients often hold implicit evaluative beliefs about each inference in the chain. These beliefs are bypassed in inference chaining, the purpose of which is to discover the most relevant inference in the chain, i.e. the one that triggers the client's irrational belief which accounts for their targeted emotional or behavioural problem at C. However, there are occasions when it is important to assess these implicit evaluative beliefs. This is particularly so in the assessment and treatment of clients' problems where distorted inferences often stem from irrational beliefs (e.g. panic disorders). The principle that unrealistic inferences stem from irrational beliefs is an important but often neglected one in REBT. As Ellis (1977, p. 9) has noted:

If you really stayed with desires and preferences, and virtually never escalated them into needs and necessities, you would relatively rarely make antiempirical statements to yourself and others. But just as soon as you make your desires into dire needs, such unrealistic statements almost invariably follow – and follow, frequently in great numbers.

In inference-evaluative belief chaining, then, therapists are advised to assess both inferences and the irrational beliefs that are held about these inferences and which, in turn, produce further distorted inferences. This pattern is particularly observable in panic disorders. Clark (1986) has outlined a cognitive approach to panic that draws upon the work of Aaron Beck. In his model, Clark argues that people who are prone to panic attacks make increasingly catastrophic interpretations of their bodily sensations. However, he does not set out to distinguish between clients' interpretations (or inferences) and their irrational beliefs about these inferences, beliefs that are held at an implicit level. In the rational emotive behavioural approach to panic disorders, these two types of cognitions are the targets for assessment and interventions. An example of inference-evaluative belief chaining is provided in Table 7.1 to illustrate this point.

Table 7.1 An example of an inference-evaluative belief chain in panic disorder

C	Feeling tense
Inference	I'm going to have trouble breathing
Irrational belief	I must be able to breathe more easily
Inference	I'm getting more anxious, I'm going to choke
Irrational belief	I must be able to control my breathing right now
Inference	I'm going to die
Irrational belief	I must not die in this fashion
C	Panic

Although it is technically correct for REBT therapists to dispute their clients' irrational beliefs about dying (see the end part of the chain in Table 7.1), the pragmatic purpose of this strategy, in such cases, is first to help clients to understand how their irrational beliefs which occur earlier in the chain actually produce their increasingly distorted inferences later in the chain and then to help them to dispute these evaluative beliefs. If this can be done in the session while the client is tense and beginning to experience the first signs of panic, then this can be a particularly powerful intervention.

At present, the relationship between distorted inferences and irrational beliefs awaits empirical enquiry and remains a fruitful area for future research in REBT.

'Disturbance about disturbance' chains

One of the unique features of REBT is the emphasis that it places on clients' tendencies to make themselves disturbed about their disturbances. This may involve exacerbation of a particular disorder (e.g. anxiety about anxiety; depression about depression) or it may involve several emotional and/or behavioural disorders within a single episode (e.g. guilt about anger; anxiety about procrastination). A typical sequence is illustrated in Table 7.2.

Table 7.2 An example of a 'disturbance about disturbance' chain

A	Sam treated me unfairly
B	He must not treat me unfairly
C	Anger
A	Anger
B	I must not get angry
C	Guilt
A	Guilt
B	There I go again experiencing needless guilt. I must not do this. I'm worthless
C	Depression

It is often quite difficult for novice REBT therapists to select the most appropriate part of the 'disturbance about disturbance' chain to target for intervention with clients. Our own practice is to keep three points in mind when making such treatment decisions. In general, we suggest that therapists work on the part of the chain that the clients want to start with and encourage their clients to do this for themselves outside the session. There are two exceptions to this general rule. The first occurs when clients actually experience in the session another unhealthy negative emotion that is part of the chain (e.g. 'It seems as if right now you are experiencing guilt about your feelings of anger. Let's first work on this until you give your full attention to working on your anger').

A second exception to the general rule occurs when clients experience outside the therapy session an unhealthy negative emotion that is also part of the chain (e.g. depression) as they attempt to work on overcoming the target emotion (e.g. guilt). In this case, we suggest that therapists encourage their clients to switch to the depression part of the chain, in the example given above, and give a plausible rationale for this (e.g. 'How can you work on your guilt when you are beating yourself over the head for feeling guilty?').

Complex chains

Clients sometimes present problems that involve a number of cognitive, emotive and behavioural components linked together in a complex chain. We have found it quite helpful to assess such chains carefully in order to help clients (1) understand the process nature of their problems and (2) identify useful points in the chain at which they can intervene to prevent the build-up of these problems. In such cases, it is usually beneficial to encourage clients to intervene at or near the beginning of these complex chains for the following reason. Towards the end of the chain these clients are so overwhelmed by the intensity of their disturbed feelings or so caught up in their self-defeating behaviours that it is unrealistic for their therapist to anticipate that they will successfully initiate a disputing intervention. To illustrate these points, we present in Table 7.3 one example of a complex chain. This arose out of my (WD) work with a female client who sought help for what she descried as 'uncontrolled binge-eating'.

Two points are worth noting with reference to this example. First, when the client had reached the end of this complex chain, she reported that it is as if she is in an altered state of consciousness. Although it is theoretically possible for her to intervene at this point and dispute her irrational belief that led her to feelings of self-loathing and binge-eating, in practice she found this enormously difficult. Thus, for pragmatic reasons, she needed to be helped to make a disputing intervention at a much earlier part of the chain. Secondly, the entire episode which has been detailed in Table 7.3 happened very quickly. The client barely noticed her tension before she headed towards the refrigerator, i.e. she was not aware of her feelings of self-anger or of discomfort anxiety. Consequently, I (WD) helped her in the therapy session to review the entire process as if it were happening in slow motion. As a result, she began to identify these implicitly felt emotions and associated irrational beliefs and began to see that psychological events (e.g. anger at self for not understanding 'simple' material) served as triggers for her subsequent irrational beliefs and more intense self-defeating emotions and behaviours. She then began to anticipate these early signs and learned to dispute the related irrational beliefs that occurred at the beginning of the chain. She became very adept at doing this and virtually eliminated her binge-eating that was previously associated with such episodes. We could then deal with her irrational beliefs that occurred later in the chain. If I had started at the end of the chain I doubt whether she would have achieved as good a therapeutic outcome as she did in this case.

Table 7.3 An example of a complex chain

A	Working on Master's thesis and experiencing difficulty with 'simple' statistics
B	I must be able to understand this. I'm a real idiot because I can't
C	Anger at self
A	Anger at self experienced as tension
B	I can't stand this tension
C	Anxious pacing around the room
A	Heightened anxiety
B	I've got to get rid of this feeling
C	Goes to the refrigerator and begins to eat a snack
A	Eating a snack
B	Oh God! What am I doing? I shouldn't be doing this
C	Guilt and increased eating (to try to get rid of the bad feeling)
A	Increased eating
B	What a pig I am. I must not binge again
C	Self-loathing and binge-eating

Outlining complex chains is particularly helpful then, when clients are barely aware of disturbed emotions and self-defeating behaviours that occur at the start of the chain and when this non-awareness leads to more intense negative and self-defeating experiences later in the chain.

Therefore, as described above, chaining is a sophisticated skill and, when used sensitively, highlights the complexity that lies behind the simple ABC formulation of clients' problems.

References

Clark, D.M. (1986). A cognitive approach to panic. Behaviour Research and Therapy, 24, 461–70.

Ellis, A. (1977). The basic clinical theory of rational-emotive therapy. In A. Ellis and R. Grieger (Eds), Handbook of Rational-Emotive Therapy. New York: Springer.

Moore, R.H. (1983). Inferences as 'A' in RET. British Journal of Cognitive Psychotherapy, 1(2), 17–23.

Chapter Eight
The Intricacies of Inference Chaining

This chapter describes some of the common errors made in inference chaining by novice as well as experienced REBTers. These errors are presented in a three stage process: first, false starts in initiating the chain; second, going deeper into the chain but following the wrong path caused by inattention to client data signposting the right one; third, stopping short of the critical A because of insufficient refinement of the activating event. Then we present the complete inference chain with annotations showing how the aforementioned mistakes can be avoided. Finally, we suggest that inference chaining does not have to be a daunting prospect but its successful execution usually requires more than just REBT training.

Since Moore (1983) formally introduced inference chaining into the literature on the ABC assessment of clients' presenting problems, it has developed into a minor art form culminating in Dryden's (1995) variations on an inference chain. Inference chaining is a technique which links the client's personally significant inferences about an activating event (A) in order to find the one (sometimes called the critical A) which triggers the client's irrational belief (B) which then, in turn, directly leads to his emotional reaction at C. This technique combines speed with depth in rapidly taking clients from the periphery to the centre of their emotional disturbance by a series of carefully crafted 'Let's assume...then what?' questions. Inference chaining can be an exceedingly difficult procedure to carry out and therefore this article will focus on the common pitfalls and errors that REBTers, novice and experienced alike, make when attempting it.

Getting started

Skimming the surface

Once the REBT therapist has a reasonably clear idea of the presenting problem, elicited an unhealthy negative emotion (in this transcript, anger) that the client experiences about the problem and has begun teaching him (in this case, example) the principle of emotional responsibility, i.e. that he largely disturbs himself about adverse events in his life or B-C thinking, she is ready to start the chain. Usual mistakes in beginning inference chaining include strengthening the client's A-C thinking, i.e. that others or events directly cause his emotional disturbance, providing reassurance prematurely, disputing the client's inferences rather than waiting for irrational beliefs to emerge, switching the focus from one disturbed emotion to another before closure has been achieved with the first one, terminating the chaining process before it has got properly underway:

Therapist: What was it that your boss said that made you angry?

Client: (clenching his teeth and fists) He said I was incompetent for failing to clinch a deal that went to a rival firm. [emphasising] He said it in front of my colleagues.

*Therapist:*And that made you angry?

Client: Yeah, that was part of it.

Therapist: What evidence do you have that your boss really believes you are incompetent? After all, you have secured many contracts for your firm.

Client: Well he said it, so he probably means it.

Therapist: He could have said it because he lost face in the eyes of the management board, or he's under too much stress. It could be anything really.

Client: I suppose so.

Therapist: How do you feel about your boss seeing you as incompetent?

Client: I feel hurt because I work so hard for my boss and therefore he shouldn't treat me like this.

In this extract, the therapist has violated the principle of emotional responsibility by reinforcing in the client's mind that his boss has caused his anger rather than his own interpretation of his boss's behaviour or remarks. In order to encourage emotional responsibility in the client, the therapist could have asked such questions as 'What's anger-provoking in your mind about your boss calling you incompetent?' or 'What were you angry about when your boss called you incompetent?'. Therefore she has to monitor her use of language during the chaining process (and, of course, throughout the course of therapy itself) in order to help the client adjust to this new view of emotional causation. Also the therapist may need to use evocative words and images in order to help the client retrieve his 'hot' cognitions (anger-charged thoughts) about the activating event and thereby move him closer to the critical A, e.g. 'So there you are in the office, surrounded by your colleagues, and your boss calls you "incompetent". Now what's anger-producing in your mind about that?'

When the client becomes visibly upset by clenching his teeth and fists as he recounts his emotional problems, it is understandable why the therapist may step in with some soothing comments in the mistaken belief that she is helping him. However, the balm she has applied is most unlikely to eradicate his disturbance-producing ideas which will probably be reactivated the next time his boss or someone else calls him incompetent. The REBT therapist is expected to assume temporarily that each inference in the chain is true in order to discover what the client is most disturbed about.

The therapist also starts to dispute the client's inferences ('What evidence do you have...?') rather than holds her fire until the client's major demand about his critical A has been revealed. Premature disputing is likely to put the client on the defensive, stop the inference chaining process in its tracks and convey to the client that inferences are crucial and not peripheral to his emotional problems (Walen et al., 1992). As with providing temporary relief, self-restraint is required in order to introduce disputing at the appropriate place in therapy.

The therapist has not pursued far enough the personal implications of the client's anger about being called incompetent in front of his colleagues. For example, does he agree that he is incompetent and if he believes that he is, how does he evaluate this view of himself? She quickly settles on the incompetence issue as the core problem and thereby brings the chaining process to an abrupt halt. The rule of thumb in inference chaining is to excavate the A and not just scratch about on the surface of it (of course, it should always be remembered that the first inference in the chain can be the critical one).

The therapist also errs in not sticking with one emotion (anger) at a time to explore and, instead, asks a question regarding feelings and receives the reply 'hurt'. Although emotions are usually linked with regard to the client's presenting problems, they are analysed separately and not in a batch as each one has a discrete cognitive structure that needs to be revealed (see 1 below). However, it is important to note that some REBT therapists would disagree with this viewpoint and suggest that sometimes an initial unhealthy negative emotion (e.g. anxiety) acts as a stepping stone or gateway to another one (e.g. guilt) that is more powerfully experienced in relation to the activating event. Therefore these therapists would shift the focus of the inference chain with a different 'driving force' emotion (see 2 below). Both REBT approaches are demonstrated in the following extract:

Therapist: What is anxiety-provoking in your mind about speaking in public?

Client: I might act foolishly.

Therapist: And if you do, what would you be most anxious about?

Client: Other people might judge me unfairly.

Therapist: Let's suppose they do, what would be anxiety-provoking in your mind about that?

Client: I'd be hurt.

1. *Therapist:* That's a separate issue because you've changed the emotional focus from anxiety to hurt. We'll deal with your feelings of hurt later. Let's stay with and continue to explore for the time being your feelings of anxiety.

2. *Therapist:* And what would you be hurt about?

Client: I'm trying my best and people are not being sympathetic to my lack of public speaking experience.

Therapist: And if they are unsympathetic to you...?

Client: I'd feel deeply ashamed.

Therapist: What would you be ashamed about?

Client: That I'd shown myself up as a weak and incompetent person. This is what worries me the most.

Therapist: So shall we tackle shame first as this appears to be the most troubling emotion at present?

Client: Yes.

With anxiety, when feared future events become actual or imagined present or past ones, the feeling will change along with the thematic content of the inference structure. In the above extract, threat or fear in anxiety; lack of fairness in hurt; revealing perceived weaknesses in shame. Therapists need to be alert to changes in the content of the inferences in order to detect an emotional shift because not all clients will explicitly signal it as the above client does. Also therapists who pursue a series of inference chains through a number of emotions are really trying to locate the supracritical A rather than a critical one because each emotion investigated will usually offer a critical A (as in the client's anxiety and hurt) but not necessarily the core one (finally identified in shame).

We find merit in both REBT viewpoints on inference chaining and will discuss this issue along with the downward arrow technique (see below) in the future.

To return to the above extract, as the therapist has elicited the unhealthy negative emotion before she initiates inference chaining, further questions to uncover more emotions will throw her off the scent in tracking down the critical A related to his anger. (It is interesting to compare inference chaining with cognitive therapy's downward arrow technique [Burns, 1980]: in the former approach, each inference is usually linked to the same disturbed emotion in order to elicit irrational ideas, while in the latter approach core beliefs are exposed by seeking the meaning of each automatic negative thought but these thoughts are not anchored in a specific feeling.)

Not paying attention

Overlooking clues

In teasing out an inference chain, the therapist has to monitor a range of verbal, affective and behavioural indicators that signal she is on the right track of the critical A, veering away from it or completely lost. The various clues offered by the client, unintentionally or not, help the therapist to formulate the next question and plot any alterations in the course of the clinical inquiry:

Therapist: Shall we return to your anger and explore that a bit more?

Client: Okay.

Therapist: Let's assume that your boss really does think you are incompetent. Then what?

Client: [with a flash of anger] It's the fact that he said it in front of the others. That's the point.

Therapist: That's understandable because no one wants to be yelled at in front of others, but what I'm trying to get you to focus on is what happens after he has called you 'incompetent'. Might you lose your job for example?

Client: Well, that could happen in the next round of redundancies if I'm seen as incompetent.

Therapist: If you lose your job, then what?

Client: Er...let me see...hmm...I suppose I wouldn't be able to keep up the mortgage and then I'd lose my house.

Therapist: And if that happened...?

Client: [indifferently] Hmm...I suppose I could be out on the street, that sort of thing.

Therapist: And if you were out on the street...?

Client: I don't know, er...would my life be shattered?

Therapist: And if your life was shattered...?

Client: [wearily] End up killing myself? I don't know.

Therapist: So are you most angry about being called 'incompetent' because it all might end in your own suicide?

Client: [frustrated] Look, what you say doesn't sound plausible to me.

Therapist: That's because this is the first time you've looked at the consequences of your anger. Also you seem to be getting angry now so it looks like we are on the right path.

Client: [unconvinced] Oh, I see.

In this extract, the therapist seems intent on following her own hunches without regard to the empirical data that the client provides for her, e.g. he stresses that the important issue for him is being called 'incompetent' in front of his colleagues but the therapist dismisses his viewpoint with false empathy and then plunges on without a backward glance that she might be taking the wrong path.

Alternatively, she could be pursuing the theoretical inference that assumes all clients' problems end in some form of personal apocalypse. Such grim events like homelessness or suicide can occur, of course, but they are not usually the clients' actual worries – these lie buried elsewhere (and probably earlier) in the chain. The therapist might have detected that she was obtaining only theoretical inferences and not clinically relevant ones if she noted the client's elongated pauses as if he is manufacturing an answer ('er...hmm...'), quizzical responses which indicate he is baffled by the therapist's questions ('End up killing myself? I don't know'), the incongruity between the increasing grimness of the inferences and the lack of any corresponding strong affect in the client which indicates his uninterest in where the therapist is taking the chain.

A third possibility is inference chaining by autopilot whereby the therapist keeps on asking 'And if that happened...?' therapy will eventually reach its destination by touching down on the critical A. This approach assumes that inference chaining follows a clear linear route and no obstacles, confusions, red herrings, uncertainties, etc. will cloud the process. The therapist obviously believes she is on target as the client displays his presenting emotion of anger; however, the anger is aimed at her for ignoring his viewpoint and not associated with locating his critical A. All three approaches fail to review the unfolding chain with the client (e.g. 'Do any of these inferences that we have uncovered so far reflect what you are most angry about?') and thereby the therapist does not gain the vital feedback necessary to abandon, make corrections in or confirm her present line of clinical investigation.

In the above extract, the therapist obviously lacks the clinical acuity to know what evidence is pertinent to the assessment of the activating event and whether she is cold, warm or hot in her proximity to the critical A. These deficiencies can be addressed in REBT training and regular supervision. What is not so easy to teach or acquire (in REBT or any other therapy) is a kind of sophisticated understanding of, a subtlety of perception about, human behaviour that the therapist uses to guide the client to the previously unfathomable core of his emotional disturbance. Such discernment may tip the balance between reaching the client's psychological epicentre and stopping several removes from it.

Stopping short

Not refining the A Enough

Sometimes the experienced therapist can be convinced that she has reached the critical A because of corroboration from the client's reactions (e.g. physical and emotional intensity) or her own hunches have been validated (e.g. the client agrees with her fear of failure hypothesis) yet, in reality, she still remains a stone's throw or even hair's breadth away from it. This usually occurs because the therapist has insufficiently refined the activating event and, as a result, has reached an illusory critical A rather than the real one (it is important to understand that each inference in a chain, with its implicit irrational belief, can create emotional distress, but REBT seeks to pinpoint the one that generates the most disturbance for the client [see Dryden, 1989]):

Therapist: So what were you angry about when he called you 'incompetent' in front of your colleagues?

Client: There's this woman I really like. I want to go out with her and she saw all this. Now I doubt if I'll have a chance with her.

Therapist: Because...?

Client: She likes men who are winners, successful, confident, all that sort of stuff.

Therapist: And how do you think she would see you at that moment?

Client: Obviously as a loser and a failure.

Therapist: Let's assume that she does see you that way, then what?

Client: [visibly tensing] She'll never consider going out with me now. I can't stand it.

Therapist: And is that what you're most angry about?

Client: Yeah, that feels right.

Although the therapist and client agree that they have got to the bottom of his anger, there still remains the troubling question of the 'it' – what precisely is the nature of the 'it' that the client cannot stand? An important task for REBT therapists is to clarify the content of the 'it' in client statements in order to better understand their evaluative beliefs. Does the client's 'it' refer to discomfort disturbance whereby he cannot tolerate working in an environment where the person he desires sees him as a loser? Or is the problem ego disturbance because the client has condemned himself on the basis of how someone else views him? Or that his romantic desires now stand no chance of being fulfilled?

Another perspective is that the 'it' represents the false bottom of the chain and therefore the way in to a subterranean stratum still to be explored. These questions are not meant to announce to the client that 'I know something you don't' but to point out to him that maybe the personal implications of his adverse activating event have not yet been fully extended.

The complete chain

Keeping one's eye on the ball at all times

We now present what we believe is a correct way of conducting inference chaining incorporating many of the points previously made.

Therapist: What is anger-provoking in your mind about being called 'incompetent' by your boss?
[The therapist establishes emotional responsibility in her opening question as well as initiating the inference chain.]

Client: [clenching his teeth and fists] I'm not incompetent just because on this occasion I failed to clinch a deal that went to a rival firm. He shouldn't have called me that in front of my colleagues.

Therapist: Would you have been just as angry if he'd said in the privacy of his office that you were 'incompetent'?
[The therapist assesses if there is any differential significance for the client in being called 'incompetent' in private or public.]

Client: No, not really because I don't value his opinion of me. He can make life more difficult for me but I can handle that.

[The therapist makes a mental note of whose opinion the client might value and therefore could be implicated in his angry reaction.]

Therapist: Okay, so what were you angry about when he called you 'incompetent' in front of your colleagues?

[The client's feedback indicates to the therapist that she should concentrate her clinical focus on the group setting aspects of the activating event.]

Client: There's this woman I really like who works in the accounts department. I want to go out with her pretty badly and she saw all this.

Therapist: 'All this' being your boss calling you 'incompetent'.

Client: Yes. Now I doubt if I'll have any chance with her.

Therapist: Because...?
[The therapist's use of a conjunction encourages the client to complete the sentence thereby helping him to develop greater cognitive awareness regarding the activating event.]

Client: She admires men who are winners, successful, confident, all that sort of stuff.

Therapist: How do you think she saw you at that moment?

Client: Obviously as a loser and a failure.

Therapist: Okay, let's pause for a moment. Is there anything we've looked at so far that you are most angry about?
[The therapist reviews the inference chain with the client in order to determine if the critical A has been located.]

Client: Well, some of those things I got pretty het up about but I'm still not sure why I got so angry when he called me 'incompetent' in front of the others. Anyway, why is it so important to find out?

Therapist: When we find your boiling point, so to speak, that's where therapeutic intervention will begin. In REBT, we believe that if clients can cope with the imagined worst in their lives, they are more likely to have less trouble tackling actual bad events. So do you think it will be to your advantage to continue the investigation?
[The therapist provides a rationale for the hunt for the critical A in order to keep the client engaged in the inference chaining process.]

Client: Okay, let's keep going. I want to find my boiling point too, as you call it.

Therapist: Now let's assume that this woman does see you as a [emphasising words] loser and a failure.

[The therapist attempts to evoke in the client the probable painful impact of those words.]

Client: [visibly tensing] She'll never go out with me now. I can't stand it.

Therapist: What's the 'it' you believe you can't stand?
[As the client has revealed the derivative part of an irrational belief, the therapist wants to check if she has reached the critical A or is near to it.]

Client: I'm not sure what you mean.

Therapist: Does the 'it' refer to your inability to stand being rejected by her?

Client: Not quite. There's something more. It's the way she sees me.

Therapist: You said earlier that you did not value your boss's opinion of you. Do you value hers?
[The therapist uses her 'mental note' to try and promote further client introspection.]

Client: Very much so.

Therapist: Her opinion of you is that you are a [emphasising words again] loser and a failure.

Client: [gripping the arms of his chair] Just like someone else's opinion I value highly.

Therapist: Who is...?

Client: [voice rising] My father. He said I'd be a loser in life. But he died before I could convince him otherwise. [banging the arms of his chair] I so desperately wanted to convince him.
[This seems like a critical A because of the intensity of the client's physical, emotional and behavioural reactions.]

Therapist: [in a quiet voice] Do you believe that you are a failure? That your father was right about you?
[The therapist checks to see if the client is ultimately disturbed by agreeing with his father's view of him or that his father's death robbed the client of the chance to change his father's opinion of him.]

Client: [tearfully] No, I don't see myself as a failure but I so desperately wanted my father to have a good opinion of me.

Therapist: If this woman at work admired you instead of seeing you as a loser, would you still be angry that your father did not have a good opinion of you?

Client: Yes.

Therapist: And if your father had a good opinion of you but this woman did not admire you, would you still be angry?

Client: No. It's my father's view of me that really matters – seeing me as a success.

[The therapist double-checks with the client that his anger is directed at his father, not the woman.]

Therapist: But as he didn't and you will never have the chance to convince him otherwise, is this the agony you cannot stand?

Client: Yes.
[The client confirms that the therapist has located the critical A.]

The therapist's next task is to help the client identify his major demand (i.e. the primary premise of the irrational belief) about the critical A and thereby connect it to the already revealed derivative from the premise, e.g. 'I absolutely should have been able to convince my father that I'm not a failure but as he's gone, I can't stand the pain of never having another opportunity to change his opinion of me'.

Conclusion

Although the inference chain presented in this article has been a complex one to tease out, it is important to remember that some chains can be relatively straightforward to unravel. We have provided some rules to follow in inference chaining (e.g. delay disputing and reassurance) as part of an REBTer's skills development. Equally important is paying close attention to the various clues, both explicit and subtle, that clients, intentionally or not, lay before the therapist. Being alert to these clues helps the therapist to formulate the next and more productive question which will draw her closer to the critical A. Those REBTers who apply a purely mechanical approach to inference chaining are much more likely to alight upon an aspect of the client's presenting problem which does not lie at the heart of his emotional distress. In the final analysis, if inference chaining is to be successfully carried out it requires a combination of rules and techniques on the one hand and an acute awareness of human behaviour on the other.

References

Burns, D.D. (1980) Feeling Good: The New Mood Therapy. New York: William Morrow.
Dryden, W. (1989). The use of chaining in rational-emotive therapy. Journal of Rational-Emotive and Cognitive-Behaviour Therapy, 7(2), 59–66.
Dryden, W. (1995). Preparing for Client Change in Rational-Emotive Behaviour Therapy. London: Whurr.
Moore, R.H. (1983). Inference as 'A' in RET. British Journal of Cognitive Psychotherapy, 1(2), 17–23.

Walen, S.R., DiGiuseppe, R. and Dryden, W. (1992). A Practitioners Guide to Rational-Emotive Therapy, 2nd edition. New York: Oxford University Press.

Chapter Nine
When Laddering and the Downward Arrow can be used as Adjuncts to Inference Chaining in REBT Assessment

This chapter looks at the ways in which laddering in Personal Construct Therapy and the downward arrow in Cognitive Therapy can be used as adjunctive techniques to inference chaining in locating a client's critical A or emotional core. We describe their use through a number of case examples and annotations. We conclude that these two methods require skilled use if they are to be integrated successfully into inference chaining and are offered as part of REBT's interest in theoretically consistent eclecticism.

The use of inference chaining in Rational Emotive Behaviour Therapy (REBT), the downward arrow in Cognitive Therapy (CT) and laddering in Personal Construct Therapy (PCT) are techniques which aim to help therapists and clients gain a rapid insight into the latters' core beliefs and values about themselves, others and the world. This chapter shows how each technique reveals underlying beliefs and then, from the REBT viewpoint, in what circumstances laddering or the downward arrow might be used as an adjunct to inference chaining in the assessment stage of therapy.

Getting to the heart of the matter

Inference chaining

This technique links the client's personally significant inferences about an activating event (A) in order to find the one (sometimes called the critical A) which triggers her irrational belief (B) which then, in turn, directly leads to her emotional reactions at C (Moore, 1983; Dryden, 1995; Neenan and Dryden, 1996). The client's inferences are linked by a series of carefully crafted 'Let's assume...then what?' questions. Before inference chaining is initiated, an unhealthy negative emotion (e.g. anxiety) about the activating event is elicited in order to anchor the chaining process in the client's emotional disturbance:

Therapist: What is anxiety-provoking in your mind about your husband dancing with another woman at the party?

Client: He might find her more desirable than me.

Therapist: Let's assume for the moment that he does find her more desirable than you. Then what?

Client: He might leave me and go off with her.

Therapist: Let's assume that he does do that. Then what?

Client: I'll be all alone in the world and worthless.

Therapist: Why would you be worthless because you're all alone in the world?

Client: Because I'm nothing without him.

Therapist: So are you most anxious about your husband leaving you because you think you are 'nothing, worthless' without him?

Client: Yes, that's what I'm afraid of [the client's critical A, her husband's departure, and her derivative irrational belief, that she will be 'nothing worthless' without him, have been revealed simultaneously].

The next step is for the therapist to help the client reveal her major demand about the critical A, e.g. 'My husband must never leave me because if he does I'll be worthless'. This irrational belief is then disputed using logical, empirical and pragmatic arguments.

Downward arrow

This method follows the logical implications of a client's key automatic thought(s) in order to discover her dysfunctional beliefs or silent assumptions (Burns, 1980; Blackburn and Davidson, 1990; Beck 1995). The client is asked for the meaning of each automatic thought in order to reveal deeper cognitive layers. Beck (1995, p. 145) suggests that 'asking what a thought means *to* the patient often elicits an intermediate belief [usually of an "if...then" construction]; asking what it means *about* the patient usually uncovers the core belief':

Therapist: Why was it upsetting for you when your husband danced with another woman at the party?

Client: He might find her more desirable than me.

Therapist: Let's suppose this is true, what would it mean to you?

Client: He might leave and go off with her.

Therapist: Okay, if he did go off with her, what would that mean to you?

Client: If he doesn't want me any more then I'll be all alone in the world [intermediate belief].

Therapist: What does that mean for you to be unwanted and all alone in the world?

Client: That I'm nothing, worthless without him [core belief].

The client is then shown how to modify her disturbance-producing beliefs by examining the evidence for and against them and questioning the utility of holding on to them.

Laddering

This technique, which is used most frequently in Personal Construct Therapy, reveals a client's personal constructs (hypotheses) at increasingly higher levels of abstraction (Hinkle, 1965; Bannister and Fransella, 1986). The client may be asked to examine a specific bipolar construct of herself (e.g. loved versus unwanted) by describing by which pole of the construct she would prefer to be described. The therapist asks 'Why?' about the preferred side of the construct which then, in turn, reveals a new construct. This procedure is repeated until the client reaches a superordinate construct which reveals a philosophy of living or core values:

Therapist: Why is it preferable for you to be loved rather than unwanted?

Client: Because that means I have importance and value to my husband rather than being all alone in the world.

Therapist: Why is it important for you to have importance and value to your husband rather than be all alone in the world?

Client: Well if he values me then he won't abandon me.

Therapist: As opposed to...?

Client: Abandoning me because he doesn't value me.

Therapist: Why is it important to you to be valued by your husband rather than not valued by him?

Client: Because that will prove I'm not worthless [superordinate construct].

The client, in the role of a personal scientist, would be helped to experiment with alternative interpretations (reconstruing) of herself and the problem in order to create a wider choice of potential behaviours that would now be available to her.

When there is no chain reaction

What's the emotion?

In the 13-step counselling sequence (Dryden and DiGiuseppe, 1990), step three is to elicit an unhealthy negative emotion about the client's presenting problem in order to initiate inference chaining at step four. However, some clients will not be able to identify a disturbed emotion and will plump for vague descriptions of their feelings like 'bad' or 'miserable'. Therapy need not be stymied because no emotions in the REBT lexicon of negative feelings have been uncovered or frustration set in because therapy cannot move on to step four (assessing the A). To find an emotion, the therapist can ask the client 'What passes through your mind when you feel bad?' and then use the downward arrow to ascertain the meaning of each cognition:

Client: I can't always afford to buy my kids the things they need for school.

Therapist: And what does that mean to you?

Client: The other kids at school will have everything and my kids will be going without.

Therapist: Let's assume they are going without, what would that mean to you?

Client: If I'm failing my children, then I'm failing as a father. Also what will the other parents think of me when they are providing adequately for their children?

Therapist: Let's suppose you are failing as a father, what would that mean about you?

Client: That I'm a very bad father.

Therapist: And if the other parents see that you are not providing adequately for your children, what would that mean to you?

Client: That the whole world can see my failings as a father.

Following this dialogue, the REBT therapist, guided by her knowledge of the themes in emotional disorders, can help the client to clarify which unhealthy negative emotions are implicated in his presenting problems: breaking his moral code as a good father by not providing what he absolutely should do for his children – this theme is usually present in guilt; revealing publicly his perceived failings as a father which he believes he must not have – this theme is usually present in shame. At this point, the therapist may want to refine further the cognitive data of each emotion at step four in order to determine if their respective critical As have been located and which emotion might be primary or secondary in the client's psychological disturbance.

Overfocusing on feelings

As mentioned earlier, inference chaining is anchored in an unhealthy negative emotion. Some REBTers, particularly novices, may become so absorbed in the textbook ordering or correct construction of the questions designed to peel away the client's layers of emotional distress that the questioning can become circular:

Therapist: What was anger-provoking in your mind when your colleague parked his car in your designated space?

Client: Well, it's my space isn't it?

Therapist: But as he didn't pay any attention to the fact that it's your space, what was anger-provoking in your mind about that?

Client: Just that – he didn't pay any attention.

Therapist: But he didn't pay any attention, did he? So let's move forward by finding out what was anger-provoking in your mind about him not paying attention?

Client: [fed up] This is getting us nowhere. We're going round in circles. I've told you the answer already!

Therapist: [sheepishly] We do seem to be stuck.

In these circumstances, the therapist can put aside the standard inference chaining format because it is being used to guide her rather than helping the client to gain greater insight into his anger. Teasing out the idiosyncratic meaning of each inference instead of hammering away at the emotion may prove more profitable for both sides:

Therapist: Can I come at this issue from another angle?

Client: Okay.

Therapist: What does it mean to you when he parks in your space?

Client: That he has no respect for me.

Therapist: Let's assume that's true, what would that mean to you?

Client: That he sees me as weak.

Therapist: And if he does see you that way, what would it mean to you?

Client: It's true, I am weak because I won't confront him over the parking. He knows that.

Therapist: And if you don't confront him because you're weak, what would that mean about you?

Client: That the whole office would know what a weak and despicable man I really am. I wouldn't be able to hold my head up at work.

Therapist: So if I can summarise: would you say that what you are most angry about is that through parking in your space and you not confronting him about it, this man has exposed you to the rest of the office as 'weak and despicable'?

Client: Yes, that's it exactly.

By changing tack and dropping the insistence on mentioning 'anger' in every sentence, the therapist is able to shift the client's attention to the private meanings he attaches to having his parking space usurped. In the therapist's final comments, she returns to the inference chaining format, without any objection from the client, to clarify with him that his critical A has been uncovered.

Ladder to the rescue

Some clients express their goals for change in very vague terms, e.g. 'I want to understand why I sit about all day doing nothing'. As Walen et al. (1992, p. 52) point out, such goals are expressed 'in terms of therapeutic process rather than outcome'. However, trying to establish what outcomes such clients would like to achieve are often met with repeated replies of 'I don't know'. As the client in the above example has intimated that he does not want to be so idle, the therapist can ask how he wants to be rather than how he actually is in order to establish a bipolar construct:

Client: Be more active, I suppose.

Therapist: Why is it preferable to be more active than idle?

Client: Well, then you get your life moving.

Therapist: As opposed to...?

Client: Being stuck.

Therapist: Why is it important to you to get you life moving rather than be stuck?

Client: Because it's better to make your mark in life than pass through unnoticed.

Therapist: Why is it important to make your mark in life rather than pass through unnoticed?

Client: Because that means you have been a somebody instead of a nobody. I want to be a somebody.

At this point, the therapist can revert to REBT to clarify the client's goal for change, target for exploration the unhealthy negative emotion associated with his presenting problem and refine further, if necessary, the client's self-depreciation:

Therapist: So is your goal of change that you become a 'somebody'?

Client: Yes, that's what I'd like.

Therapist: And what does becoming a 'somebody' actually mean?

Client: Filling my life with purposeful things like having a job and a social life.

Therapist: And how do you feel when you sit around all day not filling your life with 'purposeful things'?

Client: Depressed. That's what holds me back.

Therapist: We may have touched on this already, but what are you most depressed about when you're sitting about all day?

Client: I've already said – I'm a nobody.

Therapist: In whose eyes: yours or other people's?

Client: Mainly mine. That's where it hurts the most.

In this exchange, the laddering technique has 'opened up' the client by elaborating the personal meaning of 'sitting about' which then elicited his counselling goals and pointed the way to his critical A. This enabled the therapist to construct eventually an ABC assessment of the client's presenting problems.

Climbing out of an impasse

Often in the inference chaining process the therapist's attempts to encourage greater client introspection falter. This is usually due to the client venturing into an unknown or previously avoided cognitive landscape. If such an impasse does occur, the REBT therapist can use laddering to escape from it by offering the client a different perspective in order to collect further assessment information:

Therapist: What were you anxious about when you were sitting at your desk trying to start your essay for college?

Client: Well, I'm not sure what is really required of the essay.

Therapist: And if you're not sure, then what?

Client: I don't know, I just feel stuck.

Therapist: Let's say you weren't stuck. Then what?

Client: I'd be able to complete the essay but I'd still be anxious.

Therapist: What would you be still anxious about?

Client: I really don't know.

Therapist: [musing] Hmm.

The therapist pauses here because she is uncertain how to formulate the next question in her attempts to draw out more client inferences. However, what does suggest itself to the therapist is to ascend the construct system that the client has partially revealed:

Therapist: What for you is the opposite of stuck?

Client: Unstuck.

Therapist: Okay, let's say you are stuck here and unstuck over here [therapist uses her hands to suggest opposite poles of the construct]. Now which side would you prefer to be?

Client: I suppose unstuck because at least I'd finish my essay.

Therapist: As opposed to...?

Client: Not finishing my essay.

Therapist: Why is it important to you to finish your essay as opposed to not finishing it?

Client: So I can get my degree.

Therapist: As opposed to...?

Client: Not getting it.

Therapist: Why is it important to you to get your degree as opposed to not getting it?

Client: To prove to my parents that I'm a success.

Therapist: As opposed to...?

Client: Proving to them that I can't cut it.

Therapist: Why is it important to prove to your parents that you are a success as opposed to that you can't cut it?

Client: Who doesn't want their parents to be proud of them? But I'd still be anxious even if they were proud of me. This is what I don't understand.

Therapist: [reverting to inference chaining] Okay, what would still be anxiety-provoking in your mind despite having your parents' approval which is something you obviously desire?

Client: They would want me to go on to do a master's degree, then probably a PhD.

Therapist: Let's assume that's true. Then what?

Client: My life would be an endless academic slog in order to keep my parents proud of me. I fear that I will fail or give up at some stage and my parents would be very upset. I couldn't bear to see them upset.

Therapist: Is that what you are most anxious about: having to see your parents upset because of your perceived failure?

Client: Yes. That's why competing this essay won't give me any real peace of mind.

Therapist: And not completing it will bring that day of failure much closer.

Client: I'm trapped both ways.

In this final section of dialogue, when the therapeutic utility of laddering has been exhausted the therapist returns to inference chaining to complete the cognitive examination of the client's anxiety. Laddering provided the organic link to keep the chain unfolding and help reveal to the client what was previously puzzling him as to why essay completion would not give him peace of mind.

Concluding comments

REBT therapists who wish to use these adjuntive techniques of laddering and the downward arrow should be skilled in their use and they should not simply be seen as afterthoughts if inference chaining becomes blocked in some way. As we hope we have shown in this chapter, these additional techniques are integrated into inference chaining rather than substitutes for it. Some REBTers, even many, may protest that there are a number of REBT methods to get inference chaining moving again when it stalls that we have not mentioned. This is true. Other REBT therapists could demonstrate this by rewriting this chapter without mentioning laddering or the downward arrow. We offer this chapter in the spirit of theoretically consistent eclecticism (Dryden, 1987; Dryden and Neenan, 1995) whereby outside borrowings can bring a fresh perspective to traditional REBT practice. We hope that REBTers will not object to having two more techniques to add to their existing armamentarium.

References

Bannister, D. and Fransella, F. (1986). Inquiring Man: The psychology of Personal Constructs, 3rd edition. London: Croom Helm.

Beck, J.S. (1995). Cognitive Therapy: Basics and Beyond. New York: Guilford Press.

Blackburn, I.M. and Davidson, K. (1990). Cognitive Therapy for Depression and Anxiety. Oxford: Blackwell Scientific Publications.

Burns, D.D. (1980). Feeling Good: The New Mood Therapy. New York: William Morrow.

Dryden, W. (1987). Current Issues in Rational-Emotive Therapy. Beckenham, Kent: Croom Helm.

Dryden, W. (1995). Preparing for Client Change in Rational Emotive Behavioural Therapy. London: Whurr.

Dryden, W. and DiGiuseppe, R. (1990). A Primer on Rational-Emotive Therapy Champaign, IL: Research Press.

Dryden, W. and Neenan, M. (1995). Dictionary of Rational Emotive Behaviour Therapy. London: Whurr.

Hinkle, D. (1965). The change of personal constructs from the viewpoint of a theory of construct implications. Unpublished PhD thesis, Columbus, OH: Ohio State University.

Moore, R.H. (1983). Inference as 'A' in RET. British Journal of Cognitive Psychotherapy, 1(2), 17–23.

Neenan, M. and Dryden, W. (1996). The intricacies of inference chaining. Journal of Rational-Emotive and Cognitive-Behaviour Therapy, 14(4), 231–43.

Walen, S.R., DiGiuseppe, R. and Dryden, W. (1992). A Practitioner's Guide to Rational-Emotive Therapy. New York: Oxford University Press.

Chapter Ten
Further Methods of
Identifying the Critical A

In the previous three chapters we have considered in detail the concept and practical complexities of inference chaining, the purpose of which is to identify the Critical A – that aspect of the A which triggers the client's irrational beliefs in a episode of psychological disturbance. However, inference chaining is not an infallible method of identifying the critical A, and competent REBT therapists need other methods of assessing the critical A in their therapeutic armamentarium if they are to assess their clients' problems accurately and efficiently. Thus, in this chapter, we will consider 11 such methods.

The 'going for broke' method

When reading our material on inference chaining, you may have noticed the similarity between this method and the children's game of skimming stones. In this game a child skims a stone across a watery surface and the stone skims several times before sinking. Each skim is akin to a link in the chain and, most frequently, the sinking of the stone is akin to discovering the critical A. If inference chaining can be likened to the game of skimming stones, the first method that we are going to discuss in this chapter, the 'going for broke' method, can be likened to another game that children play on the beach. This involves the child throwing the stone as far as he or she possibly can without, of course, skimming it. In REBT, where the stone drops is the critical A. We call this method 'going for broke'; because you are trying to identify the critical A at the first attempt. As such it is something of a risky procedure. Let me (WD) use the example of Sue, a client who is anxious about speaking in public, to demonstrate the 'going for broke' method.

Windy: So when did you become anxious?

Sue: Well, I was all right until I got up on the platform.

Windy: Now think carefully, Sue. What do you think you were most anxious about?

Sue: [pause] I was scared that the audience would laugh at me if I did not give a good talk.

[In this scenario, Sue in fact did provide the critical A; however, I do not know this at this point. So I use inference chaining to check.]

Windy: And what would be anxiety-provoking in your mind about being laughed at?

Sue: Oh! I couldn't bear to be laughed at.

[As Sue provides an irrational belief in response to my request for a further inference, I make the assumption that 'being laughed at' is her critical A.]

However, what if Sue does not provide a critical A in response to my 'going for broke' question? Because I do not know whether or not her response is a critical A, I again use inference chaining to check, as follows:

Windy: So when did you become anxious?

Sue: Well, I was all right until I got up on the platform.

Windy: Now think carefully, Sue. What do you think you were most anxious about?

Sue: That the audience would be expecting a lot from me.

Windy: And if they expected a lot from you, what would be scary about that?

Sue: That I might not give a good talk.

Windy: And that would mean...?

Sue: That they would laugh at me.

Windy: And if they laughed at you, what would be scary about that?

Sue: Oh! I couldn't stand that.

In conclusion, even though you may ask a 'going for broke' question, it is still important to use inference chaining to check whether or not the client's inference is her critical A. In our experience, clients do sometimes provide you with their critical A in response to a 'going for broke' question. But, more frequently, they provide an inference located in the middle of the inference chain. So, do not assume that your client has provided you with a critical A just because you have asked for it. As a general rule use inference chaining after your 'going for broke' question as a check.

The listing approach

The second approach to finding the critical A is called the listing approach. Here, you ask your client to list all the possible As that she may have been disturbed about in the example being assessed. As your client lists the possible As, write these down on a sheet of paper or on a white board. Then, ask your client to imagine that she is actually in the situation and ask her what she thinks she was most disturbed about. Then take this A and use inference chaining as a check. Here is how I (WD) might have used the listing approach with Sue.

Windy: So when did you become anxious?

Sue: Well, I was all right until I got up on the platform.

Windy: Now see if you can list all the things you may have been anxious about. Don't worry about getting them in any kind of order, just list them.

Sue: Let me see. I was anxious about giving a poor talk...the audience seemed to expect a lot from me, I remember being anxious about that...I was scared about them laughing at me if I screwed up...and I first got anxious when I looked down and saw faces looking up at me.

Windy: Right. Now I'm going to recap on your list. As I do so, think carefully which of the items you were most anxious about at the time. Okay?

Sue: Okay.

Windy: (1) Giving a poor talk; (2) the audience expecting a lot from you; (3) the audience laughing at you; (4) seeing the faces looking up at you. Which of those were you most anxious about?

Sue: Definitely, the audience laughing at me.

Windy: Can you think of any other issue that you were more anxious about than the audience laughing at you?

[This is an additional approach to checking whether the client has provided you with the critical A. Alternatively, I could have initiated inference chaining as another way of initiating this check.]

Sue: No.

The subtraction method

The third way of determining whether or not a particular A is critical is the subtraction method. To use this method you first need to employ inference chaining or the listing method to develop a number of As that your client is anxious about. You then ask your client to rank the listed As according to how anxious she would be if she actually faced them; the highest ranked item is at the top of the list and the lowest at the bottom. In many cases, inference chaining provides you with a list of As that has already been rank ordered. However, as this is not invariably the case, we advise you to ask your client to rank order the list of As derived from inference chaining.

You then take the first, top-ranked item and ask the client whether she would still be anxious, for example, if she could cope productively with it if it happened. If the client says that she would not be anxious under these circumstances or that she would be significantly less anxious, then you have probably identified a critical A. However, if your client states that she would still be significantly anxious, then that A is probably not critical and you proceed to the next item, subtract that A from the list and assess the effect of that subtraction. Here is how I (WD) would have used the subtraction with Sue.

Windy: So when did you become anxious?

Sue: Well, I was all right until I got up on to the platform.

Windy: Now see if you can list all the things you may have been anxious about. Don't worry about getting them in any kind of order, at this point. Just list them.

Sue: Let me see. I was anxious about giving a poor talk...the audience seemed to expect a lot from me, I remember being anxious about that... I was scared about them laughing at me if I screwed up...and I first got anxious when I looked down and saw their faces looking up at me.

Windy: Right. Now I'm going to recap on your list and then I am going to ask you to rank order them in terms of how anxiety-provoking they were for you in your mind at that time. Okay?

Sue: Okay.

Windy: (1) Giving a poor talk; (2) the audience expecting a lot from you; (3) the audience laughing at you; (4) seeing the faces looking up at you. Now I am going to ask you to rank order them. Which of those were you most anxious about?

Sue: The audience laughing at me.

Windy: And then?

Sue: Giving a poor talk.

Windy: And then?

Sue: The audience expecting a lot from me.

Windy: And finally, their faces looking up at you?

Sue: Yes.

Windy: Now I want you to imagine that the audience laughing at you was not an issue for you. You could handle it successfully if it happened. Can you imagine that?

Sue: Yes.

Windy: Good. How anxious, if at all, would you feel about not giving a good talk then?

Sue: Well, I still wouldn't like it, but I wouldn't be nearly so anxious.

[This response makes it clear that Sue's critical A was the audience laughing at her. However, it would not have been the critical A, if she replied as follows:]

Sue: I would still be very anxious.

Windy: Now I want you to imagine that giving a good talk was not an issue for you. If you did not give a good talk, you could handle that quite well. How anxious, if at all, would you feel about the audience's high expectations of you?

Sue: If I could handle not giving a good talk, then I would not be that anxious about their expectations of me.

[This response makes it clear that in this scenario Sue's critical A was not giving a good talk.]

The '2x2' method

When you are working to identify your client's critical A in the ABC you are assessing, you may well find that there are two main elements in the A that the client is disturbed about. Although you could choose to make both elements the critical A, this may lead to other problems because the client may have different beliefs about each element. How can you tell which element may be more critical? By using what we call the '2x2' method. Those of you who are familiar with statistics may also think of it as the 'chi-square' method. Let us give an example of this method which will make clear what it is and how to use it.

Ian is seemingly anxious about both gaining people's approval and the uncertainty that he experiences whenever he is unsure about others' opinion of him. I (WD) am not clear whether the prospect of disapproval or the uncertainty is his critical A. So I decided to use the '2x2' method to clarify this.

Windy: So, Ian, you are anxious about being disapproved of and about not knowing how people think of you. I want to find out whether you are most anxious about disapproval or uncertainty. Are you clear about this?

Ian: No, I'm not.

Windy: Let me draw you a diagram which will help us both determine the answer to this question.

[NB The diagram that appears in Figure 10.1 is best drawn on a large whiteboard. The numbers that appear on Figure 10.1 represent a rank ordering of the scenarios thus depicted and are entered as the client answers the therapist's questions.]

	Approval	Disapproval
Certainty	4	3
Uncertainty	2	1

Figure 10.1. The '2x2' method of uncertainty/certainty and approval/disapproval as the two variables.

Windy: As you see there are four possible scenarios. Let me outline them one by one and as I do so I want you to consider which scenario you would be most anxious about, which the next, etc. Okay?

Ian: Okay.

Windy: Now in the first scenario you know that people approve of you; in the second scenario you know that people disapprove of you; in the third scenario, you suspect that people like you, but you are unsure; whereas in the final scenario, you suspect that people disapprove of you, but again you are unsure about this. Now which of these scenarios would you be most anxious about?

Ian: Well clearly, I would be most anxious about thinking that people disapprove of me, but not being sure [Square 1]. Also, obviously, I would not be anxious at all if I knew that people approved of me [Square 4].

Windy: Right. Now we have two scenarios left. Would you be more anxious if you knew for sure that people disaproved of you or if you suspected that they approved of you, but you were basically uncertain about this?

Ian: I know it sounds strange, but I would be more anxious in the uncertainty scenario [Square 2].

[This response shows that Ian's critical A involves uncertainty. If he had chosen the scenario where he knew for certain that others disapproved of him then his critical A would involve disapproval.]

The hypothesis-advancing method

In the hypothesis-advancing method, the therapist puts forward a hypothesis about the client's critical A based (1) on the information that the client has already provided about the ABC episode in question and about himself in general and (2) on the therapist's knowledge about REBT theory as it pertains to the relationship between unhealthy negative emotions and inferences. Generally, the therapist advances a hypothesis in this way when the client has provided limited information about the A despite the fact that the therapist has employed some of the other methods designed to elicit a critical A discussed in this chapter.

In general then, this method is used after such methods as inference chaining and 'going for broke' have been employed. It is used particularly when the client has provided the therapist with some information about the A, but where this information is sketchy. When this happens the therapist uses this sketchy information, considers the unhealthy negative emotion in the episode under consideration and refers back to previous ABCs the client has discussed. The therapist takes all this information and advances a hypothesis concerning the possible nature of the critical A. In doing so, the therapist needs to make clear to the client that his hypothesis is just that and if he is wrong the client should indicate so. The task of the therapist is to put this in such a way that the client is able to say 'no'. Here is how I (WD) might have used this method with Sue, if the information she had provided me with was sketchy.

Windy: So, Sue, we know that you were anxious while you stood on the platform and you think that your anxiety had something to do with the audience. Is that right?

Sue: Yes. That's right.

Windy: Okay. Now I have a hunch what you might have been anxious about and I'm going to put this to you in a moment. But let me make it clear that it is only a hunch and I may well be wrong. If I am wrong or off beam please tell me and we can take it from there. Okay?

Sue: Okay.

Windy: Based on what you've told me about this incident and from what you've told me about other incidents, my guess is that you were most anxious about the audience laughing at you if you didn't perform well. What do you make of that?

Sue: Yes! That's it. That's what I was anxious about.

[The definite quality of Sue's response is, I would argue, an indication that my hypothesis can be confirmed. The following is an example where my hypothesis can be rejected.]

Windy: Okay. Now I have a hunch what you might have been anxious about and I'm going to put this to you in a moment. But let me make it clear that it is only a hunch and I may well be wrong. If I am wrong or off beam please tell me and we can take it from there. Okay?

Sue: Okay.

Windy: Based on what you've told me about this incident and from what you've told me about other incidents, my guess is that you were most anxious about not giving a good talk. What do you make of that?

Sue: ...(pause)...Well...I suppose it could be.

Windy: It sounds to me as if my hunch doesn't ring a bell for you.

[The tentative nature of Sue's response is, I would contend, sufficient evidence to reject the hypothesis that I have put to her, and in my following response I say as much. Sometimes, however, an incorrect therapist hypothesis can be a stimulus for the client to identify the critical A for herself. This happens in the following interchange.]

Windy: Based on what you've told me about this incident and from what you've told me about other incidents, my guess is that you were most anxious about not giving a good talk. What do you make of that?

Sue: ...(pause)...Well...No, I don't think it's that. It's more how they will respond to me. Yes, that's it. I'm scared that they will laugh at me.

The theory-derived method

In the theory-derived method, the client has provided the therapist with an unhealthy negative emotion (e.g. anxiety), but cannot give any clue to what she may have been anxious about other than the broad situation she was in. In this case, the therapist uses his general knowledge about the kind of things people who find themselves in the same broad situation as the client are anxious about. The therapist then provides a verbal list of these possibilities and asks the client to indicate which item the client thinks may apply to her. The therapist then uses imagery to create an A featuring the chosen item and encourages the client to report on her response. This is how I (WD) would have used the theory-derived method with Sue.

Windy: Okay, Sue. So you know that you became anxious while you were standing on the platform, but you don't know what you were anxious about? Have I understood you correctly?

Sue: Yes, you have.

Windy: As I need to know more precisely what you were anxious about, do you think it might help if I list the kind of things that people become anxious about when in the same situation that you were in; namely, standing on a platform about to give a talk?

Sue: Yes, I think it might help.

Windy: Okay. I'll mention them one by one and as I do so, I'd like you to think which, if any, of the items on my list you may have been anxious about. Don't make any decision until you have heard the entire list. Okay?

Sue: Okay.

Windy:

(1) Some people become anxious about the prospect of giving a poor talk. Here they have some standard of performance that they believe they must live up to and they get anxious in case they don't live up to this standard. They are anxious about disappointing themselves rather than disappointing their audience.

(2) Other people are more anxious about how the audience will respond to them. They are anxious in case the members of the audience display their boredom, show overt hostility, ridicule or laugh at them, walk out or throw things.

(3) Yet other people are frightened of making fools of themselves. Here, they are scared of saying or doing something which in their minds reveal how shameful they are. This group of people are more focused on the prospect of their own foolish behaviour than they are on the reactions of the audience.

(4) The final group of people are anxious about features of their own anxiety. They are scared of the symptoms of their anxiety and thereby increase the likelihood in their minds of losing control of themselves. For example, such people are scared of such things as their mind going blank, fainting and being unable to speak.

Now do you think you may have been anxious about any of the items that I listed?

Sue: Well, when you mentioned the audience laughing that seemed to provoke a reaction in me.

Windy: Well, let's test that out. Close your eyes for a moment and imagine that you are standing on the platform ready to begin your talk. Can you picture that?

Sue: Yes, I can.

Windy: Now keep imagining that you are on the platform. As you do so start to think that you may say something that the audience finds funny that you do not intend to be humorous. They are laughing at you, not with you. How do you feel?

Sue: Well, as soon as you said that the audience were laughing AT me, I could tell that this is what I've been scared about all along.

[Sue's response indicates that I have managed to identify her critical A.]

Identifying the critical A by assessing B

We have found that sometimes we have been able to identify a client's critical A while assessing her irrational beliefs. As such, we occasionally make deliberate use of this method with the intention of identifying a critical A. Let us demonstrate how to use this method by showing how I (WD) would have employed it with Sue.

Windy: So when did you become anxious?

Sue: Well, I was all right until I got up on the platform.

Windy: What do you think you were anxious about?

Sue: I'm not sure.

Windy: Well, do you remember what mainly determines the way we feel?

Sue: Yes, our beliefs.

Windy: Right, so what do you think you were telling yourself about standing on the platform that led to your anxiety?

[Note here that having failed to find any kind of specific A above, I switch my attention to the client's beliefs. I thus work with a broad A, but as you will soon see I identify more specific As by focusing on B, not A.]

Sue: That the audience were expecting a lot from me.

[Note that in response to my deliberately vague question about her beliefs, i.e. what do you think you were telling yourself about...?, Sue provided me with an inference. Because I am primarily interested in identifying her critical A and not her irrational beliefs, I do not correct her here. I would do so if my purpose was actually to discover her irrational beliefs.]

Windy: And what were you telling yourself about the audience expecting a lot from you that led to your anxiety?

Sue: That I might not give a good speech.

[Note again that Sue provides me with another inferred A rather than an irrational belief.]

Windy: And what were you telling yourself about not giving a good speech that led to your anxiety?

Sue: That the audience will laugh at me.

[Yet another inference.]

Windy: And again what were you telling yourself about the audience laughing at you that led to your anxiety?

Sue: Oh! I couldn't bear that.

[Finally, Sue has provided me with an irrational belief about an A (the audience laughing at her). This is a probable sign that this A is critical. This still needs to be checked out and I refer you to the section on inference chaining for how to carry out such a check.]

You will note the similarity between this method and inference chaining. However, there is a crucial difference. In inference chaining you are using the C (e.g. anxiety) to discover a critical A. Thus you will ask questions like: 'What was anxiety-provoking in your mind about A...?' to go deeper into the person's chain of inferences until the critical A is discovered. However, in the present method you are using a general B-directed question to identify the critical A, e.g.: 'What were you telling yourself about this broad A to make yourself feel...?' The information that you obtain is the same, but the focus of the questions is different. Some clients respond very well to inference chaining, whereas others will provide you with inferences only when you ask about their beliefs or thoughts. As mentioned earlier, the more methods of identifying critical As you can become proficient in the better, so that if you draw a blank with inference chaining you can switch to another method such as the current one of identifying the critical A by assessing B.

Identifying the critical A by disputing musts

It is also possible to identify a client's critical A while disputing one of his musturbatory beliefs. Here, you have tried to identify your client's critical A by using one of the other methods already described in this module. However, you have only succeeded in identifying an A that is probably not critical. What you do then is identify a musturbatory belief about that A and dispute it. In response to your disputing questions, your client may take you deeper into his chain of inferences until you identify the client's critical A. Here is how I (WD) would have used this method with Sue.

Windy: So when did you become anxious?

Sue: Well, I was all right until I got up on the platform.

Windy: What was scary about standing up on the platform?

Sue: I could see people's faces looking up at me.

Windy: What was scary about them looking up at you?

Sue: ...[pause]...I don't know...

[After several different attempts to identify the client's critical A, I switch the focus of my questioning to identify the client's irrational demanding belief.]

Windy: Well, what were you demanding about the audience looking up at you that led you to feel anxious?

Sue: I was demanding that the people in the audience must not look up at me like that...

[There follows a gap where I explained the nature and purpose of disputing to the client. The dialogue continues after this point.]

Windy: Why must the audience not look up at you?

Sue: Because if they do they will expect a lot from me.

[Here Sue provides an inferred A in response to my disputing question. My purpose is to identify a critical A rather than helping her to dispute her irrational beliefs, so I take this new A and ask another disputing question of her implied must.]

Windy: And why must they not expect a lot from you?

Sue: Because I may not give a good talk.

[This is another inferred A and serves as the trigger for the next disputing question.]

Windy: Why must you give a good talk?

Sue: Because the audience will laugh at me if I don't.

Windy: And why must the audience refrain from laughing at you?

Sue: Because it would be terrible if they did laugh at me.

[The evaluative irrational belief 'it would be terrible...' provides a clue that the client may have referred to a critical A. Reviewing the chain would be a useful check here.]

You will again note that I am developing an inference chain, not by using inference chaining but by seeming to dispute must statements. As noted above, I am not actually disputing such beliefs, I am challenging them in order to elicit inferences that I have failed to elicit using more rational methods.

The 'relive it now' method

In the 'relive it now' method of identifying a critical A, you attempt to have the client relive the experience that you are assessing as if it were happening to her now. While you do so, encourage your client to verbalise any thoughts that go through her mind. Keep your own interventions to a minimum, but verbally encourage the client to go on with her account if she gets stuck (e.g. by asking 'What is happening now?' or by saying 'go on'). Many clients find this task easier if (1) they close their eyes and (2) they have had an opportunity to describe the environment in which the event took place. However, this is not true for all clients and if your client, for instance, wants to relive his experience with his eyes open by all means encourage him to do so. Before you ask your clients to undertake this reliving experience, it is important that you explain why you are asking him to do it. If he agrees, encourage him to describe the experience as if he is going through this now. Have him slow down the 'action' if his thoughts come too quickly for him to report. This method can well elicit strong affect in the session and it is best to inform your client of this. Indeed, the sudden shift of affect from weak to strong is one indicator that your client is encountering a critical A.

There are two ways in which your client can use this method. First, he can do it as if he is going directly through the experience. Second, he can do it as if he is experiencing indirectly it by seeing himself go through the experience on video, for example. Here is an example of how I (WD) would have used the 'relive it now' method with Sue.

Windy: So when did you become anxious?

Sue: Well, I was all right until I got up on the platform.

Windy: What was scary about standing up on the platform?

Sue: ...[pause]...I really don't know.

Windy: Well, it's important that we find out because knowing what you were most anxious about will enable us to help you deal with it effectively. Can you see that?

Sue: Yes, I can.

Windy: One way that we can find out what you were anxious about would be for you to relive the experience in imagination as it were and give me an ongoing account of what is going through your mind. What do you think?

Sue: I'm not sure I can do it, but I'll give it a try.

[At this point I give Sue some 'warm-up' imagery exercises so that she doesn't begin the method 'cold'. Then I proceeded as follows, with Sue electing to keep her eyes closed.]

Windy: Now you may experience strong emotion as you do this, but that is a good thing because it may well mean that we have discovered what you are anxious about. Is that okay?

Sue: Yes.

Windy: Let me start by asking you to describe the hall where you are giving the talk.

[Sue provides the description.]

Windy: You are now being introduced to the school by the headmistress. Take it from there.

[It is useful to have the client begin the 'relive it now' exercise at a time before he began to experience the target unhealthy negative emotion This 'lead in' time helps to orient the client to the broad A.]

Sue: I have begun to stand up...

Windy: I am beginning to stand up. Describe it as if it is happening now.

[At the beginning you will need to interrupt the client a few times so that he reports on his current experience.]

Sue: I am beginning to stand up. The room is quiet and I am looking down. I can see all those eager faces looking up at me. I am thinking: 'They expect a lot of me.' I am looking down at my notes. I've got to give a good talk. My anxiety is beginning to build. I suddenly picture them laughing at me and my anxiety soars... I am beginning my talk. I somehow find myself talking but I'm so anxious.

[At this point I can use a number of methods already described to review the As Sue came up with and select her critical A. I think it is already apparent from her account what this is.]

The 'relive it now' method is a good example of what is called 'vivid REBT'. For more vivid ways of identifying the critical A see Dryden (1986).

In addition to using the 'relive it now' method in the consulting room, you can also employ it with your client outside in a relevant aspect of his environment. You can accompany the client and encourage him to report his inferences in an ongoing manner. Sacco (1981) develops this method in an interesting way and his chapter is worth reading.

The opposite of the client's most cherished desire

Another way of determining the client's critical A, but one that is perhaps less vivid than the 'relive it now' method involves you first identifying the client's most cherished desire relevant to the situation in which her problem appears. Second, you ask the client what the opposite of this desire would be and how this would be manifest in the situation. The client's response may well represent the client's critical A. Let's see how I (WD) would have used this method with Sue.

Windy: So when did you become anxious?

Sue: Well, I was all right until I got up on the platform.

Windy: What were you anxious about at that point?

Sue: I'm not too sure.

Windy: Let me put this another way. What did you really want to happen in that situation – your most cherished desire, so to speak?

Sue: I would have wanted to be admired for giving a great talk.

Windy: And what would be the anxiety-provoking opposite of this for you?

[Note that I say 'anxiety-provoking' here because anxiety is the client's target emotion.]

Sue: To be ridiculed.

Windy: And how may the audience have shown that?

[Here I ask for the specific manifestation of the client's general fear that is relevant to the example that we are assessing.]

Sue: By laughing at me if I didn't give a good talk.

Windy: And if they did laugh at you, what would be scary about that in your mind?

[Note here that I ask an 'inference chaining' question to determine whether or not being laughed at is the critical A in this emotional episode.]

Sue: I'd just want to rush off the stage.

Windy: Why?

Sue: Because I couldn't bear to be laughed at.

[Here it is reasonable to conclude that being laughed at is Sue's critical A. First, it is the embodied opposite of the client's most cherished desire in the situation and the use of inference chaining does not reveal a more critical inference.]

The 'take a wild guess' method

If you have drawn a blank after using the above methods, you may still be able to identify your client's critical A by asking him or her to 'take a wild guess'. We have listened to many of Albert Ellis's therapy sessions and I have been struck by the positive response he has had to this method. You might use this technique in its own right or as part of another method (e.g. 'going for broke' or inference chaining). However, you should use it sparingly and only when your client is stuck.

This chapter completes a series of four devoted to assessing a critical A. In the following two chapters we consider another core REBT technique: disputing irrational beliefs.

References

Dryden, W. (1986). Vivid RET. In A. Ellis and R. Grieger (Eds), Handbook of Rational-Emotive Therapy. Volume 2. New York: Springer.

Sacco, W.P. (1981). Cognitive therapy in vivo. In G. Emery and R.C. Bedrosian (Eds), New Directions in Cognitive Therapy. New York: Guilford.

Chapter Eleven
Blundering into Disputing: The Perils of Inadequate Assessment, Overzealousness and Insensitivity

Introduction

Disputing clients' irrational and self-defeating beliefs is a principal activity of REBT therapists. These beliefs are deemed to be absolute and dogmatic and come in the form of unconditional musts, shoulds, oughts, have tos and got tos, e.g. 'I must never fail', and their three main derivatives of awfulising, low frustration tolerance and damnation of self and/or others, e.g. 'I'm worthless for failing my driving test'. Disputing is both an art and a science: an art because it relies upon the continual creativity of REBTers in applying or developing disputational techniques; and a science because it follows a scientific paradigm in applying logic, empiricism and utility to a client's irrational and rational belief systems. We would also add tact and sensitivity to the disputing process: clients' irrational ideas are not to be shot down like targets at a fairground rifle range.

Before an REBTer can practise the art, science and sensitivity of disputing, he or she needs to have identified an irrational belief(s) that largely (but not totally) creates the client's current emotional distress and agreed on the goals for change. It is this area of assessment that inexperienced REBTers often stumble around in, not sure of how to proceed with analysing the client's problems but their ears pricking up when the client utters a supposedly disturbance-producing word or phrase. This lack of clinical discernment means that the wrong beliefs (often rational ones) are disputed. In doing so, the therapist is deceiving himself into thinking that he has located the cognitive causes of the client's apparent emotional disturbance and the client is left bewildered.

The following excerpts from therapy are those taken from supervisees' audiotapes over the last decade and highlight the above points.

'Aha! A "must"'

Neophyte REBTers (though some experienced ones too) consider that any must or should statement uttered by the client denotes irrational thinking and therefore needs to be immediately disputed. Ellis (1977, 1980a, 1994) has repeatedly emphasised that musturbatory thinking is usually to be found at the root of emotional disturbance but the REBTer should target only absolute and dogmatic musts and shoulds, not conditional ones. Failing to heed this injunction, some REBTers pounce on the first 'must' or 'should' they hear:

Client: I'm fed up sitting at home alone, no friends, no romance. I lead a boring life.

Therapist: What do you want to do to change this situation?

Client: Well, obviously sitting at home all the time is not the answer.

Therapist: So what steps do you need to take to get some fun into you life?

Client: Well, I must have a social life, that's certain.

Therapist: But why must [emphasises word] you have a social life?

Client: I've just said: my life is dull and boring without one.

Therapist: I can understand how nice it would be to have a social life but why must you have one? There's no evidence for musts.

Client: I'm afraid you've lost me. I just told you what my problem is and the solution to it. Now you tell me I can't have a social life. How am I supposed to meet people and get some romance into my life otherwise?

Therapist: I'm not against you having a social life, just why must you have one?

Client: [exasperated] I must have one if I want to meet some desirable men. I won't meet them otherwise. I thought you were supposed to be helping me.

Therapist: I do want to help you and that's why I'm trying to get you to focus on your irrational demands that you must have a social life. The demands will block you from achieving your goal.

Client: What's irrational about wanting a social life? It's hardly going to come to my front door so I've got to get out there and find it.

Therapist: Ah, but you said 'want' not 'must'. There's a great difference between these two words.

Client: I'm sorry but I don't understand what's going on here. Every time I mention 'social life' you attack me.

This excerpt is an example of what Dawson (1991) calls 'mad dog disputing': usually, newly qualified REBTers, as he once was, are 'so well trained to "look for the should's, look for the must's" that I tended to attack them as soon as they reared their irrational heads' (p. 111). As Walen et al. (1992, p. 212) point out, 'this reaction frequently misses the target. Remember that these words are harmful because of the concepts that they stand for, not their face value.' In the above extract, the therapist is not trying to elicit the concept behind the client's 'must' and automatically assumes it is disturbance-creating. If the therapist had paid more attention to what the client actually said, he would have noticed that the client's 'must' was conditional – 'I must have one if I want to meet some desirable men'. The therapist's pseudo-triumph in locating a non-absolute must and doggedly hanging on to it leads to client bewilderment and the feeling that she is under attack from the therapist. This is hardly the best way to construct a therapeutic alliance.

What the therapist should (preferably) have done is to discover what prevents the client from developing a social life. This is more likely to yield an unconditional must:

Client: Well, I must have a social life, that's for certain.

Therapist: What prevents you from socialising?

Client: I'm worried.

Therapist: What about?

Client: Well, if I meet a man...

Therapist: What's worrying about that?

Client: I might like him but he might not like me.

Therapist: And if that happens...?

Client: Then he'll reject me.

Therapist: And if that happens...?

Client: That will prove how worthless I am.

Therapist: In order to avoid that happening, what are you telling yourself about the prospect of socialising?

Client: I must be certain that I won't be rejected.

Therapist: And as that can't be guaranteed...

Client: That's what keeps me stuck indoors.

In this extract, the therapist has uncovered a true irrational belief: 'I must be certain that I won't be rejected because if I am this will prove I'm worthless.' The client is now more likely to see what is blocking her from developing and enjoying a social life than the previous therapist's fixation on disputing the first 'must' she uttered. Disputing in the first extract was goal-blocking and disorientating for the client; disputing in the second extract, when the therapist embarks on it, is more likely to prove goal-attaining and plausible for her.

'He said a "should"'

The word 'should' can prove particularly difficult to inexperienced REBTers as it has several non-dogmatic meanings (Dryden, 1995): (1) recommendatory – 'You should have a sauna because you'll feel great afterwards'; (2) predictive – 'My mother should phone me tomorrow as she usually does on a Friday'; (3) ideal – 'I think people should be more courteous to each other as it would help to create a nicer society'; (4) empirical – 'Now that I've mended the plug, the table lamp should come on.' The potentially disturbance-inducing should represents demandingness and needs to be discriminated from the aforementioned shoulds. This has not been done in the following dialogue:

Client: I'm having problems with my wife.

Therapist: In what way?

Client: She should pay more attention to me. She spends a lot of time watching the television, reading her women's magazines, always on the phone talking to her friends. That sort of thing.

Therapist: Why should she pay more attention to you?

Client: Well, I'd feel a whole lot better and then we might have a better relationship. Seems reasonable to me.

Therapist: Well you're actually unreasonable because you're demanding how she should be behaving.

Client: I'm not sure I'm demanding it. I just want to try and understand what's going on between us. If I can achieve that then our relationship should improve.

Therapist: But there you go again with the 'should'. You're being inflexible with how your future should turn out. There's no room for manoeuvre if things don't turn out in your favour.

Client: Look, I just want things to be better between me and my wife. If we can work things out, then our relationship should go back to the way it used to be.

Therapist: I doubt it will with all those 'shoulds' in the way.

Client: I don't understand why you keep on taking me to task every time I say 'should'. Can't I speak freely in therapy?

The therapist appears to be the dogmatic one in the above exchange by assuming that every 'should' uttered by the client is pathological and thereby sidetracking, or even wrecking, therapy by unnecessary disputing. The client's last comment indicates he might be falling prey to a therapist-induced irrational belief: 'I shouldn't use the word" should"' (Dryden and Neenan, 1995). The therapist should, if she wishes to improve her clinical skills, pay attention to the client's verbal, behavioural and affective responses when the word is used as well as how the word is employed in describing his problems. In order to distinguish between rational and irrational shoulds, Walen et al.(1992, p. 116) suggest 'it would be wise for the therapist who hears a "should" to rephrase the sentence and feed it back, to ensure that it represents demandingness':

Therapist: When you say 'she should pay more attention to me' are you actually laying down the law as to how she absolutely [emphasises word] should behave?

Client: No, I'm not doing that. I just want some more attention from her. If I can understand what's going on between us, then our relationship should improve.

Therapist: Would you say that your relationship has got to, must improve otherwise it will be the end of your world or some other calamity?

Client: That's a bit dramatic. I wouldn't put it like that. I'll certainly do my best to try and rectify things but I know there are no guarantees in life. I hope we can put things right though and then our relationship should go back to the way it used to be.

Therapist: Does the relationship have to be the way it was before?

Client: That's what I want...but on second thoughts, if we get over this bad patch and find out what's wrong, our relationship can't really be exactly the same as before, can it?

Therapist: Well, relationships evolve like everything else in life.

By feeding back the client's 'shoulds', the therapist discovers that they are non-pathological and therefore not implicated in the client's emotional problems. Careful assessment has avoided wasting valuable therapy time. So what is the client's disturbance-producing should(s)?

Therapist: We've been talking about how you believe that your wife does not pay enough attention to you. How do you feel about that?

Client: I get a bit irritable sometimes.

Therapist: Anything stronger than that?

Client: Well, I do get angry about it occasionally.

Therapist: Would you like to explore what's going on in your head when you get angry?

Client: Yes, that might be helpful.

Therapist: What do you say to yourself when she doesn't pay you much attention? She would rather do anything else than talk to you [the therapist uses evocative language to try and elicit 'hot' or emotionally charged cognitions].

Client: [showing signs of agitation, voice rising] I've done everything for her, tried to make her happy, given her anything she wants. And this is the way she treats me.

Therapist: And as she does treat you in this uncaring and dismissive way, what then?

Client: [gripping the sides of his chair] Who the hell does she think she is?

Therapist: She obviously believes she has a good reason for doing it.

Client: [angry] She shouldn't bloody well treat me like this! It's not fair. I'm not a piece of shit she's stepped in!

Therapist: Is that what you are most angry about: that you absolutely should not be treated like this after all you've done for your wife?

Client: Yes, but I don't understand why she does it.

Therapist: Maybe we can throw some light on that when you're in a calmer frame of mind.

The therapist has uncovered a proper disturbance-creating should and linked it to the client's anger. Once the client is shown and accepts that his anger is counterproductive in trying to resolve his current problem with his wife, then genuinely therapeutic disputing can commence.

Disturbance-producing? Yes; relevant to therapy? No

In the above dialogues, we have shown misguided efforts to dispute harmless musts and shoulds and thereby created counsellor-induced blocks in therapy In the following extract, the client does offer irrational ideas but they are irrelevant or peripheral to her presenting problems:

Client: Sorry I'm late. I got delayed washing my hair. I always have to look my best.

Therapist: Hmm. Well, we can get down to business straightaway.

Client: Good.

Therapist: Why do you always have to look your best?

Client: [puzzled] That's just the way I am. Do you want me to talk about my problems?

Therapist: We seem to have one already.

Client: I haven't started yet.

Therapist: You see in REBT we believe that irrational ideas can be emotionally harmful. You can detect these ideas when people use words like 'must, should, have to'. In your case, you always have [emphasises word] to look your best.

Client: But I don't want to talk about that.

Therapist: Let me ask you this: how would you feel if you left your house not looking your best?

Client: I'd feel bloody awful but it's not something I ever do. I always look my best when I go out.

Therapist: But don't you see the problem there – this demand that you have to leave your house looking your best?

Client: I've never seen it as a problem before. My doctor referred me to you because he said you could help me with stress at work. I hope he hasn't made a mistake.

The client apparently has irrational ideas, in the REBT sense, regarding her appearance when she leaves the house, but the client does not see any problem with her attitude and wants to get on with discussing her presenting complaints. As Beck (1976, p. 218) points out: 'It is obvious that not all people who think erroneously need or want to get their thinking straightened out. When a person's erroneous ideation disrupts his life or makes him feel miserable, then he becomes a candidate for some form of help.' In this case, the client's life is being disrupted by stress at work. Even if it did emerge later in therapy that there was a pathological link between having to appear always at her best and stress at work, it still remains the client's choice whether or not she wants explore this link.

'Nothing is awful'

Dryden and Yankura (1995, p. x) state that awfulising beliefs 'are rigidly located on a "magical" continuum ranging from 101% badness to infinity...when a person is awfulising, she literally believes at the moment that nothing could be worse'. Whatever happens in life, from failed relationships to genocide, empirically happens–the clock cannot be wound back to make these events disappear. When a client disturbs herself through awfulising she is demanding that bad events should not have occurred or should not be as bad as they are.

While acceptance of grim empirical reality is a key component of REBT theory and practice, it is important that this concept is used with great care otherwise it can appear that the therapist is belittling or even ignoring the client's real suffering:

Client: I still can't believe that it happened: my mother and boyfriend dying in the same week. She died of cancer and he was killed in a car crash. It's absolutely awful. I still can't believe it happened. I refuse to believe it. My life has been devastated.

Therapist: These events are very sad indeed but not awful.

Client: What? I don't understand what you mean.

Therapist: Well, these very bad events have occurred but occur they did. When you start awfulising, as we say in REBT, you refuse to accept reality and thereby get stuck in unhealthy grief and suffering.

Client: Is there healthy suffering? My life has been destroyed and you expect me to accept it just like that. You have no idea of what I feel or what I'm going through.

Therapist: I think I can understand but I'm trying to show you a healthy and rational way of coming to terms with these tragedies.

Client: I don't want to come to terms with them – I want to feel the way I feel and not be lectured about it. Have you ever had two people whom you loved dying in the same week?

Therapist: No, but the principle of not awfulising about it would apply equally to me or anyone else in your situation.

Client: I can't believe you're saying this. You're just a walking textbook. You have no understanding whatsoever of what I'm going through. I can't talk to you.

In the above extract, the therapist is not choosing his comments carefully in the light of the client's reaction. He just drones on telling her that awfulising is wrong and not the 'correct' response to grief. The client is right to call him a 'walking textbook'. REBT concepts are certainly not blunt instruments therapists use to beat their clients into submission with and thereby grudgingly accept the REBT viewpoint (not that this is working in the above dialogue). REBTers should try to determine the most clinically beneficial time to introduce the concept of awfulising instead of rushing headlong into it. Sometimes the term can be dropped altogether while the principles underlying it are still explained:

Client: I still can't believe that it happened: my mother and boyfriend dying in the same week. She died of cancer and he was killed in a car crash. It's absolutely awful. I still can't believe it happened. I refuse to believe it. My life has been devastated.

Therapist: How can I be of help?

Client: I need to talk to someone so badly. I just want to pour everything out that I feel. I don't know what else to do.

Therapist: Do you think that talking about it will eventually help you to come to terms with these tragedies?

Client: I think so, I hope so. I'm just so numb with grief. How can these things happen?

Therapist: All I can say is that they do. Maybe not much of an answer, but the great struggle ahead is for people to learn how to cope with it.

Client: But what if I can't, if I don't want to?

Therapist: Then you might get stuck in unhealthy grief which is being depressed for a long period. That usually occurs when people refuse to accept what has happened in their lives.

Client: What happens then?

Therapist: Then I would try to help you develop some attitudes that accept the painful reality of loss while at the same time encouraging you to start getting on with your life again.

Client: It's too early for that. I'm not ready yet.

Therapist: Let's take it one step at a time.

The therapist is obviously not disputing the client's thinking but pointing out some of the pitfalls of unhealthy grief. He also suggests how he would help her if she got 'stuck' in this reaction. With clients who have suffered personal tragedies and whose grief is dysfunctional – defined in REBT as 'persistence over time of dominant irrational beliefs regarding the loss event, the deceased and the self' (Malkinson, 1996, p. 166) – gentle challenging of such beliefs is called for rather than the usual force and vigour that drives traditional REBT disputing. Also, as Dryden (1995) points out, REBTers should avoid labelling painful activating events as a 'hassle not a horror' or 'unfortunate but not awful'. Such trivialisation of the client's suffering will probably destroy any burgeoning therapeutic relationship.

You've got low frustration tolerance

The powerful concept of discomfort disturbance or low frustration toler-ance (LFT) (Ellis, 1979, 1980b) stems from an individual's demands that life conditions must be easy and comfortable otherwise he or she will not be able to endure any discomfort or hardship. In therapy, this usually translates as clients should not have to work too hard in the process of change because they cannot stand or bear the struggle required to reach their goals. Ellis (1985) suggests that LFT is probably the most common reason why clients resist change. Therefore any form of foot-dragging in therapy is usually hypothesised to be due to LFT ideas. As with awfulising, care should be taken in assessing and understanding the severity of the client's problem:

Client: I'm still getting the nightmares, panic attacks, feeling on edge all of the time. I can't get the assault out of my head. He nearly killed me.

Therapist: Well I have suggested that by repeatedly exposing yourself in your imagination to the assault is usually an effective way to help you become less disturbed about it.

Client: I get so anxious just thinking about doing that. I don't think I could cope with that.

Therapist: That's because you're blocking yourself with something called low frustration tolerance. This means that you're telling yourself that you can't stand the discomfort and upset in carrying out this procedure.

Client: I've suffered enough. I just want it to go away.

Therapist: I'm afraid it won't go until you start facing your fears. And that won't happen unless you overcome these low frustration tolerance ideas. It's important that you start telling yourself that you can stand the pain involved in reliving the assault.

Client: I do want to do what you say but...

Therapist: ...but what?

Client: Maybe I should take lots of tranquillisers to blot it out. Then I would have some peace.

Therapist: An untranquil peace. That won't help. If you can learn to tolerate what lies ahead, this will be more effective than handfuls of tablets.

Muran and DiGiuseppe (1994, p. 166) maintain that suggesting to clients who have suffered greatly already that they have a low tolerance for frustration because they resist 'recounting the trauma may be perceived as an invalidation of the traumatic experience'. The therapist in the above dialogue is very close to doing just that because, as in previous examples in this chapter, she is not employing the term with sufficient care or looking at modifying it based upon the client's reaction – the client might believe he is being assaulted for a second time because of the therapist's relentless approach. Clients who have experienced prolonged suffering, e.g. post-traumatic stress disorder (PTSD), physical disabilities or chronic illness, are 'just willing to experience a *high enough* frustration level that is required to complete the desired task' and therefore the goal for therapists is to help such clients 'develop *greater* frustration tolerance' (Muran and DiGiuseppe, 1994, p. 167):

Client: I'm still getting the nightmares, panic attacks, feeling on edge all of the time. I can't get the assault out of my head. He nearly killed me. It shattered my life.

Therapist: Are your symptoms getting worse?

Client: Yes, I don't have much control over them.

Therapist: One of the most effective long-term methods of control over and eventual reduction of your symptoms is prolonged exposure in imagery to the assault and examination of your ideas associated with it – like, are you able to rebuild a shattered life? This may help you to look at and deal with the assault differently so you become much less upset when you think about what happened to you.

Client: I don't think I can face it. I've suffered enough already.

Therapist: You have been through a tremendous ordeal. You have put up with a lot of pain and suffering that most people wouldn't begin to understand or even cope with.

Client: I just want everything to go away so I can feel better.

Therapist: I understand that but, unfortunately, in order to get better and suffer less in the long-term, you will experience more anguish and upset in the short-term through this and other methods to tackle your flashbacks and nightmares. I'm afraid I'm asking you to suffer a bit more temporarily.

Client: Haven't I suffered enough? I know you're trying to help me but isn't there another way like more tablets?

Therapist: Let me ask you this: your symptoms are getting worse, you have no peace of mind at present, do you think things will get harder or easier for you if you avoid focusing on these painful memories of the assault by taking more tablets?

Client: I know things will get worse – they are getting worse. I suppose I'll have to make an extra effort if I want to get better, to put this thing behind be. I'll just have to learn reluctantly to put up with whatever lies ahead with this treatment. I'll keep my fingers crossed.

Therapist: That's good. I'm sure you'll find the extra effort now worth the eventual gains.

Instead of 'accusing' the client of having LFT and therefore blocking his recovery, the therapist, in the above dialogue, emphasises the pain and suffering he has already endured. Therefore she encourages him to endure more discomfort for therapeutic purposes – prolonged imaginal exposure to the assault coupled with cognitive restructuring 'help clients work through their traumatic event, discover and revise meanings associated with it, and develop more adaptive responses to it' (Warren and Zgourides, 1991, p. 161).

'Part of me still feels worthless'

One of the two meanings of acceptance in REBT is that individuals learn to accept themselves and others unconditionally as fallible human beings who do not have to act other than they do and are too complex to be legitimately given a global rating such as 'worthless' or 'perfect' (Dryden and Neenan, 1995). Unconditional self-acceptance is the elegant solution to the problem of self-worth as Ellis (1976, p. 6) advises individuals 'to abolish most of what we normally call your human ego and retain those parts of it which you can empirically verify and fairly accurately define'. Because so many clients have problems based on conditional self-acceptance or self-esteem, some REBTers automatically and dogmatically assume that the only solution to the client's ego disturbance is to strive for unconditional self-acceptance:

Client: I know you keep on telling me to learn to accept myself for my five wasted years on drink and drugs but I don't think I'll ever be able to do that. I'll always see part of myself as worthless for what I did during those years.

Therapist: (emphatically) Well you'd better learn to accept yourself if you don't want to go back to drink and drugs. Whenever you condemn yourself for your bad or obnoxious actions you're going to feel depressed, angry, ashamed, guilty, and then return to the drugs to blot out these feelings.

Client: That's largely how it used to work. But if I learn to be more self-accepting from now on this is less likely to happen when things go wrong in my life.

Therapist: You want it both ways: self-condemning for past actions and self-accepting for future ones. That won't work. There's an irreconcilable tension between these two concepts – no matter how stable your life becomes there will always be a part of you that could destabilise it because you don't think you're worthy enough to achieve success, happiness or whatever based on your past behaviour. Unconditional self-acceptance is the only reliable basis for change. Anything else is strictly short-term.

Client: I don't agree my way is short-term. I am ashamed of my past behaviour but that certainly doesn't mean it will destabilise my future. How can you be so sure of how my life will turn out? I still think about those wasted years and how worthless I was for leading that kind of life. I don't get particularly upset or reach for a drink to comfort myself. I can accept myself for my worthlessness in that area of my life.

Therapist: That's not the REBT view: self-acceptance is unconditional in all areas of one's life – past, present and future. This can have a dramatic effect on how you deal with emotional crises.

Client: I don't think I want to be totally self-accepting or could ever achieve it. There will always be things in my life which I'll condemn myself for but that doesn't mean my life will fall apart.

Therapist: But it increases the chances that it might and this is the danger.

Client: Look, can we talk about something else? I don't want to spend the rest of my life in therapy going on about this issue.

Therapist: Okay, but I will come back to it again as I don't think you've really grasped what I'm saying to you.

Teaching clients to internalise the 'attitude of unconditional self-acceptance is probably the most important variable in their long-term recovery [from substance abuse]' (Ellis et al., 1988, p. 71); however, in the above exchange, the therapist is insisting that the client has to internalise this attitude. The client is trying to put forward what she considers to be a realistic way of change but the therapist is deaf to her viewpoint because of his own irrational ideas. As Neenan (1997) points out, many clients find the concept of greater self-acceptance (GSA) easier to grasp than unconditional self-acceptance (USA): 'It is part of the human condition never to be completely satisfied with ourselves and this will inevitably involve some form of self-judgement. This certainly does not mean that we cannot lead happy, productive and efficient lives because we also carry within us a measure of self-discontent or disturbance (p. 32).' If a client is not persuaded by the idea of USA then the therapist should switch to GSA:

Client: I know you keep on telling me to learn to accept myself for my five wasted years on drink and drugs but I don't think I'll ever be able to do that. I'll always see part of myself as worthless for what I did during those years.

Therapist: Okay, well let's look at greater self-acceptance in your life. This means that a lot of the time you can strive for and succeed in divorcing your actions from yourself – label the action as 'helpful' or 'unhelpful' but don't label yourself. Obviously this is something that will not happen over night but will evolve in our life if you continually practise it.

Client: I understand that and I do want to be more self-accepting.

Therapist: Now, these ideas like worthlessness are light sleepers and can be easily woken or activated when you're under some kind of emotional stress. How are you going to deal with these ideas if you lack self-acceptance at that point?

Client: I admit that might be difficult but I'm going to do my best to compartmentalise it to the specific problem at that time without letting it spill over into other areas of my life.

Therapist: Easier said than done.

Client: True, but it's my struggle, not yours. I don't want to be totally self-accepting because I don't think it's either desirable or possible. There will be some things in my life that I will condemn myself for but that doesn't mean my life has to fall apart because of it.

Therapist: I'm not trying to talk you out of your viewpoint but just curious how you would cope with a problem when you were in a self-damning frame of mind. I will certainly show you a number of methods to strengthen your commitment to greater self-acceptance.

Client: Thanks. That will help me a lot.

In determining whether to teach USA or GSA, REBTers should keep in mind the intellectual capabilities of their clients, often their more modest goals for change and the limited time they are prepared to spend in therapy rather than automatically assuming that what is best for them is to achieve a egoless state of being. How can the REBTer ultimately know that USA rather than GSA will bring clients greater happiness, stability and fulfilment in their lives?

Conclusion

In this chapter, we have tried to convey some of the blunders that particularly inexperienced REBTers commit when they rush into disputing clients' presumed irrational beliefs or goals for change. Clinical discernment comes before disputing: the therapist needs to agree with the client the target of the dispute; in some cases, when the target has been agreed, gentle discussion or light disputing is called for with sensitive issues (e.g. rape) or certain groups (e.g. the elderly). The eagerness of some REBTers to get 'stuck into' the client's irrational ideas must always be tempered with or restrained by the knowledge of the possibly irreparable harm they could inflict on the therapeutic alliance.

Finally, we have shown that these blunders come from a variety of sources. First, they often occur because the therapist is clinically inexperienced and tries to fit the client to the REBT model rather than tailoring the REBT to suit the uniqueness of the client. Second, these blunders are made because the therapist is employing REBT either too literally or unthinkingly. REBT concepts are deceptively simple in theory. In practice, they are complex, and the focus should be on the meaning of words rather than on the words themselves. Effective REBT therapists focus on meaning and encourage their clients to do the same. Lastly, these blunders are made because some therapists do not take the time and trouble to understand their clients' problems in depth. At the first sign of a must or should, assessment stops. Good REBT is based on accurate and thoughtful assessment. Novice REBTers easily forget this. We hope this chapter gives them a gentle reminder of this clinical fact of life.

References

Beck, A.T. (1976). Cognitive Therapy and the Emotional Disorders. New York: International Universities Press.

Dawson, R.W. (1991). A counselling and educational model for using RET effectively. In M.E. Bernard (Eds), Using Rational-Emotive Therapy Effectively: A Practitioner's Guide. New York: Plenum.

Dryden, W. (1995). Facilitating Client Change in Rational Emotive Behavviour Therapy. London: Whurr.

Dryden, W. and Neenan, M. (1995). Dictionary of Rational Emotive Behaviour Therapy. London: Whurr.

Dryden, W. and Yankura, J. (1995). Developing Rational Emotive Behaviour Counselling. London: Sage.

Ellis, A. (1976). RET abolishes most of the human ego. Psychotherapy: Theory, Research and Practice, 13, 343–8. (Reprinted New York: Albert Ellis Institute for Rational Emotive Behaviour Therapy.)

Ellis, A. (1977). The basic clinical theory of rational-emotive therapy. In A. Ellis and R. Grieger (Eds), Handbook of Rational-Emotive Therapy, Vol. 1. New York: Springer.

Ellis, A. (1979). Discomfort anxiety: a new cognitive-behavioural construct (Part 1). Rational Living, 14(2), 3–8.

Ellis, A. (1980a). An overview of the clinical theory of rational-emotive therapy. In R. Grieger and J. Boyd (Eds), Rational-Emotive Therapy: A Skills-Based Approach. New York: Van Nostrand Reinhold.

Ellis, A. (1980b). Discomfort anxiety: a new cognitive-behavioural construct (Part 2). Rational Living, 15(1), 25–30.

Ellis, A. (1985). Overcoming Resistance: Rational-Emotive Therapy with Difficult Clients. New York: Springer.

Ellis, A. (1994). Reason and Emotion in Psychotherapy, 2nd edition. New York: Birch Lane Press.

Ellis, A., McInerney, J.F., DiGiuseppe, R. and Yeager, R.J. (1988). Rational-Emotive Therapy with Alcoholics and Substance Abusers. New York: Pergamon Press.

Malkinson, R. (1996). Cognitive behavioural grief therapy. Journal of Rational-Emotive and Cognitive-Behavioural Therapy, 14(3), 155–71.

Muran, E.M. and DiGiuseppe, R. (1994). Rape. In F.M. Dattilio and A. Freeman (Eds), Cognitive-Behavioural Strategies in Crisis Intervention. New York: Guilford Press.

Neenan, M. (1997). Reflections on two major REBT concepts. The Rational Emotive Behaviour Therapist, 5(1), 31–33.

Walen, S.R., DiGiuseppe, R. and Dryden, W. (1992). A Practitioner's Guide to Rational-Emotive Therapy, 2nd edition. New York: Oxford University Press.

Warren, R. and Zgourides, G.D. (1991). Anxiety Disorders: A Rational-Emotive Perspective. New York: Pergamon Press.

Chapter Twelve
Structured Disputing of
Irrational Beliefs

Until recently, there has been little written in the non-textbook REBT literature on disputing irrational beliefs. This is surprising since disputing is
such a central part of the REBT process. The notable exceptions to this
neglect are DiGiuseppe's (1991) important chapter where he broke down
disputing into its component parts and Beal et al.'s (1996) article applying
DiGiuseppe's schema to a single irrational belief.

DiGiuseppe's (1991) contribution

DiGiuseppe's (1991) and his students listened to many of Albert Ellis's
therapy tapes and focused on his disputing work with clients. Their
purpose was to develop a comprehensive taxonomy of the different
elements of disputing. This taxonomy described the following elements:

The target of the dispute

Disputes can be directed at the following targets: demands, awfulising
beliefs, low frustration tolerance (LFT) beliefs and depreciation beliefs
(where self, others and life conditions are being depreciated). An important point stressed by DiGiuseppe is that helping clients to construct
rational beliefs is an integral part of the disputing process. In so doing,
DiGiuseppe argues that it is important to use the same disputing
questions targeted at the alternative rational beliefs. Here the targets of
the dispute are preferences, anti-awfulising beliefs, high frustration tolerance beliefs and acceptance beliefs (where self, others and life conditions
are being accepted).

The nature of the dispute

DiGiuseppe argued that disputes fall into one of three categories. First,
there are empirical disputes which ask clients to put forward evidence
attesting to the truth or falsity of the belief. Second, there are logical
disputes which ask clients to consider whether the target belief is

logical or not. Third, there are heuristic disputes which ask clients to consider the functionality of the target belief. As argued above, these different disputes are targeted at both irrational beliefs and newly constructed rational beliefs. As is well accepted in REBT, irrational beliefs are inconsistent with reality, illogical and yield dysfunctional results while rational beliefs are consistent with reality, logical and yield functional results.

Level of abstraction

Both irrational beliefs and rational beliefs can be placed along a specificity-abstractness continuum. DiGiuseppe provides an example where a client was angry with his wife for not behaving as he thinks she 'should' and shows that this client could have several beliefs ranging from the very specific: 'My wife must make dinner when I want her to make it' to the very abstract: 'The world must be the way I want it.'

It follows that disputes can be directed at beliefs that range along this continuum. Therapists can make two major errors here. First, they can direct their disputes at beliefs that are too abstract and second, they can fail to help their clients to dispute core irrational beliefs by disputing only very concrete irrational beliefs.

Disputing styles

DiGiuseppe (1991) identified four major disputing styles. These are

Socratic disputing

Here therapists dispute their clients' irrational beliefs and help them to test out their newly constructed rational beliefs by asking them questions designed to make them think for themselves about the empirical, logical and heuristic status of both sets of beliefs. When clients provide the incorrect answers to these open-ended questions their Socratic therapists follow up with more open-ended questions and this process continues until the clients are helped to arrive at the correct responses (correct, that is, according to REBT theory).

Didactic disputing

Didactic disputing involves therapists directly explaining to their clients why their irrational beliefs are inconsistent with reality, illogical and dysfunctional and why their alternative rational beliefs are, by contrast, consistent with reality, logical and functional. When using this disputing style, therapists are advised to check whether or not their clients understand and agree with the points being made. The purpose of didactic disputing is client learning not just the therapist teaching.

Metaphorical disputing

In this style of disputing, therapists tell their clients a metaphor which is designed to show clients why their irrational beliefs are irrational and/or why their rational beliefs are rational. As with didactic disputing, when using a metaphorical dispute it is important that the therapist ensures that the client has understood and concurs with the point that the metaphor is designed to make.

Humorous disputing

Ellis and other experienced therapists often show clients that their irrational beliefs are irrational in a very humorous manner. Here they make clear that the target of the humour is the clients' beliefs, not the clients themselves.

Other styles

There are two styles of disputing that DiGiuseppe (1991) does not discuss. These are self-disclosure and enactive disputing. When therapists question their clients' beliefs using self-disclosure, they draw upon their own personal experiences of thinking irrationally, challenging these irrational beliefs and eventually thinking rationally (Dryden, 1990). In enactive disputing, therapists challenge their clients' irrational beliefs through action. An example of this style of disputing is found when a therapist throws a glass of water over himself in the session to demonstrate that one can act foolishly without being a fool.

Structured disputing

What neither DiGiuseppe (1991) nor Beal et al. (1996) have addressed is the issue of bringing structure to the disputing process. This will be the focus for the remainder of this chapter. There has been very little discussion in the REBT literature of the importance of structure in disputing irrational beliefs and questioning rational beliefs. Through listening to Ellis's therapy tapes it is not clear that his disputing interventions are guided by any obvious structure. Indeed, he seems to be guided by his clients' responses to his previous disputing intervention when making follow-up interventions. This flexible and relatively unstructured approach is fine in the hands of seasoned REBT therapists, but it is likely that for novice REBT practitioners, lack of structure when disputing will frequently lead to therapist confusion and the breakdown of the disputing process. Consequently, it is advisable for novice REBT therapists to use a structured approach to disputing irrational beliefs and questioning rational beliefs until they have honed their disputing skills to a high level.

In what follows, four approaches to structured disputing will be presented and discussed. In doing so, the focus will be on the nature of the dispute and the target of the dispute. What will be discussed applies to whichever style of disputing is used and it is assumed that disputes are made at the most appropriate level of specificity.

Approach 1: Disputing focused on separate components of a belief

In disputing that is focused on separate components of a belief, the therapist focuses on one component of an irrational belief at a time and directs the three main arguments towards that component before moving on to the next component. Following DiGiuseppe, the therapist also directs the same arguments against components of the client's rational beliefs, again one at a time. There are actually two ways of doing this. In the first version, the therapist moves on to questioning a component of the client's rational belief (e.g. his preference) as soon as she has disputed the relevant component of his irrational belief (i.e. his demand).

In the second version, the therapist disputes all components of the client's irrational belief (i.e. his demand and its appropriate derivatives) before questioning all the components of the client's rational belief (i.e. his preference and its appropriate derivatives).

The two versions of this approach will now be illustrated. In the chosen example, the components of the client's irrational belief are as follows:

Demand: I must be approved by my girlfriend's parents.

Awfulising belief: It would be awful if I were not approved by my girlfriend's parents.

LFT belief: I couldn't stand it if I were not approved by my girlfriend's parents.

Self-depreciation belief: If I am not approved by my girlfriend's parents, it means that I am an unworthy person.

The components of the client's rational belief are as follows:

Preference: I would like to be approved by my girlfriend's parents, but this is not essential.

Anti-awfulising belief: It would be bad if I were not approved by my girlfriend's parents, but it would not be awful.

HFT belief: It would be difficult for me to tolerate not being approved by my girlfriend's parents, but I could stand it.

Self-acceptance: If I am not approved of my girlfriend's parents, it does not mean that I am an unworthy person. It means that I am a fallible human being who is facing a difficult situation.

In version 1 of this approach the therapist proceeds as follows:

Demand: I must be approved by my girlfriend's parents.

[empirical dispute, logical dispute, heuristic dispute]

Preference: I would like to be approved by my girlfriend's parents, but this is not essential.

[Empirical dispute, logical dispute, heuristic dispute]

Awfulising belief: It would be awful if I were not approved by my girlfriend's parents.

[Empirical dispute, logical dispute, heuristic dispute]

Anti-awfulising belief: It would be bad if I were not approved by my girlfriend's parents, but it would not be awful.

[Empirical dispute, logical dispute, heuristic dispute]

LFT belief: I couldn't stand it if I were not approved by my girlfriend's parents.

[Empirical dispute, logical dispute, heuristic dispute]

HFT belief: It would be difficult for me to tolerate not being approved by my girlfriend's parents, but I could stand it.

[Empirical dispute, logical dispute, heuristic dispute]

Self-depreciation belief: If I am not approved by my girlfriend's parents, it means that I am an unworthy person.

[Empirical dispute, logical dispute, heuristic dispute]

Self-acceptance belief: If I am not approved by my girlfriend' parents, it does not mean that I am an unworthy person. It means that I am a fallible human being who is facing a difficult situation.

[Empirical dispute, logical dispute, heuristic dispute]

Please note it is assumed here (and elsewhere in this chapter) that the client understands and agrees with the therapist's argument before the therapist moves on to the next argument. Thus, the therapist ensures that the client understands and agrees with the idea that there is no empirical evidence in favour of his demand that he must have the approval of his girlfriend's parents, but there is such evidence in favour of his preference (empirical arguments) before disputing this demand logically. Thus, the therapist persists with a line of argument within each element of the above structure before moving on to the next element. However, if a client just cannot resonate with a particular argument after an appropriate period of the therapist's persistence, the therapist is advised to move on as indicated in the structure.

Also, please note that it is not being advocated that REBT therapists should adopt the following target order that was presented above, i.e. musts, preferences; awfulising, anti-awfulising; LFT, HFT; self-deprecation, self-acceptance, or the following argument order that was again used above, i.e. empirical, logical, heuristic. The question of order within the structure is a matter for future consideration. However, it is argued that within a structured approach to disputing, whichever order is selected should be consistently applied.

In version 2 of this approach, the therapist targets her disputes against all four components of the client's irrational belief before questioning all four components of his rational belief. Thus, the therapist proceeds as follows:

Demand: I must be approved by my girlfriend's parents.

[Empirical dispute, logical dispute, heuristic dispute]

Awfulising belief: It would be awful if I were not approved by my girlfriend's parents.

[Empirical dispute, logical dispute, heuristic dispute]

LFT belief: I couldn't stand it if I were not approved by my girlfriend's parents.

[Empirical dispute, logical dispute, heuristic dispute]

Self-depreciation belief: If I am not approved by my girlfriend's parents, it means that I am an unworthy person.

[Empirical dispute, logical dispute, heuristic dispute]

Preference: I would like to be approved by my girlfriend's parents, but this is not essential.

[Empirical dispute, logical dispute, heuristic dispute]

Anti-awfulising belief: It would be bad if I were not approved by my girlfriend's parents, but it would not be awful.

[Empirical dispute, logical dispute, heuristic dispute]

HFT belief: It would be difficult for me to tolerate not being approved by my girlfriend's parents, but I could stand it.

[Empirical dispute, logical dispute, heuristic dispute]

Self-acceptance belief: If I am not approved by my girlfriend's parents, it does not mean that I am an unworthy person. It means that I am a fallible human being who is facing a difficult situation.

[Empirical dispute, logical dispute, heuristic dispute]

Approach 2: Disputing focused on paired components of irrational and rational beliefs

In this approach the therapist questions paired components of the client's irrational belief and rational belief at the same time. The following structure shows how this step-by-step approach can be used by clients on their own.

Questioning demands and preferences

Step 1: Take your demand and identify the alternative to this belief which is a preference. Write them side by side on a sheet of paper under the following appropriate headings.

Demand	*Preference*
I must be approved by my girlfriend's parents.	I would like to be approved by my girlfriend's parents, but this is not essential.

Step 2: Ask yourself the following question: 'Which belief is true and which is false?'

Step 3: Write down the answer to this question and provide written reasons for your answer.

Step 4: Ask yourself the following question: 'Which belief is sensible/logical and which doesn't make sense or is illogical?'

Step 5: Write down the answer to this question and provide written reasons for your answer.

Step 6: Ask yourself the following question: 'Which belief is helpful/yields healthy results and which is unhelpful/yields unhealthy results?'

Step 7: Write down the answer to this question and provide written reasons for your answer.

Step 8: Ask yourself the following question: 'Which of the two beliefs do you want to strengthen and act on?'

Step 9: Write down the answer to this question and provide written reasons for your answer.

Questioning awfulising beliefs and anti-awfulising beliefs

Step 1: Take your awfulising belief and identify the alternative to this belief which is an anti-awfulising belief. Write them side by side on a sheet of paper under the following appropriate headings.

Step 2: Ask yourself the following question: 'Which belief is true and which is false?'

Step 3: Write down the answer to this question and provide written reasons for your answer.

Awfulising belief

Anti-awfulising belief

It would be awful if I were not
approved by my girlfriend's
parents.

It would be bad if I were not
approved by my girlfriend's
parents, but it would not be awful.

Step 4: Ask yourself the following question: 'Which belief is sensible/
logical and which doesn't make sense or is illogical?'
Step 5: Write down the answer to this question and provide written
reasons for your answer.
Step 6: Ask yourself the following question: 'Which belief is helpful/yields
healthy results and which is unhelpful/yields unhealthy results?'
Step 7: Write down the answer to this question and provide written
reasons for your answer.
Step 8: Ask yourself the following question: 'Which of the two beliefs do
you want to strengthen and act on?'
Step 9: Write down the answer to this question and provide written
reasons for your answer.

Questioning LFT beliefs and HFT beliefs

Step 1: Take your LFT belief and identify the alternative belief which is an
HFT belief. Write them side by side on a sheet of paper under the
following appropriate headings.

LFT belief

HFT belief

I couldn't stand it if I were not
approved by my girlfriend's parents.

It would be difficult to tolerate not
being approved by my girlfriend's
parents, but I could stand it.

Step 2: Ask yourself the following question: 'Which belief is true and
which is false?'
Step 3: Write down the answer to this question and provide written
reasons for your answer.
Step 4: Ask yourself the following question: 'Which belief is sensible/
logical and which doesn't make sense or is illogical?'
Step 5: Write down the answer to this question and provide written
reasons for your answer.
Step 6: Ask yourself the following question: 'Which belief is helpful/yields
healthy results and which is unhelpful/yields unhealthy results?'
Step 7: Write down the answer to this question and provide written
reasons for your answer.
Step 8: Ask yourself the following question: 'Which of the two beliefs do
you want to strengthen and act on?'

Step 9: Write down the answer to this question and provide written reasons for your answer.

Questioning self-depreciating beliefs and self-acceptance beliefs

Step 1: Take your self-depreciation belief and identify the alternative to this belief which is a self-acceptance belief. Write them side by side on a sheet of paper under the following appropriate headings.

Self-depreciation belief	*Self-acceptance belief*
If I were not approved by my girlfriend's parents, it means that I am an unworthty person.	If I am not approved by my girlfriend's parents, it does not mean that I am an unworthy person. It means that I am a fallible human being who is facing a difficult situation.

Step 2: Ask yourself the following question: 'Which belief is true and which is false?'

Step 3: Write down the answer to this question and provide written reasons for your answer.

Step 4: Ask yourself the following question: 'Which belief is sensible/logical and which doesn't make sense or is illogical?'

Step 5: Write down the answer to this question and provide written reasons for your answer.

Step 6: Ask yourself the following question: 'Which belief is helpful/yields healthy results and which is unhelpful/yields unhealthy results?'

Step 7: Write down the answer to this question and provide written reasons for your answer.

Step 8: Ask yourself the following question: 'Which of the two beliefs do you want to strengthen and act on?'

Step 9: Write down the answer to this question and provide written reasons for your answer.

The advantages to this approach to structured disputing is that it helps the client to see the falseness, illogicality and dysfunctionality of an irrational belief target and the truth, logic and functionality of its rational alternative more clearly because these targets are considered together. If evaluating irrational and rational beliefs together is more effective than evaluating them separately (i.e. Approach 2 is more effective than Approach 1), it would also follow that within Approach 1, version 1 would be more effective than version 2. These are, of course, empirical questions that could easily be investigated.

Approach 3: Disputing focused on arguments: One belief at a time

In this approach, the focus of the disputing is on the arguments (empirical, logical and heuristic) and this focus guides the process. Thus, the therapist proceeds as follows:

Are the following ideas true or false? Give reasons for your answer:

Demand: I must be approved by my girlfriend's parents.

Awfulising belief: It would be awful if I were not approved by my girlfriend's parents.

LFT belief: I couldn't stand it if I were not approved by my girlfriend's parents.

Self-depreciation belief: If I am not approved by my girlfriend's parents, it means that I am an unworthy person.

Preference: I would like to be approved by my girlfriend's parents, but this is not essential.

Anti-awfulising belief: It would be bad if I were not approved by my girlfriend's parents, but it would not be awful.

HFT belief: It would be difficult for me to tolerate not being approved by my girlfriend's parents, but I could stand it.

Self-acceptance belief: If I am not approved by my girlfriend's parents, it does not mean that I am an unworthy person. It means that I am a fallible human being who is facing a difficult situation.

Are the following ideas logical or illogical? Give the reasons for your answer:

Demand:

Awfulising belief:

LFT belief:

Self-depreciation belief:

Preference:

Anti-awfulising belief:

HFT belief:

Self-acceptance belief:

Are the following ideas helpful or unhelpful? Give the reasons for your answer:

Demand:

Awfulising belief:

LFT belief:

Self-depreciation belief:

Preference:

Anti-awfulising belief:

HFT belief:

Self-acceptance belief:

Approach 4: Disputing focused on arguments: One paired set of components at a time

Here the focus of the disputing is again on arguments used, but this time each paired set of components relating to the irrational and rational belief is considered together. The therapist proceeds as follows:

Demand	*Preference*
I must be approved by my girlfriend's parents.	I would like to be approved by my girlfriend's parents, but this is not essential.

Awfulising belief	*Anti-awfulising belief*
It would be awful if I were not approved by my girlfriend's parents.	It would be bad if I were not approved by my girlfriend's parents, but it would not be awful.

LFT belief	*HFT belief*
It couldn't stand it if I were not approved by my girlfriend's parents.	It would be difficult to tolerate not being approved by my girlfriend's parents, but I could stand it.

Self-depreciation belief	*Self-acceptance belief*
If I were not approved by my girlfriend's parents, it means that I am an unworthy person.	If I am not approved by my girlfriend's parents, it does not mean I am an unworthy person. It means that I am a fallible human being who is facing a difficult situation.

Which of the following ideas is logical and which is illogical? Give reasons for your answer

Demand–Preference

Awfulising belief–Anti-awfulising belief

LFT belief–HFT belief

Self-depreciation belief–Self-acceptance belief

Which of the following ideas yields healthy results and which yields unhealthy results? Give reasons for your answer

Demand–Preference

Awfulising belief–Anti-awfulising belief

LFT belief–HFT belief

Self-depreciation belief–Self-acceptance belief

As argued above, our hypothesis is that approach 4 will be more effective than approach 3 because in approach 4 the irrational beliefs and their rational alternatives are considered at the same time, whereas in approach 3 they are considered separately. Again this is a matter for empirical enquiry.

In each of the four approaches to the structured disputing discussed in the chapter, it has been assumed that all four components of an irrational belief and its rational alternative will be disputed. However, in clinical practice, it may well be the case that the therapist will dispute only the client's demand and one major derivative (e.g. a self-depreciation belief in ego disturbance and an LFT belief in discomfort disturbance) and question only the client's preference and one major derivative. This can be reflected in the structured approaches to disputing discussed here by omitting the derivatives that are not targeted for disputing.

It was argued earlier in this chapter that a structured approach to disputing helps novice REBT therapists to dispute effectively. It is also probably the case that structured disputing also helps clients to practise disputing their irrational beliefs and questioning their rational beliefs on paper between sessions and to internalise the disputing process so that after a while they are able to dispute irrational beliefs in their heads. If this assumption is correct, then it may well be the case that therapists who bring structure to the disputing process in sessions help clients to be structured in their disputing between sessions. Again this awaits empirical enquiry.

References

Beal, D., Kopec, A.M. and DiGiuseppe, R. (1996). Disputing clients' irrational beliefs. Journal of Rational-Emotive and Cognitive-Behaviour Therapy, 14, 215–29.

DiGiuseppe, R. (1991). Comprehensive cognitive disputing in RET. In M. Bernard (Ed), Using Rational-Emotive Therapy Effectively: A Practitioner's Guide. New York: Plenum.

Dryden, W. (1990). Self-disclosure in rational-emotive therapy. In G. Stricker and M. Fisher (Eds), Self-disclosure in the Therapeutic Relationship. New York: Plenum Press.

Index

'2x2' method, 133–134
ABCDE model, 1–2, 12, 30, 31
Abrams, M., 46
acceptance of self and others, 2, 96–97
    see also self-acceptance
activating events (As)
    critical, *see* critical activating events
    inference chaining, 107, 113–114
    problem-solving focus, 5
    trends in REBT, 12, 23
adolescent clients, 9, 17
agoraphobia, 85–86
Alcoholics Anonymous (AA), 29
alcoholism, 29, 39–41
aloneness intolerance, 88, 89
ambiguity intolerance, 82–83
anger, 54–55
anti-awfulising beliefs, 2
    full vs. partial, 95
    questioning, 167–168
anxiety, 9, 55
applications of REBT, 9
appropriate negative emotions, 12, 30
Aurelius, Marcus, 1
autonomy, dire need for, 83
avoidance
    behaviour intolerance, 74
    cognition intolerance, 74
    physical illness-related disturbances,
        71
awfulising beliefs, 2
    disputing errors, 151–153
    questioning, 167–168
    trends in REBT, 20

background to REBT, 1
basic theory of REBT, 1–2
Beck, Aaron T., 13, 20, 24, 103
    downward arrow technique, 120
    erroneous ideation, 151
behavioural methods in REBT, 16
behavioural therapy, 8
behaviour intolerance, 74
behaviourism, 12
beliefs (Bs)
    assessment to identify critical A,
        138–139
    basic theory, 2
    ego disturbance, 53–54
    inference chaining, 107
    problem-solving focus, 5
    trends in REBT, 12, 23
Berlin, I., 50
Bernard, M.E., 48
bibliotherapy, 8
bonds in therapeutic alliance, 27
Bordin, E., 27
boredom intolerance, 78
Boyd, J., 23, 45, 53
brevity in therapy, 24
business applications of REBT, 9

certainty, dire need for, 82
chaining, 101
    complex, 105–106
    'disturbance about disturbance',
        104–105
    inference, see inference chaining
    inference-evaluative belief, 103–104

change intolerance, 79
children, 9, 17
chi-square ('2x2') method, 133–134
Clark, D.M., 103
claustrophobia, 86
code violations by others, intolerance of,
        84–85
cognition intolerance, 73–74
cognitive-behaviour therapies (CBT), 24
    consumerism, 28
    post-traumatic stress disorder, 31–32
cognitive–emotive dissonance, 7
cognitive psychotherapy, 29–30
cognitive revolution in psychotherapy, 14
cognitive therapy, 13
    downward arrow, 111, 119, 120–121,
        127
        emotions, finding, 122
        feelings, overfocusing on, 123–124
completion, dire need for, 87–88
complex chains, 105–106
comprehensive cognitive disputing,
        30–31
compulsive wanderlust, 86
conflict intolerance, 84
consequences (Cs)
    inference chaining, 107
    trends in REBT, 12, 23
constructivist cognitive psychotherapy, 29
consumerism in psychotherapy, 28
control, dire need for, 81
couples therapy, 9
course of therapy, 8–9
critical activating events (critical As)
    dealing with, 5–6
    identifying, 5–6, 129
        by assessing beliefs, 138–139
        by disputing musts, 139–140
        'going for broke' method, 129–130
        hypothesis-advancing method,
            135–136
        inference chaining, 107
        listing approach, 130–131
        opposite of client's most cherished
            desire, 142–143
        'relive it now' method, 141–142
        subtraction method, 131–133
        'take a wild guess' method, 144
        theory-derived method, 136–138
        '2x2' method, 133–134
critical realism, 19

damnation, 2, 20
Dawson, R.W., 147
death-related disturbances, 71, 73
debating of irrational beliefs, 21
de Botton, A., 50
defining of irrational beliefs, 21
denial
    behaviour intolerance, 74
    physical illness-related disturbances,
        71
depression, 55–56
deprivation intolerance, 76–77
depth-centredness of therapy, 24
deservingness philosophy, 75
detection of irrational beliefs, 21
determinism, 37–38, 50
DIBS (Disputing Irrational Beliefs), 21
didactic disputing, 162
DiGiuseppe, R.
    disputing, 30–31, 161–162
    emotional responsibility, 43
    low frustration tolerance, 154, 155
discomfort anxiety, 61
discomfort disturbance, 2–3, 61
    vs. ego disturbance, 62–63
    trends in REBT, 22–23
    varying levels of, 64
discomfort intolerance, 77
discriminating between irrational and
        rational beliefs, 21
disgust, 70
disorder intolerance, 89–90
disputing (D), 161
    abstraction, level of, 162
    errors, 145, 158–159
        awfulising beliefs, 151–153
        conditional musts, 146–148
        conditional shoulds, 148–150
        irrelevant irrational beliefs,
            150–151
        low frustration tolerance, 153–156
        unconditional self-acceptance,
            156–158
    to identify critical A, 139–140
    inference chaining, 109
    nature of, 161–162
    structured, 163–164
        focus on arguments, one belief at a
            time, 170–171
        focus on arguments, one paired set
            of components at a time, 171–172

focus on paired components,
167–169
focus on separate components,
164–166
styles, 162–163
didactic, 162
humorous, 163
metaphorical, 163
Socratic, 162
targets, 161
trends in REBT, 12, 30–31
Disputing Irrational Beliefs (DIBS), 21
disturbance, 5–8
see also discomfort disturbance; ego
disturbance
'disturbance about disturbance' chains,
104–105
disturbed emotions, 12
doing things quickly, dire need for,
86–87
downward arrow technique, 111, 119,
120–121, 127
emotions, finding, 122
feelings, overfocusing on, 123–124
Dryden, Windy
awfulising beliefs, 151–152, 153
ego disturbance, 52–53
free will, 38, 43
inference chaining, 107
trends in REBT, 27, 28, 30, 33
unhealthy and healthy negative
emotions, taxonomy of, 12

education, 15, 17
effective philosophy (E), 12
efficient therapy, characteristics of,
24–25
effort intolerance, 80
ego disturbance, 2–3, 52–53, 59–60
beliefs, themes and emotions, 53–54
vs. discomfort disturbance, 62–63
framework
anger, 54–55
anxiety, 55
depression, 55–56
envy, 56–57
guilt, 57
hurt, 57–58
jealousy, 58–59
shame, 59
vs. non-ego disturbance, 63

trends in REBT, 22, 23
Ellis, Albert
background to REBT, 1, 11
change, 7–8
cognition intolerance, 74
discomfort anxiety, 61, 62
discomfort disturbance, 62
disputing, 161, 163
ego disturbance, 52
free will, 37–38, 39, 41, 46
Gloria, 15
inference-evaluative belief chains, 103
low frustration tolerance, 154
musturbatory thinking, 146
rational beliefs, 93, 94, 99, 100
sex therapy, 13
'take a wild guess' method, 144
trends in REBT
1955–61, 11–12, 13, 14
1961–93, 14–17
1970s, 17–18, 19–22, 23
1980s, 24–25, 26–27, 28, 29
1990s, 29–30, 31
1993–, 31–32
unconditional self-acceptance, 156,
157
emotional control, 48
emotional episode, 23
emotional insight, 14
emotional responsibility, 3, 41–43
emotion intolerance, 68
emotions
ego disturbance, 53–54
lack of, 122
emotive-evocative methods in REBT, 16,
18
emotive therapy, 8
empathy in therapeutic alliance, 27
empirical disputes, 161
enactive disputing, 163
envy, 56–57
Epictetus, 1, 11
e-prime, 19
Erhard Seminars Training (est)
movement, 26
excitement, dire need for, 78
existential aspects of REBT, 3
extensiveness of therapy, 24

failures in REBT, 25
familiarity, dire need for, 78–79

family therapy, 9
feedback from client, 8
feelings, overfocusing on, 123–124
Foulkes, P., 37
freedom, dire need for, 83
free will, 37–38, 50
    benefits, doubts about, 48–50
    emotional responsibility, 41–43
    past, influence on present, 43–45
    stress, 45–48
    susceptibility vs. excitability, 39–41
frustration-aggression hypothesis, 76
frustration intolerance, 76
full rational beliefs, 93–97

genetic factors, 39
genuineness, 27
geography, disturbances related to,
    85–86
Gloria, 15
goals, 27–28
'going for broke' method, 129–130
Golden, W.L., 27
greater self-acceptance, 157–158
Grieger, R., 23, 45, 53
group therapy activities, 26
guides for REBT practitioners, 29
guilt, 57

Hauck, Paul, 8, 24, 75
health, psychological, 26–27
healthy negative emotions, 12, 30
hell disturbances, 73
heredity, 39
heuristic disputes, 162
high frustration intolerance (HFI), 63
high frustration tolerance (HFT) beliefs,
    2, 64
    full vs. partial, 95–96
    questioning, 168–169
homework tasks, 8, 25
humanistic aspects of REBT, 13
humour in therapy, 21
    disputing, 163
hurt, 57–58
hypochondria, 70, 71, 79
hypothesis-advancing method, 135–136

identity, 'the is of', 19
imagery, 8, 18
immediate gratification, dire need for, 86

'I'm not me' syndrome, 7
impasses, climbing out of, 125–127
inaction intolerance, 74–75
inappropriate negative emotions, 12, 30
industry applications of REBT, 9
inevitability vs. susceptibility, 39–41
inference chaining, 5, 101–103, 107, 117
    assessing beliefs compared to, 139
    complete chain, 114–117
    'going for broke' method, 129, 130
    laddering and downward arrow as
        adjuncts to, 119–120, 127
    feelings, overfocusing on, 123, 124
    impasses, climbing out of, 125,
        126–127
    not refining the A enough, 113–14
    overlooking clues, 111–113
    skimming the surface, 107–11
    subtraction method, 131–132
inference-evaluative belief chains,
    103–104
injustice intolerance, 75
Institute for Rational Living/Institute for
    Rational-Emotive Therapy, 13, 15,
    16, 17
intellectual insight, 14
intolerance of others, intolerance of, 90
irrational beliefs, 2, 92–93
    assessment to identify critical A,
        138–139
    development, and existence of
        rational beliefs, 100
    disputing, see disputing
    inference-evaluative belief chains,
        103–104
    introjected false preferences as signs
        of, 99
    irrelevant, 150–151
    probing for, 98
    trends in REBT, 12, 14, 19–21
'is of identity', the, 19

jealousy, 58–59
Journal of Rational-Emotive and
        Cognitive Behaviour Therapy, 15
Journal of Rational-Emotive Therapy, 15
'just world' hypothesis, 75

Kushner, Rabbi Harold, 75
laddering, 119, 121, 124–125, 127

impasses, climbing out of, 125–126, 127
lateness disturbance, 85
listing approach, 130–131
Living School, 17
logical disputes, 161–162
logical positivism, 19
looked after, dire need to be, 83
loss intolerance, 87
low frustration intolerance (LFI), 63
low frustration tolerance (LFT) beliefs, 2, 61–62
  change as cause of, 7, 14
  disputing errors, 153–156
  questioning, 168–169
  trends in REBT, 14, 20, 22–23
  varying levels of, 63–64

'mad dog disputing', 147
maintenance of therapeutic progress, 24–25
Malkinson, R., 153
Maultsby, M.C. Jr., 79
mental illness, disturbance related to, 71–73
metaphorical disputing, 163
moderate frustration intolerance (MFI), 63
moderate frustration tolerance (MFT), 64
Moore, R.H., 101, 107
most cherished desire, opposite of, 142–143
Muran, E.M., 154, 155
musts, 2
  disputing
    errors, 146–148
    to identify critical A, 139–140
  trends in REBT, 20–21

Neenan, M., 52–53, 157
negative external conditions, 66
  ameliorating, 67–68
  eliminating, 67
  maintaining, 67
negative internal states, 66
  eliminating, 67
  maintaining, 66
  reducing, 66–67
non-disturbed emotions, 12
non-ego disturbance, 61, 62
  vs. ego disturbance, 63

future directions, 90–91
taxonomy, 68
  aloneness intolerance, 88
  ambiguity intolerance, 82–83
  autonomy and freedom, dire need for, 83
  behaviour intolerance, 74
  boredom intolerance, 78
  certainty, dire need for, 82
  change intolerance, 79
  code violations by others, intolerance of, 84–85
  cognition intolerance, 73–74
  completion, dire need for, 87–88
  conflict intolerance, 84
  control, dire need for, 81
  death-related disturbances, 73
  deprivation intolerance, 76–77
  discomfort intolerance, 77
  disgust, 70
  disorder intolerance, 89–90
  doing things quickly, dire need for, 86–87
  effort intolerance, 80
  emotion intolerance, 68
  excitement, dire need for, 78
  familiarity, dire need for, 78–79
  frustration intolerance, 76
  geography, disturbances related to, 85–86
  immediate gratification, dire need for, 86
  inaction intolerance, 74–75
  intolerance of others, intolerance of, 90
  looked after, dire need to be, 83
  loss intolerance, 87
  novelty, dire need for, 78
  pain intolerance, 70
  persistence intolerance, 79–80
  physical illness-related disturbances, 70–71
  psychological problems and mental illness, disturbances related to, 71–73
  repetition intolerance, 79
  right, dire need to be, 75–76
  safety, dire need for, 89
  sensation intolerance, 69
  solitude, dire need for, 88–89
  task difficulty intolerance, 81

time, disturbances related to, 85
transition intolerance, 84
understanding, dire need for, 82
unfairness and injustice intoler-
    ance, 75
valence issue, 64–68
varying levels of, 63–64
non-philosophical approach, 28
novelty, dire need for, 78
'nowism', 86

obsessive-compulsive disorder (OCD),
    32
opposite of client's most cherished
    desire, 142–143
other-pity, 75

pain intolerance, 70
panic disorders, 103–104
partial rational belief, 93–97
past, influence on present, 43–45
'Perfect Rationality', 21
Perls, Fritz, 15, 16
persistence intolerance, 79–80
Personal Construct Therapy (PCT), 119
    laddering, 119, 121, 124–125, 127
        impasses, climbing out of,
            125–126, 127
personality disorders, people with, 32
personality formation, theory of, 22
pervasiveness in therapy, 24
Phares, E.J., 89
philosophical change, 28
phrenophobia, 72
physical illness-related disturbances,
    70–71
Popper, Karl, 19
positive external conditions, 64, 66
    finding, 65
    increasing or intensifying, 65
    maintaining, 65
positive internal states, 64, 66
    establishing, 64
    intensifying, 65
    maintaining, 64
post-traumatic stress disorder (PTSD),
    31–32
practice of REBT, 3–4
    course of therapy, 8–9
    disturbances, identifying and dealing
        with, 5–8

early problem-solving focus, 4–5
practitioner guides, 29
preferences, 2
    distinguishing between true and
        introjected, false, 99
    distinguishing between two different
        types of, 98–9
    partial
        vs. full, 93–94
        strength, and transformation
            process, 97
    questioning, 167
prevention in therapy, 25
primary rational beliefs, 94
'Problems of Daily Living' workshops, 15
problem-solving focus, 4–5
psychoanalysis, 12
    cognitive revolution, 14
    consumerism, 28
    Ellis's disenchantment, 1, 11, 24
    trends in REBT, 13, 14
psychological health, 26–27
psychological problems, disturbances
        related to, 71–73

Raimy, Victor, 72
rational beliefs, 2, 92
    disputing, 161
    escalation vs. transformation, 93
    full vs. partial, 93–97
    and irrational beliefs, development of,
        100
    nature, characteristics and types, 92
    preference
        distinguishing between true and
            introjected, false, 99
        distinguishing between two
            different types of, 98–99
    probing for possible irrationalities, 98
    trends in REBT, 12
rational derivatives, 94–97
rational-emotive therapy, 14–17
rational encounter marathons, 16–17
rationalist cognitive psychotherapy,
    29–30
Rational Living, 15
rational recovery (RR), 29
rational therapy (RT), 11–14
rational training, 15–16
reactance, 83
'relive it now' method, 141–142

repetition intolerance, 79
research findings on REBT, 9
resistance in therapy, 26
responsibility
    emotional, 3, 41–43
    therapeutic, 3
right, dire need to be, 75–76
Rogers, Carl, 12, 15
Rothschild, B.H., 70

safety, dire need for, 89
Schutz, Will, 16
scientific debate, 21
secondary problems, 14
secondary rational beliefs (rational
        derivatives), 94–97
self-acceptance, 2, 96–97
    greater, 157–158
    questioning, 169
    unconditional, see unconditional self-
        acceptance
self-defeating beliefs, see irrational
        beliefs
self-defeating emotions, 12
self-depreciating beliefs, questioning,
        169
self-disclosure, 163
self-fulfilling prophecies, 14
self-helping beliefs, see rational beliefs
self-helping emotions, 12
self-help literature, 29
Self-Management and Recovery Training,
        29
self-pity, 75
semanticists, 18–19
sensation intolerance, 69
shame, 59
shame-attacking exercises, 8, 16
shithood, 52–53
shoulds, 148–150
Socratic disputing, 162
solitude, dire need for, 88–89
songs, rational humorous, 21
Stoics, 1, 11
stress, 45–48
structured disputing, 163–164
    focus on arguments, one belief at a
        time, 170–171
    focus on arguments, one paired set of
        components at a time, 171–172
    focus on paired components, 167–169

focus on separate components,
        164–166
substance abuse, 9
subtraction method, 131–133
susceptibility vs. inevitability, 39–41

'take a wild guess' method, 144
task difficulty intolerance, 81
tasks in therapeutic alliance, 28
temperament, 38
themes, 53–54
theory-derived method, 136–138
therapeutic alliance, 27–28
therapeutic approach, 21–22, 23
therapeutic progress, maintenance of,
        24–25
therapeutic responsibility, 3
thoroughgoingness of therapy, 24
time, disturbances related to, 85
tinnitus, 69
training, rational, 15–16
transition intolerance, 84
trends in REBT, 11, 33
    1955–61 (rational therapy), 11–14
    1961–93 (rational-emotive therapy),
        14–17
    1970s, 17–23
    1980s, 23–29
    1990s, 29–31
    1993– (rational emotive behaviour
        therapy), 31–32
Trimpey, J., 29
'2x2' method, 133–134

unconditional positive regard in thera-
        peutic alliance, 27
unconditional positive self-rating, 96, 97
unconditional self-acceptance, 96–97
    disputing errors, 156–158
    trends in REBT, 13, 17–18
understanding, dire need for, 82
undeservingness philosophy, 75
unfairness intolerance, 75
unhealthy negative emotions, 12, 30

valence issue, non-ego disturbance,
        64–68
Vernon, Ann, 17
Vesey, G., 37
vivid REBT, 27, 142
vocabulary, emotional, 3

Walen, S.R.
  emotional responsibility, 43
  musts, 147
  phrenophobia, 72
  shoulds, 149
  trends in REBT, 23–24
  vague goals, 124
wanderlust, compulsive, 86

Wessler, R.A., 23, 82
Wessler, R.L., 23, 82
'wild guess' method, 144
will-power, 38

Yankura, J., 38, 151–152
Young, H.S., 53